RELIGION, MORALITY, AND THE LAW

NOMOS

XXX

NOMOS

Harvard University Press

The Liberal Arts Press

Atherton Press

Aldine-Atherton Press

Lieber-Atherton Press

New York University Press

NOMOS XXX

Yearbook of the American Society for Political and Legal Philosophy

RELIGION, MORALITY, AND THE LAW

Edited by

J. Roland Pennock, *Swarthmore College*

and

John W. Chapman, *University of Pittsburgh*

New York and London: New York University Press · 1988

Religion, Morality, and the Law: Nomos XXX
edited by J. Roland Pennock and John W. Chapman
Copyright © 1988 by New York University
Manufactured in the United States of America

Library of Congress Cataloging-in-Publication Data

Religion, morality, and the law.

(Nomos ; 30)
Outgrowth of a meeting of the American Society for
Political and Legal Philosophy held in conjunction with
the Association of American Law Schools in New Orleans,
Jan. 1986.
Bibliography: p.
Includes index.
1. Religion and law—Congresses. 2. United States—
Religion—Congresses. 3. Religion and politics—
United States—Congresses. 4. Church and state—
United States—Congresses. I. Pennock, J. Roland
(James Roland), 1906–   . II. Chapman, John
William, 1923–   . III. American Society for
Political and Legal Philosophy. IV. Association of
American Law Schools. V. Series.
BL65.L33R45 1988   344'.09   87-28150
ISBN 0-8147-6606-4   342.49

CONTENTS

CONTRIBUTORS

ROBERT M. COVER
Law, Yale University

RONALD R. GARET
Law and Religion, University of Southern California

STANLEY HAUERWAS
Religion, Duke University

LOUIS HENKIN
Law, Columbia University

STEPHEN HOLMES
Political Science, University of Chicago

GEORGE A. KELLY
Political Science, The Johns Hopkins University

JOHN LADD
Philosophy, Brown University

ERIC MACK
Philosophy, Tulane University

JOHN H. MANSFIELD
Law, Harvard University

LISA NEWTON
Philosophy, Fairfield University

DAVID A. J. RICHARDS
  Law, New York University

DAVID G. SMITH
  Political Science, Swarthmore College

PREFACE

This thirtieth volume of NOMOS grows out of the meetings of the American Society for Political and Legal Philosophy held in conjunction with the Association of American Law Schools in New Orleans in January 1986. The topic, "Religion, Morality, and the Law," selected as usual by vote of the membership of our Society, was thought to be timely in view of current controversies over the proper interpretation of the religion clauses in the First Amendment to the Constitution. R. Kent Greenawalt, serving as chairman of the program committee, wisely arranged a program of much wider ambit than one confined to matters of constitutional interpretation, a policy that has been continued by the editors in their selection of authors not represented in the program of the meetings. Readers, we believe, will find in these contributions a diet calculated to enrich and stimulate discussion of this important subject.

Roland Pennock, editor of the Society for many years, has resigned that office as of December 31, 1986, except for seeing this volume to the press. At its 1986 meeting, ASPLP elected its associate editor John W. Chapman as the new editor. Pennock will act as associate editor for its successor, after which a new policy will be inaugurated: the chairman of the program Committee for each year will be asked to serve as associate editor for the resulting volume.

J.R.P.
J.W.C.

INTRODUCTION

J. ROLAND PENNOCK

Religion, morality, and the law are said by one of our authors
(George Kelly) to comprise a three-legged stool, upon which
the state rests. Force and authority are not mentioned, but perhaps authoritative force is considered to be a derivative of law
in its provisions for sanctions; and all three of the "legs" entail
authority in at least one of its varied senses. (See NOMOS I
and NOMOS XXIX.) At first glance, it might appear that the
relation of law to the state is not on all fours with the relation
between the state and religion or that between the state and
morality. In a Kelsenian sense, law and state, if not identical,
are at least coterminous. A state without law would not be a
state according to usual definitions of those terms, although it
is at least arguable that the converse does not hold. As David
Richards points out in a different context, however, these entities and their mutual relations are constantly changing. A
modern state without law would indeed be a contradiction in
terms, while the same can hardly be said of a state without religion. Morality stands in a still different relation. It is not integral to the state in the way that law is, yet we can hardly
conceive of a state existing, let alone enduring, without morality—and this not only because we can hardly conceive of a people without a morality of some kind. Nor is it only because
without "constitutional morality" a constitution would be
worthless. No, it is even more because all politics, and so all
government, must rely on a pervasive *trust;* and for trust morality is essential.

1

The further question, to which I shall return, is whether morality itself can survive without the support of religion, at least in some form. The ways in which law, morals, and religion are intertwined and how these interconnections complicate the problems the courts face in interpreting the Establishment Clause are discussed in Louis Henkin's subtle consideration of these and related problems, including the not yet fully explored difficulties in distinguishing between religious and social purposes. Is giving pleasure, including religious pleasure, or protecting the sensibilities of certain groups a "secular purpose?" he asks.

Returning for a moment to the relation between state and the law, one puzzle underlines Richards's point about change. Custom, customary law, and the law of a fully developed state are not identical, but it is often difficult to draw the lines between them. One grows out of the other. Magic and religion are also deeply involved in this sociopolitical development. Moreover, both law, in the form of customary law, and religion, each infused with morality, are essential to the creation, development, and support of the state. So we come back to Kelly's three-legged stool.

Questions can be raised about the proposition that these three institutions, political law, morality, and religion are united at least in that they serve as supports for the state. Each has its own body of law and they are by no means always mutually harmonious. "Render unto Caesar that which is Caesar's, and unto God that which is God's"; the Church doctrine of the two swords: These formulas serve to remind us, if reminder is necessary, that organized religion and the law of the state have often been in sharp conflict. As Stephen Holmes remarks, we did not wait for modern liberalism to introduce the doctrine of state neutrality in religious matters. It was not to uphold liberty but to avoid civil strife that that principle was proclaimed. It may well be, as Mansfield argues, that official neutrality as between contending religious factions and movements is not enough for this purpose; but whereas the Shah's secularism failed to maintain the peace, the union of religion and politics practiced by his successor has destroyed peace both *in* other nations and *with* other nations. In the light of these facts it is not strange that our First Amendment enshrined both the guarantee of religious liberty and the principle of state neutrality with regard to religious matters (or whatever was meant by the non-Establishment Clause).

Neither is it a matter for surprise that the attempt thus to avoid violent or at least disruptive internal conflict has not been completely successful. The tension between freedom of religious exercise and the prohibition of state action that can be thought (especially by the Supreme Court) to support religion (on the theory that religious liberty entails the obligation of the state to show no favoritism between believers and nonbelievers) has created its own conflicts. On the one hand we have Jerry Falwell and many others urging the state to support the morality that their religious beliefs entail, while many strongly protest the actions of the "moral majority"—some on the political grounds that motivated the framers and others, like Stanley Hauerwas in this volume, on theological grounds. Eric Mack takes a contrasting position on the neutrality issue, arguing that moral prescriptions are essential for political debate and accordingly that neutrality will not do the job the liberals want. At this point, from a still different point of view, David Smith, invoking the insights of Tocqueville, protests Hauerwas's position on political grounds. Civil religion, he contends, has proved itself, as both Rousseau and Tocqueville believed, a valuable, perhaps invaluable support to the democratic state.

In this increasingly secularized world (which is what it seems to be in spite of the revitalization of religion as a powerful force in some quarters), it might seem to be religion that is least vital to the support of the state, barring Iran and perhaps some of the other Muslim states. But this immediately raises the question of the relation between religion and morality. Is morality dependent upon religion?—a question that is discussed by more than one of our authors. Lisa Newton gives the common position regarding this question a new twist, arguing that the church today, as "theorist, leader, and enabler of a self-defense pact for the private sector" against state expansion that threatens both liberty and democracy. (p. 197)

In a sense reversing the order just discussed, the tragically uncompleted paper of the late Robert Cover provides us with a fascinating case study of an attempt to bring the Messiah through law.[1]

Even as Kelly notes that religion, morality, and the law converge in their support for the state, Ronald R. Garet calls attention to another convergence. These three bodies of ideas and precepts, he argues, intersect in a version of natural law theory, which he terms a "human-nature-naturalist" theory. He pursues his study through an examination of theological "creation" theories, showing, among other things, that theories of this *genre* have greater variety and richness than the inclusion among them of "creation science" would suggest.

A part of a problem already adverted to here and there throughout the foregoing rather rambling remarks calls for further attention. Why are the issues to which the religion clauses of the First Amendment to the United States Constitution are directed the object of so much difficulty? Is it strange that the authors of that amendment combined two clauses often found in conflict with each other? In the concluding essay in this volume, John Ladd argues that the fault lies in the absoluteness of the claims of all religions in the midst of religiously pluralistic societies. If only the believers (and the nonbelievers) in the various religions would accept the proposition that those who hold beliefs other than theirs (although obviously mistaken by their own lights) would admit that perhaps all of these systems of thought and belief contain some element of truth—something of value—then the problems would at least be ameliorated.

With these introductory remarks I commend you to the real thing, the substantive essays themselves. But not before expressing my appreciation to Kent Greenawalt, for arranging the program of the meetings that provided the major part of the meat of this volume, and to Despina Gimbel for her skill and patience in handling its publication, as she has for many of its predecessors. Finally, Eleanor Greitzer, Assistant to the Editor, deserves more thanks and praise than I can express for the alertness, efficiency, accuracy, and tact with which she has aided me in my editorial functions for lo these many years!

NOTE

1. This study is at once a condensation and a continuation of Cover's well-received article, Robert M. Cover, "Nomos and Narrative," *Har. L. R.* 97 (1983): 4–68.

1

JEAN BODIN: THE PARADOX OF SOVEREIGNTY AND THE PRIVATIZATION OF RELIGION

STEPHEN HOLMES

Nothing can be public, where nothing is private.—Bodin[1]

Liberal beliefs about the proper relation among law, morality, and religion first acquired distinct contours during the wars of religion that ravaged France between 1562 and 1598. While recent commentators on the state's obligatory "neutrality" toward conflicting moral ideals often refer to this bloodily traumatic period,[2] they usually do so only in passing. We can shed considerable light, however, upon our constitutionally mandated separation of political and religious spheres as well as upon the uneasy relation between law and morals typical of the liberal tradition if we exhume and reexamine one deeply influential argument for religious toleration advanced in late sixteenth-century France.

I. Toleration and *Raison d'État*

Generalizing from the English and American cases, we ordinarily assume that liberal ideals initially emerged in a struggle against the politics of absolutism. Rights, we tend to think, are shackles imposed upon a restive sovereign. The relation between power and freedom, however, was never so unequivocally antagonistic as the storybook account makes it appear. In crucial cases, rights were created and maintained *by* the modern state to promote the goals *of* the modern state. The slow and irregular advance of religious freedom, in particular, was inextricably entwined with the consolidation of dynastic rule, especially in France. The subsequent conflict between liberalism and absolutism should not be allowed to obscure their common filiation in this respect. By the 1570s, a disjunction of temporal and spiritual domains was already being advocated as a technique for strengthening the sway of secular rulers over nonreligious matters. Privatization of religious disputes or the withdrawal of public officials from theological controversies was acclaimed as sovereignty-enhancing. Important theorists urged the government to steer clear of "the religious thicket," so to speak, in order to augment effectiveness and credibility in other domains. With benefit of hindsight, a cynic even might claim that the cause of religious toleration succeeded chiefly because it proved advantageous to power-wielders, humane respect for rights of conscience providing little more than a figleaf of morality for an otherwise self-interested policy. Be this as it may, advocates of toleration *were* prudently solicitous of political authorities. As a result, they placed uncommon emphasis on the state-building function of the depoliticization of religion.

Accustomed by historical accident to an alliance between toleration and antiroyalism, American scholars tend to slight the decisive role played by absolutism in establishing throughout Europe a taken-for-granted separation of religious and political domains. French political theory provides a useful corrective here because so many of its major representatives presuppose a mutually supportive relation between state power and individual freedom. To mention a very late instance: Emile Durkheim argued explicitly that the modern state, far from being an implacable enemy of individual rights, actually created and sustained such rights by dissolving the oppressive "communal" bonds of clan, caste, sect, and parochial village.[3] In advancing this to-Americans-paradoxical argument, Durkheim was simply reiterating a central tenet of French political theory: Liberty and sovereignty, individualism and community, far from being hostile alternatives, can enliven and reinforce one another.[4] An important variation on this general theme is the hypothesis of a mutually supporting relation between public authority and the privatization of religion. To reconstruct the arguments that were originally adduced to bolster this paradoxical thesis, we can do no better than to examine Jean Bodin's *Les six livres de la république* (1576), written to support state authority on the one hand and the toleration of sectarian diversity on the other. Before turning directly to the *République*'s discussion of religion, however, we must clarify Bodin's theory of sovereign power.

II. The Bodin Problem

Sovereignty is "the most high, absolute, and perpetual power over the citizens and subjects of a commonweal." It is quite simply "the greatest power to command" (I, 8, 84). This superiority is not merely relative but absolute: "It behooveth him that is sovereign not to be in any sort subject to the command of another" (I, 8, 91). Terrible concentration of power is justified as the one acceptable alternative to religious civil war. Mutual butchery of citizens was Bodin's *summum malum,* the uttermost evil to be avoided at all costs. In a startlingly pagan phrase, he defines "civil war" as "the only poison to make empires and states mortal, which else would be immortal" (V, 5, 602). An absolute sovereign alone can put an end to the fratricide devastating France since the early 1560s.

His authoritative pronouncements about authority have established Bodin's reputation as a self-appointed spokesman for centralizing monarchs who "put to sleep" representative bodies inherited from the Middle Ages and eventually drew all political power into their own hands. Absolute sovereigns, as Bodin described and admired them, were both internally supreme and externally independent. These two characteristics were complementary sides of the same coin, for a king typically had to assert his authority against unruly forces, such as the Catholic League, that were simultaneously localist and internationalist.

When Bodin contends that "the marks of sovereignty are indivisible," he is not making the merely conceptual point that, by definition, sovereignty ceases to be sovereignty once it is divided. Rather, he is advancing a causal generalization about the viability of internally divided political institutions. For example:

"Where the rights of sovereignty are divided betwixt the prince and his subjects: in that condition of the state, there are still endless stirs and quarrels for the superiority, until some one, some few, or all together have got the sovereignty" (II, 1, 194). Or again: States in which lawmaking authority is divided "find no rest from civil wars and broils, until they again recover some one of the three forms," that is, until they settle down as either democracies, aristocracies, or monarchies (II, 1, 195). Far from being definitionally impossible, divided sovereignty episodically crops up; but whenever it does, it proves radically unstable.[5]

Bodin carries this argument to its logical conclusion and thus subverts his own assertion that sovereign power can be stably located in either one, a few, or the majority. He ends up alleging, in fact, that a monarch alone can be an effective sovereign: "The chief point of a commonweal, which is the right of sovereignty, cannot be, nor subsist (to speak properly) but in a monarchy: for none can be sovereign in a commonweal but one alone" (VI, 4, 715). His fundamental premise, here and throughout, is that an absolute king is best equipped to prevent the sedition, faction, and civil war that are perpetual threats to every commonwealth and that have become particularly perilous to France during the Catholic-Huguenot struggles. Because of this general line of argument, the *République* is usually, and not unjustly, described as an early statement of the absolutist political program.

Partly accurate, this interpretation is nevertheless incomplete. For one thing, Bodin appears to be a traditionalist as well as an innovator. Alongside his advocacy of radically centralized sovereignty, we find him praising, or seeming to praise, institutions usually associated with the ancient "polity of estates." On the one hand, as his reputation would lead us to expect, he repeatedly emphasizes that obedience to the sovereign is not based on consent: "So we see the principal point of sovereign majesty, and absolute power, to consist principally in giving laws unto the subjects in general, without their consent" (I, 8, 98).[6] Because it may be whimsically or unpredictably withdrawn, "consent" provides an unstable foundation for political authority. Moreover, if subjects have discordant aims, consent-based authority will be paralyzed or fall into conflict with itself. Hence, every effective sovereign is, and must be, an independent, uninfluenced, uncommanded commander.

At least Bodin *sometimes* argues this way. At other times, he forcefully stresses the quid-pro-quo arrangement whereby citizens voluntarily exchange obedience for protection.[7] In the relevent passages, he writes unambiguously that the duties of princes are just as binding as the duties of subjects: "As the subject oweth unto his lord all duty, aid, and obedience; so the prince also oweth unto his subjects justice, guard, and protection: so that the subjects are no more bound to obey the prince, than is the prince to administer unto them justice" (IV, 6, 500). The prince, too, has unbreakable obligations. While legally unaccountable, he is nevertheless duty-bound. But what does Bodin mean here? How can an uncommanded commander nevertheless be subject to binding obligations? How is this seeming inconsistency to be resolved?

The tension here is pivotal and relevant to Bodin's justification of religious toleration, as we shall see. To cite another case: Bodin simultaneously says that the sovereign is both above the law and yet subject to the law, that "the prince is acquitted from the power of the laws" and that "all princes of the earth are subject unto the laws of God, of nature, and of nations" (I, 8, 91 and 90). Here Bodin appears to use the word *law* equivocally, referring to man-made law in one case and natural law in another. But we must not erase the verbal "contradiction" too hastily. Indeed, the drama of Bodin's position lies precisely here, in this systematic oscillation between two not-quite-compatible claims.

A sovereign is above the law because he makes the law. Indeed, "the law is nothing else but the commandment of a sovereign, using his sovereign power" (I, 8, 108). A command theory of law is therefore built into the foundations of Bodin's concept of sovereignty:

> Under this same sovereignty of power for the giving and abrogating of the law are comprised all the other rights and marks of sovereignty, so that (to speak properly) a man may say, that [legislative power is the] only mark of sovereign power, considering that all the other rights thereof are contained in this, *viz.*, to have power to give laws unto all and every one of the subjects and to receive none from them (I, 10, 161–162).

Most striking is Bodin's radical claim that a law acquires its validity solely from its source and not at all from its content. Even

if a law corresponds to reason, it is valid *only* because it is promulgated by the proper authority: "The laws of a sovereign
prince, although they be grounded upon good and lively reasons, depend nevertheless upon nothing but his mere and frank
good will" (I, 8, 92). This is pure voluntarism: *voluntas non ver-
itas facit legem,* a doctrine tailored to the needs of a faction-riven
society. The "justice" of any law is open to dispute, particularly
if citizens cultivate inconsistent religious beliefs. By contrast, even
implacably hostile groups can be brought to admit that a law
has been officially promulgated by a *de facto* sovereign. Thus, it
has sometimes been argued that legal positivism first emerged
as a strategy for stabilizing the ship of state in a turbulent religious war.[8]

III. Limits on Sovereign Power

Sovereignty is strictly unconditional. Rather than law's establishing authority, authority establishes law. The king is *absolu-
tus,* utterly absolved from legal accountability. He is unre-
stricted by custom, the consent of subjects, or even his own laws.
These assertions are radical and striking, and Bodin means them
to be. Throughout the *République,* however, every such assertion is balanced by a reassuring counterclaim: Sovereignty is
conditional, limited, accountable, and surprisingly unfree. Bodin's unbound sovereign is restricted in a number of ways.

First, and fundamentally, the sovereign is limited by divine
and natural law: "No more also can the laws of sovereign princes
alter or change the laws of God and nature" (I, 8, 104). Indeed,
Bodin upbraids political writers who accentuate the legally unconditional status of the sovereign: "They that generally say
that princes are not subject unto laws nor to their own conventions, if they except not the laws of God and nature, and the
just contracts and conventions made with them, they do great
wrong both unto God and nature" (I, 8, 104). True, Bodin does
not assign to any earthly agency the power to enforce divine
and natural law upon a reigning sovereign. But his stress on
the total subjection of sovereign princes to a higher law is much
too relentless to be treated as marginal or secondary. The laws
of God and nature are essential to his theory of political sovereignty. But questions remain: What are these laws of nature?

How do we recognize them? What sort of binding authority do they have? Why should a prince, subject to no one's command, acquiesce in annoying restraints?

Bodin also insists that his unbound sovereign is nevertheless tightly bound by the constitutional rules of the kingdom, the *leges imperii* or *lois royales*. The sovereign must passively submit, first of all, to the tradition of passing the crown to the male heir: "Touching the laws which concern the state of the realm, and the establishing thereof; for as much as they are annexed and united to the crown, the prince cannot derogate from them, such as is the law Salique" (I, 8, 95). Even absolute power is powerless in some respects. The prince's word may be law; but he dare not choose his own successor.

Despite the unboundness of sovereignty, moreover, the prince is explicitly barred from treating the royal domain as his private property: "It is certain by the edict and laws concerning the public domain, that it is not to be alienated" (I, 10, 182). *These* laws are quite unlike the commands of a sovereign. Indeed, they are commands to which the sovereign must submit. The domain lands belong to the commonwealth and cannot be sold—not at least by an act of royal will and not without the consent of the Estates.

Similarly, while the king is allowed to make laws without consent, he is forbidden to levy taxes without it: "It is not in the power of any prince in the world, *at his pleasure* to raise taxes upon the people, no more than to take another man's goods from him" (I, 8, 97). The Estates have the right to decline subsidies. The shockingly constitutionalist flavor of this arrangement is emphasized by Bodin's reference to Philippe de Commynes who, earlier in the century, had been imprisoned by the crown for making a similarly seditious suggestion. Bodin is scathing about writers who incite the king to tax without consent. This, he claims, "is as much as if they should say it to be lawful for them to rob and spoil their subjects, oppressed by force of arms; which law, the more mighty use against them that be weaker than themselves, which the Germans must rightly call the law of thieves and robbers" (I, 8, 109). In passages such as these, the royalist Bodin echoes the language of anti-royalism.

Furthermore: While "the prince is not subject to his laws, nor to the laws of his predecessors," he is nevertheless subject "to his own just and reasonable conventions, and in the observation whereof the subjects in general or particular have interest" (I, 8, 92). The sovereign is especially bound, says Bodin, by covenants issued not of his own free will but rather at the request of his subjects.

It is not wholly correct to say that Bodin empowers no worldly agency to enforce these limits upon the king. The power of the Estates to refuse subsidies is an obvious counter-example. Moreover when Bodin asks whether a magistrate may resign rather than enforce a law perceived to be unjust, he answers that such a magistrate *can* resign if a majority of his fellow magistrates agree that the law violates natural equity (III, 4, 316). Bodin does not elaborate; but one implication might be that a majority of dissenting magistrates could justly resign as a body. If they did this, however, the king would have no means for enforcing his own laws. So here, too, at least by implication, Bodin grants *de facto* veto power to men operating independently of royal control.[9]

Here is our philological and theoretical puzzle: The sovereign is both bound and unbound.[10] It is a genuine mystery. And scholars have adopted a variety of attitudes toward it. Some simply diagnose Bodin as inconsistent, arguing that he negligently combines the old and the new, medieval constitutionalism with modern absolutism, without making any effort at synthesis.[11] Others skirt the problem, suggesting that, in the *République*, "The rights of absolute sovereignty must always be tempered by the laws of nature."[12] While true, this analysis does not go very far. Why is sovereignty tempered by higher law? What is the force of this "limit"? Can a sovereign still *be* sovereign if his power is limited in this way? Nannerl Keohane does better, advancing the intriguing claim that the "limits" on sovereign power are "most accurately understood as conditions for its exercise."[13] Unfortunately, this promising suggestion remains undeveloped. While endorsing the commonplace notion of Bodin's basic "inconsistency,"[14] Julian Franklin, too, suggests *en passant* that Bodin embraced limitations on state power as techniques for enhancing state power.[15] In my view, this lucid paradox explains the underlying unity of the *République*.

IV. SOVEREIGNTY-REINFORCING RESTRAINTS

The *République* is, in many ways, a diffuse and slippery work. Its fundamental argument, however, can be restated with some precision. To approach the book as a coherent set of doctrines, we must first notice that Bodin is chronically addicted to paradoxes. He amusingly stresses, for example, both the advantages of deprivation and the disadvantages of overendowment. He notes, echoing classical sources, that "Men of a fat and fertile soil, are most commonly effeminate and cowards; whereas contrariwise a barren country makes men temperate by necessity, and by consequence careful, vigilant, and industrious" (V, 1, 565). And this observation about inferior soil is juxtaposed to another about superior intelligence: "The Florentines in their assemblies spoil all through the subtlety of their wits" (V, 1, 563). A relish for paradox, notable in Bodin's illustrations and asides, also inspires his entire argument about sovereignty. His basic idea, put simply, is that *limits strengthen* or that, under certain circumstances, *rigidities produce flexibilities*.

Bodin is far from being a pure decisionist or voluntarist. But neither is he a traditional moralist or pious exponent of natural law. To comprehend the peculiar structure of his argument, we must first set aside our intuitive sense that restrictions inhibit. Limitations may enable as well as disable. Indeed, limits can well be enabling *because* they are disabling. Consider grammar. Rules governing the use of language cannot be adequately conceived as pure prohibitions on, or obstacles to, speech. By submitting ourselves to constraints, we gain the capacity to do many things we would otherwise never be able to do. Philosophers distinguish between regulative and constitutive rules: the former, such as a sign forbidding smoking, place a limit upon a pre-existent activity, while the latter, such as the rules of chess, make an activity possible for the first time. Rules of grammar, in fact, are *possibility-creating rules* and therefore cannot be accurately described as manacles clamped upon a pre-existent freedom.[16]

Bodin's massive treatise is much too sprawling and loose-knit to be completely summarized in any single thesis. Nevertheless, this argument does stand out: Laws of nature, laws of succession, nonalienability of the domain lands, immemorial customs, a prohibition on taxation without consultation, and the informal prerogatives of parlements and Estates can substantially *increase* the power of a prince. Bodin treats restrictions on power, rather unconventionally, as a set of authority-reinforcing, will-empowering, and possibility-expanding rules. Meinecke was therefore quite right to describe him as an early proponent of anti-Machiavellian *raison d'état*.[17]

To deal with the problem of religious civil war, Bodin argues that law is valid solely when promulgated by an authority with the capacity to enforce it. While a "positivist" strategy might stifle dispute about which laws deserve obedience, it raises other difficulties, particularly the problem of the self-binding of the supreme power. How can the wielder of the highest authority be compelled to compel himself? An all-powerful monarch can prevent his subjects from acting unjustly and destroying the peace, but who can prevent the monarch from behaving in this way? Bodin had to devise a method of coercing the king that did not simultaneously destroy the advantages of radically centralized royal power. His solution was to rethink traditional limits on royal power as conditions for the *successful* exercise of royal power. Successful does not mean just, or right, or in accord with God's law, but simply capable of preventing civil war and keeping domestic peace.

Bodin sought to reconceptualize traditional restraints as instruments of princely authority. He rethought disabling rules as enabling ones. As a result, he was not an imperfect Hobbes who spoiled his otherwise-modern doctrine of sovereignty with a vestigial medievalism. Bodin's natural law, for example, should be just as attractive to an unvirtuous as to a virtuous prince. A worst-case approach, the gloomy assumption that enlightened statesmen will not always be at the helm, is only reasonable because "There have been but few princes for their virtues famous" (IV, 1, 414). Continuing in a Madisonian vein, Bodin adds: "Fear . . . is the only controller of virtue" (V, 5, 603). Accepting this rather pessimistic premise, he focuses almost exclusively on rules that would be self-enforcing, which presuppose no motive nobler than the self-interest of the prince. Neither moral nor religious motives can be relied upon:

> There is nothing more true, than what was spoken by Brutus the Tribune of the people unto the nobility of Rome, that there was one only assurance for the weak against the mighty, which was that if the mighty would, they could not hurt them: for that ambitious men that have power over another, never want will (V, 6, 619).

Institutional arrangements can make it difficult, although not strictly impossible, for the all-powerful sovereign to abuse his power. In any case, a prudent sovereign will relinquish some power voluntarily when he learns that limitations on his caprice increase his capacity to govern.

Earlier exponents of natural law had periodically drawn attention to the political advantages of moral self-restraint.[18] But Bodin focuses almost exclusively on the secular side-effects of the prince's virtues. True, the suggestion that he "secularized" natural law to make it appealing even to princes of low moral character confronts an obvious objection: Seemingly sincere references to God's will abound throughout the *République*. This is disturbing counter-evidence. But not decisive. For one thing, "It is better to have an evil commonwealth than none at all" (IV, 3, 469). Furthermore, even "The tyrant is a sovereign" (I, 8, 87). Tyrants frequently violate justice. But Bodin acknowledges their sovereignty because oppression is preferable to civil war. Avoidance of civil war is primarily a secular goal, even though it is also good for religion and pleasing to God. Preventing subjects from slaughtering one another is the immediate purpose of all political authority. This negative goal takes precedence over all rival aims, including the most inspiring religious objectives.

Bodin's main argument is structured to convince unvirtuous rulers that submitting to natural law and other restraints has significant strategic advantages. If a sovereign breaks his word too often, for example, his word will become useless as a tool for mobilizing cooperation. Activity and passivity, influence and adaptation, are not mutually exclusive. Only by *adapting* to nature, can a prince exert power over it (V, 1, 545, 558, 564). To arrive at the port of his choice, a pilot must not imperiously ignore natural limits, but must instead "yield unto the tempest" (VI, 4, 720) and know how to ride out the storm. Similarly, by adapting diplomatically to his subjects' habits and beliefs, the prince can increase his ability to influence their behavior. In the "Preface" to the first edition, Bodin attacks Machiavelli for having taught that commonwealths could be stably founded on injustice (A70). To refute this crude Machiavellism, Bodin points to the political harvest to be reaped by a prince who respects limitations on his power. He even redescribes natural law as a set of prudential maxims for avoiding revolution. In general,

> A commonweal grounded upon good laws, well united and joined in all the members thereof, easily suffer not alteration: as also to the contrary we see some states and commonweals so evil built and set together, as that they owe their fall and ruin unto the first wind that bloweth or tempest that ariseth (IV, 1, 434).

A tyrant may be a sovereign; but his position is precarious. Cruel princes "hazard their whole states" (III, 7, 373). A tyrant is always terrified: "If he be cruel, he will stand in fear that some one in so great a multitude will take revenge" (VI, 4, 721). Tyrannicide will occur, whether it is legally allowed or disallowed. Constitutional prohibitions on the right of violent resistance are but parchment barriers. By contrast:

> Fear I say of death, of infamy, and of torture: these be the revenging furies which continually vex tyrants, and with eternal terrors torment them both night and day: then envy, suspicion, fear, desire of revenge, with a thousand contrary passions at variance among themselves, do so disquiet their minds, and more cruelly tyrannize over them, than they themselves can over their slaves, with all the torments they can devise (II, 5, 226).

Tyrants are not punished in the afterlife alone, but also in the here-and-now. The laws of revenge and revolution, now christened laws of nature, provide a this-worldly seat of judgment. They help rulers focus their minds and provide them with a keen incentive to embrace some form of limited government.

All temporal jurisdiction belongs to the sovereign, except for paternal power. At first, Bodin's proposal to share the prince's authority with the head of the domestic household seems surprising for:

> The last and highest degree [of authority] is of such as have the absolute power of life and death; that is to say, power to condemn to death, and again to give life unto him which hath deserved to die; which is the highest mark of sovereignty . . . proper *only* unto sovereignty (III, 5, 326–327, my emphasis).

But despite Bodin's avowal that "the marks of sovereignty are indivisible," he makes an exception in this case: "It is needful in a well-ordered commonweal to restore unto parents the power of life and death over their children" (I, 4, 22). But why? Why should the prince divest himself of a crucial mark of sovereignty, the monopoly on punishment by death? Bodin's answer is that, by so doing, the king will be better able, in the long run, to exact obedience from his subjects: "Domestical justice and power of fathers [are] the most sure and firm foundation of laws, honor, virtue, piety, wherewith a commonweal ought to flourish" (I, 4, 23). Here we have a case of giving away power to gain power: *reculer pour mieux sauter*. If you take one step back, you can bound two steps forward. Governance is eased by a sharing of burdens. Authority is strengthened when its jurisdiction is narrowed. The public realm becomes easier to govern if something is taken out of it. This pattern of argument reappears countless times throughout the *République*. That it forms the centerpiece of Bodin's argument for religious toleration will not, therefore, be altogether surprising.

V. THE SELF-BINDING OF THE SOVEREIGN

Consider now the prohibition Bodin places upon self-binding. In his chapter "Of Sovereignty," he writes:

> If then the sovereign prince be exempted from the laws of his predecessors, much less should he be bound unto the laws and ordinances he maketh himself; for a man may well receive a law from another man, but impossible it is in nature for [him] to give a law unto himself, no more than it is to command a man's self in a matter depending of his own will (I, 8, 91–92).

This argument is significant, not least of all because of its subsequent history. Thomas Jefferson, among others, took up Bodin's proposition and applied it to the democratic sovereignty of the people.[19] In the course of the *République,* however, initial objections to binding precommitments are severely qualified. Ultimately, Bodin comes closer to Madison, who fiercely defended constitutional precommitment, than to Jefferson, who attacked it. To understand how Bodin accomplishes such a reversal, we must discover the purpose he believes served by an injunction against self-binding.

A prohibition upon self-binding is itself a restriction on the king's freedom of action. This is only logical: To be free in some respects, a king must be unfree in others. For example, the king cannot refuse in advance to hear the complaints of his subjects: "The prince cannot so bind his own hands, or make such a law unto himself [or] prohibit his grieved subjects from coming unto him with their humble supplications and requests" (I, 10, 169). Once he has heard a complaint, the prince can do as he wishes; but he cannot refuse to listen beforehand because this would be an act of self-destruction, a relinquishing of supreme power to decide what to do.

More profound than the self-binding taboo, and underlying it, is the self-destruction taboo. Self-binding is illicit when it entails a diminution of royal power. For the same reason, self-binding is permissible and even obligatory when it helps maintain or increase royal power. If the king can retain or extend his authority only by tying his hands, then tie his own hands he must. The sovereign "ought to take away all occasion of discontentment that men might have against him; and better means is there none, than to leave all that may be to the disposition of the laws and customs, no man having just cause to complain of the prince" (IV, 4, 490). Abdication of power is not always an infringement of the prince's will. It can also be a technique for asserting his will.

A concrete example occurs in Bodin's discussion of coinage. One of the main powers of the sovereign, he says, is to "appoint the value, weight, and strength of the coin" (I, 10, 175). But this, too, is a right that the king must never exercise, and for his own good:

> The prince may not make any false money, no more than he may kill or rob, neither can he alter the weight of his coin to the prejudice of his subjects, and much less of strangers, which treat with

him, and traffic with his people, for that he is subject to the law
of nations, unless he will lose the name and majesty of a king (VI,
3, 687).

Public credit is a vital resource for the crown. By committing
himself in advance to coins of fixed value, the king can success-
fully resist pressures to depreciate, cultivate the confidence of
creditors, and retain better control of the economy in general.
Self-binding is an effective technique for indirectly increasing one's power. Once we have grasped this paradox, we will
have no trouble explaining how Bodin can both advocate absolute sovereignty and argue that a commonwealth "should by
laws, and not by the prince's will and pleasure, be governed"
(IV, 4, 490). After all, there are only twenty-four hours in a
sovereign's day. General laws are much less time-consuming,
yield greater return per unit of effort, than particular proclamations and decrees. A king is not legally obliged to lay down
general rules and keep them; but if he has a grain of sense, he
will do so (IV, 4, 486). Utterly self-interested princes, if they
see clearly, will make substantial concessions to their subjects.
The sovereign aristocracy of Venice provides a revealing example. Their willingness to relinquish small bits of privilege and
power is neither altruistic, nor pious, nor required by law:

> The Venetians, to maintain their Aristocratical estate, impart some
> small offices unto the people, contract alliances with them, borrow
> of them to bind them to the maintenance of the state; and disarm
> them quite: and to make them more mild and pliable, they give
> them full scope and liberty to all sorts of pleasures: and some-
> times they make their rich citizens burgesses (VI, 4, 711).

Voluntary sharing of privilege and power is neither legally nor
morally required. It is a shrewd bargain negotiated to win cooperation. Constitutions *are* bargains. Even absolute kings, usually considered the arch-enemies of constitutionalism, can see
the advantage of striking a deal. The slyly manipulative strategy of the Venetian oligarchy included disarming the common
citizenry and, more subtly, making them creditors to give them
a stake in the state's stability. The freedoms and minor powers
devolved upon the commoners, in any case, were justified as
serving the interests of the sovereign. This is the central para-

dox of Bodin's theory of sovereignty: Less power is more power. He says it quite explicitly: "The less the power of the sovereign is (the true marks of majesty thereunto still reserved) the more it is assured" (IV, 6, 517). In other words, by limiting himself, the sovereign is able to preserve and even strengthen himself.

The *République* endorses all strategies for maintaining and increasing royal power, which is, in turn, the sole guarantor of civil peace. The political demand to maintain power overrides legal taboos against accepting limitations on power. Traditional prohibitions against alienating the domain lands fit perfectly into this pattern. The force behind these restrictions does not derive from any conventional moral precept, such as: "*regnum* is not *dominium*," or "The goods of the community must not be treated as if they were the prince's private property." Rather, selling the domain is impermissible because it would undermine the king's independence and freedom of action. Stripped of an independent source of revenue, the prince would be forced to irritate and estrange the public by imposing onerous taxes:

> To the end that princes should not be forced to overcharge their subjects with imposts, or to seek any unlawful means to forfeit their goods, all monarchs and states have held it for a general and undoubted law, that the public revenues [e.g., from the domain lands] should be holy, sacred, and inalienable, either by contract or prescription (VI, 2, 651).

To prevent monarchs from acting in a self-destructive manner, it is indispensable to tie their hands, to withdraw their income from their own control.

Bodin uniformly justifies prohibitions and entitlements by adducing their beneficial consequences for royal power. To tax without consent is, in principle, a violation of the rights of subjects. But it is also, and far more importantly, a danger to the stability of the regime. Writers who encourage the prince to tax without consent are counseling self-destruction:

> Now certainly it is a greater offense to infect princes with this doctrine than it is to rob and steal. . . . They that maintain such opinions, show the lion his claws. . . . [M]ade worse by instruction [the prince proves] to be a tyrant . . . and break[s] all the laws

both of God and man: and afterward enflamed with corrupt desires and affections, which altogether weaken the more noble parts
of the mind, he quickly breaketh out from covetousness to unjust
confiscations, from lust to adultery, from wrath to murder (I, 8,
109).

Loss of self-control is breakdown of power. Contrariwise, by
voluntarily accepting stabilizing constraints, a prince can increase his capacity soberly to achieve his ends. Even if the sovereign were not legally obliged to consult the Estates before
levying a tax, he could increase his revenues by granting the
Estates a role in the taxing process. Voluntary compliance is the
most efficient method for extracting resources from tight-fisted
subjects.

The command theory of law sounds advantageous for the
sovereign. But the power to *make* law is only valuable to the
extent that law is *obeyed*. Even if there were not formal or legal
conditions on his lawmaking authority, the prince must in fact
share power with others and accept limits on himself if only to
secure obedience. Traditions are valid only if they are permitted to remain in effect by the king's will: "Custom hath no force
but by suffrance, and so long as it pleaseth the sovereignty" (I,
10, 161).[20] Predictably, however, Bodin proceeds to cast doubt
on the superiority of prince-made law over inherited custom.
Interested in obedience, no ruler will casually dissolve customs
and promulgate unheard-of laws: "Newness in matter of law
is always contemptible, whereas to the contrary, the reverence
of antiquity is so great, as that it giveth strength enough unto
a law to cause it to be of itself obeyed without the authority of
any magistrate at all joined unto it" (IV, 3, 469–470).[21] Lawmaking power is not self-sufficient. To ensure obedience to his
laws, the sovereign must rely on custom.

He must also rely on the cooperation of the Estates, general
and provincial, of the parlements, and of the officers of the
realm. Similarly, "There is nothing that giveth greater credit
and authority unto the laws and commandments of a prince, a
people, or state, or in any manner of commonweal, than to
cause them to pass by the advice of a grave and wise Senate or
Council" (III, 1, 254).[22] While legally independent, the sover-

eign lacks a professional civil service and is therefore politically dependent on nonappointed officials who make his laws acceptable.

The king is not formally obliged to bow to the wishes of magistrates, for instance. While retaining the right of remonstrance, parlements cannot finally refuse to register royal edicts. Nevertheless, the magistrate is the "living and breathing law" (III, 5, 325), and ignoring his wishes may result in the total nullity of the king's most cherished commands. In other words, the *informal power* of judges is enormous. While the king is officially an uncommanded commander, he must clearly, if he wants to achieve his own goals, expose himself to considerable influence from below:

> Neither ought the prince . . . knowing the magistrates to be of contrary opinion unto his, to constrain them thereunto: for the ignorant and common people is no ways more moved to disloyalty, and contempt of their prince's edicts and laws, than to see the magistrates hardly dealt withall, and the laws by them contrary to their good liking published and enforced (III, 4, 323).

Rather than combining medieval natural law and modern absolutism in a thoughtlessly eclectic fashion, Bodin focuses single-mindedly on the varieties of informal rights and powers that any calculating monarch must grant his subjects if he is to exert his authority effectively.

In justifying the separation of powers, too, Bodin emphasizes its power-enhancing function. An independent judiciary increases the king's capacity to govern. Malefactors must be punished; but if the king exacts penalties personally, he will create resentments that may, in turn, weaken his authority. Thus, a clever sovereign will reserve to himself the distribution of rewards while delegating to independent magistrates the job of issuing condemnations and exacting fines: "In which doing, they who receive the benefits shall have good cause to love, respect, and reverence the prince their benefactor; and those who are condemned shall yet have no occasion at all to hate him, but shall still discharge their choler upon the magistrates and judges" (IV, 6, 512). The separation of powers, according to this analysis has serious resentment-deflecting and responsibility-ducking functions. An independent judiciary, in any case, is not meant to paralyze power but, on the contrary, to increase the government's capacity to do its job.[23]

In general, absolute power is less powerful than limited power because power-wielders need cooperation not just compliance.[24] In both democracy and monarchy, power-sharing is prudent:

> If the prince or the people shall take upon themselves the authority of the Senate, or the commands, offices, or jurisdictions of the magistrates; it is much to be feared, lest that they, destitute of all help, shall at the length be spoiled of their own sovereign majesty also (IV, 6, 518).

Because he needs voluntary cooperation, a prince cannot safely engross control of all political functions.

The basic "dialectic" in Bodin's argument can be illustrated in a number of other ways. While any attempt to subordinate the king to the Estates will lead to chaos,[25] "a combining of a monarchy with a popular government" is "the most assured monarchy that is" (II, 7, 250).[26] In the same vein:

> how necessary the assemblies and meeting of the whole people for to consult of matters are is hereby perceived, in that the people which may so call together such counsels, with them all things go well: whereas others which may not so do, are oppressed with tributes and servitude (III, 7, 385).

If the king ignores the Estates, civil war will ensue; if he consults the Estates he can stabilize and enlarge his authority: "so far it is from that such an assembly in any thing diminisheth the power of a sovereign prince, as that thereby his majesty is the more increased and augmented" (II, 1, 192). By stressing that consultation is not required legally, Bodin emphasizes how indispensable it is politically.

Ultimately it is contrary to the king's interest to "put to sleep" the old representative assemblies:

> The just monarchy hath not any more assured foundation or stay than the Estates of the people, communities, corporations, and colleges. For if need be for the king to levy money, to raise forces,

to maintain the state against the enemy, it cannot be better done than by the estates of the people, and of every province, town, and community (III, 7, 384).

The sovereign should retain these traditional bodies not because he is "just," and not because of the sanctity of tradition, but for purely calculating and self-interested motives.[27] The prince's power cannot be measured by his capacity to command a bending of the knee. More significant is his ability to solve whatever problems are at hand. If the problems he faces are exceptionally difficult, he will need a great deal of help. While the "rights" of subjects are not guaranteed constitutionally, as a result, they may be secured by the needs of power:

> For where can things for the curing of the diseases of the sick commonwealth, or for the amendment of the people, or for the establishing of laws, or for the reforming of the state, be better debated or handled, than before the prince in his Senate before the people (III, 7, 384)?

For subjects aiming to extract political concessions from the king, the threat of violent resistance is less effective than the threat to withdraw cooperation. Commands-backed-by-force are too crude to mobilize cooperation. Self-interest alone will thus lead a rational prince to establish or retain some kind of representative assembly.

In general, a people free to express itself is more tractable and forthcoming than one compelled to remain silent. A wise prince will realize that he can personally benefit from whatever freedom of speech he concedes. A king who repressed the Estates would deprive himself of a vital source of information. When the prince appears at the meeting of the Estates, he acquires substantial useful knowledge:

> There [the representatives] confer of the affairs concerning the whole body of the commonweal, and of the members thereof; there are heard and understood the just complaints and grievances of the poor subjects, which never otherwise come unto the prince's ears; there are discovered and laid open the robberies and extortions committed in the prince's name; whereof he knoweth nothing (III, 7, 384).

By granting freedom to his subjects, the monarch can gain control over his own inferior agents. In some cases, moreover, criticism strengthens the monarch; and therefore an intelligent king "refuseth not to be freely and discreetly reproved for that he hath done amiss" (II, 4, 212). Before he can correct his own mistakes, a prince has to learn about them, and where can he acquire this knowledge, if not from a free-spoken assembly?

VI. Religion

Bodin's views on religious persecution and state power naturally allied him with the *politiques*. Unlike the *dévots* or Catholic extremists with whom the *politiques* are usually contrasted, he preferred civil peace to religious uniformity and was thus accused of abandoning "noble" for "base" aims. Toleration was difficult because "the people everywhere [are] most jealous of their religion" and "cannot . . . endure any rites and ceremonies, differing from the religion by themselves generally received." Neither laws nor magistrates can restrain "bands of men" whose "rage will oft times most furiously break out" (III, 7, 381). Ordinary men and women in sixteenth-century France did not understand the need for separating religious and political allegiances. Many preferred civil war to sharing their country with heretics. First-hand experience of self-destructive dispositions on the part of the people may have made Bodin somewhat less scornful of paternalism than we tend to be today.

The unsuccessful Colloquy of Poissy (1561) put an end to hopes for doctrinal reconciliation. Because Calvinists were too numerous, well-armed, and committed to be reconverted, attempts to suppress dissent by force would have imposed unacceptable costs on all Frenchmen. The situation was unprecedented. Faced with what he saw as intractable sectarian divisions, Bodin responded in an appropriately radical way. He abandoned the traditional view that social cohesion required all subjects to share religious beliefs. As a deputy at the Estates-General of 1576, the very year his great political work first appeared, he vigorously advocated a policy of toleration and conciliation with Huguenots. Compromise was the only feasible alternative to civil war.[28]

The *République* issues in a plea that "no man be forbidden the private exercise of such his religion" (IV, 7, 539). The king should cease attempting to save souls, punish heretics, or eliminate religious dissonance. Such efforts only undermine political order and provoke rebellion. Sovereign authority should lower its sights, resting satisfied with the lesser goal of establishing a *modus vivendi* between conflicting groups. Bodin praises one ancient emperor for enacting a "law of forgetfulness" and another for issuing an edict of "union and tranquillity or quietness," both aiming "to reconcile the companies of all sorts of religions among themselves" (III, 7, 382). This is essentially the policy he favors for France. Subjects owe obedience to their sovereign on the secular ground that he, in turn, guarantees internal and external peace. Peace is not an end-in-itself, to be sure, any more than food or shelter are; but it is an essential precondition for every worthwhile goal: "It is impossible for a commonweal to flourish in religion, justice, charity, integrity of life, and in all the liberal sciences and mechanic arts, if the citizens enjoy not a firm and lasting peace" (V, 5, 598).

In rejoinder to his *dévot* critics, Bodin could well have said: Lower goals serve higher ones. Instead of futilely attempting to confer moral perfection or Christian redemption on his subjects, the monarch should attempt to "avoid commotions, troubles, and civil war" (IV, 7, 537). If the king keeps the peace, his subjects can pursue a wide variety of spiritual objectives. The state is a legal framework in which moral antagonists can coexist and cooperate in secular undertakings. Sectarian religions can also flourish, but only so long as they adapt themselves to the rules of peaceful coexistence.

No sooner was the *République* published than it was attacked. In *dévot* circles, at least, it was viewed as a scandalous defense of religious pluralism and, by implication, as an impious condemnation of the St. Bartholomew's day massacre.[29] It is crucial to keep these hostile reactions in mind when examining Bodin's statements that religion is essential to the state (e.g., "Preface," A70; and VI, 1, 645). Consider this frequently cited and potentially misleading passage:

> There is nothing which doth more uphold and maintain the states
> and Commonweals than religion and . . . it is the principal foun-

dation of the power and strength of monarchies and Seignories
as also for the execution of justice, for the obedience of the subjects, the reverence of the magistrates, for the fear of doing evil,
and for the mutual love and amity of every one towards other
(IV, 7, 536).

To understand what Bodin is saying, we must focus on what
he is denying. Remarkable for contemporaries was his refusal
to endow the state with an overriding obligation to establish
true religion. Even a false religion, he says, is better than none.
To pre-empt or outbid the *dévot* opposition, he sometimes declares that the ultimate goal of every commonwealth is religious. But, in fact, the state's real goal is nothing holier than
social peace.

Bodin admits that religion is "a matter very considerable" (VI,
1, 648). But the *République* is fundamentally nonreligious: "I
here speak not but of temporal sovereignty, which is the subject
that I entreat of" (I, 9, 137). As J. W. Allen wrote: "You can
eliminate from Bodin's *Republic* all his references to God, and
to Princes as the lieutenants of God, and the whole structure
will stand unaltered."[30] Although it has frequently been dis-
puted, Allen's analysis seems basically correct. At several points,
for example, Bodin emphasizes the nonidentity of religious and
political change.[31] Concerned with maintenance of *political*
communities, he attends exclusively to religion's secular effects.
History shows that foul conspiracies against the commonwealth
have often been hatched "under shadow of religion" (III, 7,
380). That religion can be a pretext was memorably demonstrated by the way secular rulers used the Reformation as an
excuse to expropriate ecclesiastical property. The Church's
enormous wealth "hath ministered occasion of troubles and se-
ditions against the clergy, throughout all Europe, when as in
show [the princes] made a color of religion" (V, 2, 575). Bodin
was especially concerned with the pretext of religion for fear
that "conspiracies and rebellions of mutinous subjects against
their sovereign princes" would be justified by an "especial commandment of God" (II, 5, 224). If used to undermine obedience, religion can plunge the state into anarchy: "But yet this
is especially to be considered, that we pretend not the vain show
of religion, or rather of superstition, against our prince's com-

mands, and so upon a conscience evil-grounded open a way unto rebellion" (III, 4, 325). Aware that religion may be adduced as a pretext for rebellion, the sovereign prince will judge every appearance of faith by a secular standard.

In the *République*, at least, religion captures Bodin's attention because of its influence on the sovereign's capacity to keep the peace. A false religion is nevertheless useful because it "doth yet hold men in fear and awe, both of the laws and of the magistrates, as also in mutual duties and offices one of them towards another" (IV, 7, 539).[32] If fear of hellfire lends credibility to the law, then religion is a welcome ally: "Neither is it to be expected that either prince or magistrate shall reduce those subjects under the obedience of the laws that have trodden all religion under foot" (VI, 1, 645). In other words, Bodin advances a social-prop theory of religion. The utility of religion does not hinge upon its truth.

The concept of sovereignty itself was profoundly anticlerical. It implied, primarily, the independence of the king from papal control. The French king was the model of an absolute sovereign because he cultivated this independence much more assiduously than his fellow monarchs:

> But howsoever the Bishop of Rome pretended to have a sovereignty over all Christian princes, not only in spiritual, but also in temporal affairs. . . . Yet could not our kings even for any most short time endure the servitude of the bishop of Rome, nor be moved with any of their excommunications, which the popes used as fire-brands to the firing of the Christian commonweals (I, 9, 145).

In the same vein, Bodin remarks that the church owns too much land, that the king's word should be sufficient without any religious oath being superadded, and that a Christian prince must keep his word to infidels (I, 8, 92 and V, 6, 628). Religion is even impiously said to vary with climate.[33] Bodin's analysis of sovereignty, in sum, is essentially nonreligious. His idea of supreme authority was designed to fit *all* states, pagan as well as Christian.

VII. Toleration and the Power of the Prince

We are now in a position to apply our analysis of Bodin's theory of sovereignty to his discussion of religion. That the state can increase its authority by restricting its jurisdiction also serves as Bodin's principal argument for toleration. The *République* counsels a propitiatory approach: "And albeit a prince had the power by force to repress and reform a mutinous and rebellious people, yet ought he not so to do, if otherwise he may appease them" (IV, 7, 532). Repression is to be avoided, if at all possible, because it is self-defeating. This brings us quite close to Bodin's central argument for toleration:

> I will not here in so great variety of people so much differing among themselves in religion, take upon me to determine which of them is the best (howbeit that there can be but one such, one truth, and one divine law, by the mouth of God published) but if the prince well assured of the truth of his religion, would draw his subjects thereunto, divided into sects and factions, he must not therein (in my opinion) use force (IV, 7, 537).

Bodin argues against slavery on the grounds that it poses a threat to slaveowners (I, 5, 32–46). In advocating toleration, he again slights the rights of the persecuted, concentrating instead upon the interests of the persecutors. From the prince's own viewpoint, violence is profoundly counterproductive. It not only fuels civil hatred and weakens authority; but it also prevents the conversion of heretics and even creates hypocrites and atheists: "The more [the minds of men] are forced, the more froward and stubborn they become" (IV, 7, 537).[34] Naturally, kings desire to secure religious homogeneity. But forcing consciences will not do: "minds resolved, the more they are crossed, the stiffer they are" (III, 7, 382). A king will have a better chance of saving souls if he simply tolerates dissenters and lives a pious life according to the teachings of his church. Example will win more conversions than force.

Against zealots of all denominations, Bodin—who was clearly a believer of some sort—argues that tolerance of religious diversity does not imply personal indifference to religion.[35] Not only political power, but even the piety of the prince, can survive a reform that leaves religion up to individuals. Even more relevant for France, perhaps, is the Roman example. The Romans, although they insisted on public worship of Roman gods, "Yet for all that did they easily suffer every man privately within the city to use his own manner and fashion, and his own religion" (IV, 7, 538). Private worship leaves the public realm untouched; indeed, it can leave it much improved.

Bodin's approach to the toleration question is consciously eclectic. To forge an alliance among anti-persecution parties, he touches all bases. He argues (1) that a man's conscience, by natural necessity, cannot be compelled, (2) that persecution leads to hypocrisy, atheism, and disobedience, and (3) that God accepts any form of worship so long as it comes from a pure heart. But his basic concern is to protect neither God nor the individual but rather the state. He never mentions that the violent suppression of dissenters might be morally wrong. But he *does* underline the wild imprudence of using violence if the sovereign is at all uncertain of success, for: "There can be nothing more dangerous unto a prince, than to make proof of his forces against his subjects, except he be well assured to prevail against them: which otherwise were but to arm a lion, and to show him his claws, wherewith to tear his master" (III, 7, 382). Here is a clear echo of Bodin's fundamental argument: A prince has a right to repress religious dissent; but if he exercises it, he risks destruction. As a self-imposed limit on the king's authority over the lives of his subjects, toleration is sovereignty-reinforcing. The very word *toleration* derives from the Latin for strength: to stand up, support, and sustain. The doctrine of toleration could thus be incorporated smoothly into the political program of absolutism. Religious liberality promotes the ascendancy of the crown.

Superficially, Bodin agrees that the ideal recipe for social cohesion remains *une foi, une loi, un roi*. Subjects have no inalienable right to freedom of conscience. But religious homogeneity is now impossible. Here, as always, the sovereign must adapt to the situation. Reconverting or suppressing dissenters would be the optimal solution,

> But it may be that the consent and agreement of the nobility and people in a new religion or sect, may be so puissant & strong, as that to repress or alter the same, should be a thing impossible, or

at leastwise marvelous difficult, without the extreme peril and danger of the whole state. . . . Wherefore that religion or sect is to be suffered, which without the hazard and destruction of the state cannot be taken away: The health and welfare of the Commonweal being the chief thing the law respecteth (III, 7, 382).

The best is the enemy of the good; piety can subvert peace. To wield power effectively, the ruler must acquiesce in irreconcilable sectarian divisions. Religious unity remains an ideal, but, in the circumstances, religious diversity is the only realistic option.

VIII. NEUTRALITY AND FACTION

Some great noblemen hoped for a *cuius regio, eius religio* solution in France, the king reduced to a figurehead and local princes ruling over semi-autonomous religious units. In other words, toleration was *not* the only available alternative to civil war: Partition was also possible. But Bodin emphatically rejects partition as a way of handling religious diversity. The dangerous side-effects of faction are best neutralized in a *large* kingdom. He asserts repeatedly that "The greater the Monarchy is, the more goodly and flourishing it is, and the subject more happy, and living in an assured peace" (VI, 4, 721). Great scale promotes peace because "'Conversions and changes of commonweals do more often happen in little and small cities or states, than in great kingdoms full of great provinces, and people." A "small commonweal," he goes on to say, "is soon divided into two parts or factions" (IV, 1, 432). Such a polarized situation is extremely dangerous. Since conciliation cannot be imposed, the only peace-promoting and union-preserving alternative is to diffuse tensions by proliferating factions. In the *Heptaplomeres*, Toralba cryptically remarks that "Many things cannot be opposite by nature to the same thing," meaning that a surfeit of sects renders two-way polarization unlikely. And Octavius adds: "For this reason, I think, the kings of the Turks and Persians admit every kind of religion in the state, and in a remarkable harmony they reconcile all citizens and foreigners who differ in religions among themselves and with the state."[36] For this reason, too, Bodin recommends increasing the size of the population in order to domesticate faction: "There is nothing more dangerous than to have the subjects divided into two factions without a mean, the which doth usually fall out in cities where there are but few citizens" (V, 2, 571). The advantage of large size is its attendant pluralism; peace can be achieved through multiplicity.[37] Civic concord can be fostered not only by religious homogeneity but also by multiplication of sects. Two denominations will inevitably be locked in war; while a promiscuous variety of religions will settle comfortably into peace. Although strikingly Madisonian, this argument is also distinctive. Bodin does not, for example, argue that a proliferation of sects will prevent a majority from imposing its wishes on minorities. Rather, "Where there be more than two sects or sorts, there must needs be some in the mean betwixt the two contrary extremes, which may set them agreed, which otherwise of themselves would never fall to agreement" (540). Large states can contain faction because they naturally produce mediators to manage and regulate conflict. A society divided along a single cleavage is unlikely to yield neutral arbiters.

Bodin's discussion of toleration in Book Four, chapter 7 deserves to be reconstructed in some detail. He begins by reiterating that, in some circumstances, religion can help quell civil war by striking fear into the hearts of citizens:

> For at such time as the Florentines were fallen out into such a fury among themselves, as the city swam with the blood and slaughter of the citizens: and that they could by no means be parted, Francis Soderin the bishop, attired in his bishoplike attire and attended upon with a company of priests, and a cross carried before him, came into the midst of the furious citizens, so bandying it one against another; at the sight and presence of whom, they all for the reverend fear of religion upon the sudden laid down their weapons, and so without more ado, got themselves home every man unto his own house (IV, 7, 534).

But why, in the 1570s and in France, would Bodin choose to expand on religion's contribution to social peace? He soon adds, again invoking the example of Florence, that "deadly broils" can be resolved only by "mediation" of a neutral bystander. Most important of all, once a cycle of revenge and counter-revenge has become established, the factions involved cannot bring it to a halt by themselves, even if they ardently wish to, so long as they are attached to an ethic of honor:

> Oftentimes it happens that the citizens, divided into factions weary at length of their murders and tumults, seek but to find an occasion for them to fall to agreement; yet being of opinion it to touch them in honor that should first seek for peace, therefore continue their bloody quarrels until they have utterly ruined one another, if some third man interpose not himself betwixt them for the making of them friends (IV, 7, 535).[38]

In popular and aristocratic commonwealths, mediation of a neutral party is difficult to come by. In a monarchy, nothing could be easier. Indeed, this is the chief advantage of the monarchical form of government. The king, so long as he remains a third man, strategically located above the battle, can impose peace on warring factions.

In Bodin's France, unlike in Soderini's Florence, the Catholic Church could not play the neutral moderator, for Catholicism was one of the partisans. Thus, Bodin's discussion of Soderini cannot be interpreted as an endorsement of religiously imposed order. Here is a danger that every prudent sovereign must avoid:

> Sometime it happeneth the sovereign prince to make himself a party, instead of holding the place of a sovereign Judge: in which doing for all that he shall be no more but the head of one party, and so undoubtedly put himself in danger of his life, and that especially when such dangerous seditions and factions be not grounded upon matters directly touching his estate, but otherwise, as it has happened in almost all Europe within this fifty years, in the wars made for matters of religion (IV, 7, 535).

Only by nonentanglement, by adopting a position of neutrality toward religious conflict, by viewing questions of religion as alien to questions of state, can the prince avoid anarchy and retain power. The Catholic-Calvinist struggle is solely a "matter of religion." When divisive and essentially nonpolitical issues are at stake, the king must remain sovereignly nonpartisan.

In apparent disregard of this concern for nonpartisanship, Bodin endorses Solon's famous "law for part-taking," whereby no Athenian citizen was allowed to remain neutral in cases of factious conflict: "which unto many seemed a thing unreasonable, considering that the greatest praise and commendation of a good subject is; to be a quite civil man, desirous and doing the best that he can to live in peace" (IV, 7, 540). This strange law, however, was not quite as unreasonable as it seems. It inhibited troublemakers hoping to reap profits from the sidelines after having fomented factional discord. And it also encouraged moderate parties to work more actively to prevent the outbreak of factional war. When conflict had already erupted, the law of part-taking was a reliable mechanism for recruiting the community's otherwise reticent élites, ensuring the presence of some relatively cool heads on each side, thereby helping bring the conflict to a speedy end. By involving everyone, a legal prohibition on neutrality provided a powerful incentive for responsible citizens to steer the community away from civil war.

How is this digression related to Bodin's central argument for a policy of religious toleration? It seems, for a moment, that he is now reversing himself and arguing *against* the neutrality of the prince. Engagement not detachment is essential. It is always advantageous, in time of war, for weaker parties to join the stronger. During the Peloponnesian War, Theramenes "had kept himself quiet, and stood still looking on, but as an idle beholder, without taking part either with the one or with the other." This was an unwise policy, for he "was himself at the last forsaken of all, and so left unto the mercy of the tyrants, who made him a miserable spectacle unto all men, and in the end most cruelly put him to death" (IV, 7, 541). Does this mean that neutrality is dangerous and partisanship wise? Is Bodin suggesting, despite his opposition to the extreme Catholics,[39] that the French king should simply side with one party, just as the League wished?

Not at all. Any monarch desiring to stay safely aloof cannot remain a passive spectator but must instead, from his position of neutrality, deliberately stage-manage the factional struggle: "He therefore which will stand as neuter, whether it be in civil war, or in wars amongst strangers, ought at the least to do his endeavor to set the rest agreed" (IV, 7, 541). Neutrality is not *fainéantise* but rather a combination of nonpartisanship and mediation. The state must adopt an active role if a stable polity is to be created. The prince of a religiously divided kingdom cannot simply dispense justice and thereby maintain the pre-existent social balance, for there is no spontaneous social balance. He must be much more dynamic, innovative, creative than traditional kings. He must be willing relentlessly to pressure and manipulate his subjects without, of course, provoking unnecessary resentments.

Book 5, chapter 6, where Bodin again appraises the politically ambiguous consequences of neutrality, provides another perspective. The topic here is the prince who adopts a stance of nonalignment toward conflicting foreign powers. But Bodin's argument mirrors the earlier passage: "It is therefore commendable for the greatest and mightiest princes to remain neuters" (V, 6, 624). This is almost always the best course if the prince has sufficient power to act as a mediator: "It is therefore more safe for him that remains a neuter to mediate a peace, than to nourish war" (V, 6, 624). This is a central tenet of *politique* thought: The state is a neutral power mediating among hostile parties all of whom will thrive best in peace but none of whom can achieve peace without help. Bodin ably summarizes this precept as follows:

> One of the most necessary things for the assurance of treaties of peace and alliance, is to name some great and mightier Prince to be judge and umpire in case of contravention, that they may have recourse unto him to mediate an agreement betwixt them; who being equal, cannot with their honors refuse war, nor demand peace (V, 6, 625).

Translated into domestic policy this means that the state can serve as an umpire between religious factions only if it refuses to identify itself too closely with the spiritual aspirations of any one of them. By subjecting himself to an extreme Catholic faction, a king who attacked the Huguenots would enfeeble the crown. The peace-keeping regime is necessarily unresponsive; or rather, the king must both represent and not represent his subjects. He must hold their loyalty but he must not reflect their uncompromising and vengeful attitudes when conducting affairs of state.[40]

IX. THE LAW OF SILENCE

In Book IV of the *Heptaplomeres* Coronaeus asks: "Is it proper for a good man to discuss religion?"[41] In general, all seven speakers agree that discussions of religion can be dangerous. By forbidding debate, many other worthwhile activities are made possible for the first time. Where nothing is private, nothing is public: The withdrawal of intractable problems from the agenda of discussion makes discussion of *other* issues more congenial, rational, and constructive. Limits strengthen; restrictions are possibility-creating. For example:

> At Siena the Senate for a long time permitted academies, but the condition was stipulated that there would be no discussions about divine matters and the decrees of the popes. Although one man foolishly violated this edict and suffered capital punishment, there have been no uprisings in that city up to this day.[42]

The *Heptaplomeres* itself contains an extraordinarily free-wheeling discussion of religious questions by a multidenominational group including a Catholic, a Calvinist, a Lutheran, a Jew, a Mohammedan, and a skeptic. Lengthy debate, however, leads no one to change his mind. The dialogue then concludes: "Afterwards they held no other conversation about religion, although each one defended his religion with the supreme sanctity of his life."[43]

The idea of imposing a law of silence upon religious controversies had already appeared in the *République*. Once a religion is established, no public disputes about doctrine or even attempts at rational demonstration should be allowed. Some of Bodin's arguments for a legally enforced policy of nondiscussion are overtly religious. Faith, which is ultimately beyond reason, can only be weakened by necessarily unsuccessful attempts to defend it rationally. Once raised, however, doubts will fester, not only to undermine religion but ultimately to destroy the state.

Bodin approves heartily of the truce between Lutherans and Catholics established by the Peace of Augsburg (1555). Strict laws should prohibit public disputations of religion, which after long civil war was by the estates and princes of the German empire provided for, and a decree made, that the princes should with mutual consent defend both the Roman and Saxon religion: whereunto that was also joined, That no man should upon pain of death dispute of the religions. Which severe punishments, after that the German magistrates had inflicted upon diverse, all Germany was afterwards at good quiet & rest: no man daring more to dispute of matters of religion (IV, 7, 536).[44]

To apply his Augsburg sympathies to France, Bodin has to shift ground slightly. Peace can be established, even in a unified kingdom containing a multiplicity of sects, so long as a strict gag rule is imposed upon questions of dogma. Especially in a pluralistic realm, public speech should be purged of doctrinal disputes. Here is Bodin's least secular argument for imposing silence on religious controversy:

> Nothing is so firm and stable, nothing so manifest and clear (except it rest upon most plain and undoubtful demonstrations) which may not by disputation and force of argument be obscured or made doubtful: and especially where that which is called into question, or dispute, resteth not so much upon demonstration or reason, as upon the assurance of faith and belief only: which they which seek by demonstrations and publishing of books to perform, they are not only mad with reason, but weaken also the foundations of all sorts of religions (IV, 7, 535).

The ecumenical appeal implicit in the last phrase is reinforced by the hint that religion cannot yield to rational consideration. Bodin is not saying that the Catholic religion is true and therefore that freedom to dispute it is inherently absurd and immoral. Rather, he is saying that rational proofs of religion are open to doubt and, to avoid the ravages of doubt, we should just cease talking about it. The limits of reason dictate removal of rationally irresolvable questions from the public agenda.

X. Bodin's Legacy

The paradox that limited power is more powerful than unlimited power, the affiliated notion that religious toleration is sov-

ereignty-reinforcing, and even the suggestion that irresolvable
disputes are best handled by methods of avoidance all play an
important role in political theory after the sixteenth century. A
few randomly chosen examples will demonstrate that the influence of these ideas was broad and deep and certainly not limited to France.

One of Spinoza's central themes is that the sovereign has no
right to destroy or even diminish his own power, and that he
must therefore tolerate religious diversity. Rulers are also re-
assured that "Liberty can be conceded to every man without
injury to the rights and authority of sovereign power."[45] Locke
not only argues that legal restraints enhance the freedom of
the constrained individual;[46] but he noticeably emphasizes the
self-defeating or power-eroding effects of religious intolerance.[47] Montesquieu stresses that too much power will make a
sovereign insecure and that, under modern conditions, even
legally unlimited rulers have an interest in being virtuous.[48] In
the *Persian Letters,* he asserts that harsh rule makes a country
ungovernable and, more pertinently, that the Revocation of the
Edict of Nantes was self-defeating: it underminded the power
of the French state by depriving the nation of some of its most
useful citizens.[49] According to Kant, finally, civil freedoms cannot be infringed without a general decline in state power: "For
this reason [i.e., to maintain state power], restrictions placed
upon personal activities are increasingly relaxed, and general
freedom of religion is granted."[50]

The mutually reinforcing relation between individual freedoms and sovereign authority was first elaborated at unforget-
table length by Jean Bodin. The opening of a legal path to
autocracy was not, therefore, the main intellectual contribution
of his great work.[51] With persistence and clarity, Bodin invoked
raison d'état to justify semi-constitutional restraints on sovereign
power. This was his most important legacy to subsequent theorists. We might, of course, conclude that he was an immoral
realist, cynically reducing the rights of subjects to the utility of
princes. Alternatively, we can judge him to be an unrealistic
moralist, naively expecting abusive regimes to collapse and authorities voluntarily to limit their own caprice. The plausibility
of both assessments testifies to the obscure but tantalizing drama
of the *République.*

NOTES

1. Jean Bodin, *The Six Bookes of a Commonweal* (Cambridge: Harvard University Press, 1962), I, 2, 11. All in-text references are to book, chapter, and page of this English translation of 1606 which was based on both the French and Latin versions of the original. Spelling and punctuation have been modernized.
2. For example, John Rawls, "Justice as Fairness: Political Not Metaphysical," *Philosophy and Public Affairs* 14 (Summer 1985): 225.
3. Emile Durkheim, "Rapport de l'Etat et de l'individu," *Leçons de Sociologie*, Paris: Presses Universitaires de France, 1950, pp. 91–99.
4. Another notable proponent of this counterintuitive thesis was Pierre Bayle. Universally acknowledged as a central figure in the history of toleration, Bayle fully supported the politics of absolutism because he believed that the state's independence from religious authorities could only be achieved if the king attained full civil supremacy. Absolutism was the only plausible remedy to clerical oppression because only an all-powerful monarch could "keep the tribe of ecclesiastics in their place," enforcing a sharp dissociation of this-worldly and other-worldly authority. Elisabeth Labrousse, *Bayle* (Oxford: Oxford University Press, 1983, p. 76). Far from being a despotic abuse of undivided power, Bayle believed, the Revocation of the Edict of Nantes symbolized Louis XIV's inability to enforce his sovereign will upon religious authorities (ibid., p. 77). While further enfeebling the state, a policy of intolerance and persecution was already a sign of crippled sovereignty.
5. Admittedly, the tautological notion that "divided sovereignty" is a logical contradiction is suggested by Bodin's remark that a mixed state "was never found" (II, 1, 194).
6. Cf., Bodin, *Six Bookes*, I, 10, 159, 160.
7. For example, "The prince is bound by force of arms and of his laws to maintain his subjects in surety of their persons, their goods, and families: for which the subjects by a reciprocal obligation owe unto their prince, faith, subjection, obeyance, aid, and succour" (I, 7, 69).
8. Being a traditionalist by training and temperament, Bodin also employs argument-by-analogy in making his case for the king's monopoly on supreme power. The universe as a whole is organized hierarchically as a great chain of being: everywhere we look, we discern "royal" authority. Nature provides the archetype which society must replicate. First of all, a family, "which is the true image of a commonweal," has but a single father. Moreover: "All the laws of nature guide us unto a monarchy, whether that we behold

[the human body] which hath . . . but one head for all the members, whereupon depends the will, moving and feeling: or if we look to this great world which hath but one sovereign God: or if we erect our eyes to heaven, we shall see but one sun: and even in sociable creatures, we see they cannot admit many kings, nor many lords, how good soever" (VI, 4, 718). To some extent, then, Bodin's political theory derives from his metaphysical views about cosmic hierarchy and stability. C. R. Baxter, "Jean Bodin's Daemon and his Conversion to Judaism," in *Jean Bodin: Verhandlungen der internationalen Bodin Tagung in München*, ed. Horst Denzer (Munich: Beck, 1973), pp. 1–21. On the other hand, the immediate occasion for his fervid endorsement of the absolutist cause was not his pious appreciation of God's handiwork, but rather the chaos of France's religious civil wars. He was more concerned to avoid murderous disorder than to achieve divinely anointed perfection. Bodin's hostility toward private armies and private justice was sharpened by personal experience: He was at Paris during the St. Bartholomew's Day massacre. A "miserable anarchy," he says, "is the plague of all states" (VI, 4, 717). True, civil war was also aesthetically displeasing, that is, discordant with the beauties of the *Stufenkosmos*. But Bodin's proposals for avoiding it were more worldly, pragmatic, crafty, and responsive to daily events than a disproportionate stress on his outmoded metaphysics would suggest. One might say, of course, that Bodin combines the classical argument that politics should *mirror* natural order with a quite distinct claim that politics must *quell* natural disorder. Nature includes sin (I, 5, 35), that is to say, man's inborn unruliness. Human nature, in all its wretchedness, is clearly revealed in primitive societies: "The first sort of men were most given to rapine, murder, and theft, delighting in nothing more, nor accounting any honor greater than to rob and kill, and to oppress the weaker sort as slaves" (III, 7, 362). At all stages of social development, human beings must be bridled by external controls. Their spontaneous wishes—for example, their desire to inflict pain on the weak—are unworthy of respect. The bestial and disorderly side of human nature finds better opportunity to express itself in some situations than in others. Denominational conflict seems particularly well-suited for releasing such primordial cruelty. To counter this contemporary version of a perennial threat, a strong ruler must take control and gain a firm monopoly on all legitimate use of violence within the realm. Ultimately, however, Bodin justified authority in a wholly secular manner, not as a punishment for sin but rather as the creation of order out of disorder. To prevent France from destroying itself in factious warfare, sovereignty must be located in a monarch whose power is formally—though not actually—unlimited.

9. Note also that the magistrate is *not* bound "to obey or put into execution the prince's commands in things unjust and dishonest" (III, 4, 312).

10. That this paradox is a general one, not limited to the *République*, is stressed by Roland Mousnier: "le concept d'absolutisme est difficile pour nous car l'absolutisme, au sens littéral, est sans limite, et l'absolutisme monarchique au contraire est limité" ("Les concepts d' «ordres» d' «états», de «fidélité» et de «monarchie absolute» en France de la fin du XVe siècle à la fin du XVIIIe," "*Revue historique* 217 [1972], p. 304).

11. J. W. Allen, *A History of Political Thought in the Sixteenth Century* (London: Methuen, 1928), p. 410; Georges Weill, *Les Théories sur le pouvoir royal en France pendant les guerres de religion* (Paris: Hachette, 1891), p. 168.

12. Quentin Skinner, *The Foundations of Modern Political Thought*, vol. 2 (Cambridge: Cambridge University Press, 1978), p. 297.

13. Nannerl O. Keohane, *Philosophy and the State in France* (Princeton: Princeton University Press, 1980), p. 74.

14. Julian Franklin, *Jean Bodin and the Rise of Absolutist Theory*, (Cambridge: Cambridge University Press, 1973), pp. 69, 87.

15. Ibid., pp. 70, 92. Franklin gestures toward a distinction between "constitutional restraints" which Bodin disallows and "institutional restraints" which he accepts (Ibid., p. 98); but a perhaps exaggerated concern with legal formalities as well as commitment to a stylized "battle" between absolutism and constitutionalism prevent Franklin from exploring this distinction in depth. John Plamenatz provides the most convincing, though still offhand, assessment along these lines. Bodin, he wrote, "appears more inconsistent than in fact he was. He thought it dangerous to allow that anyone had a legal right to set a limit to royal authority, but he knew that the king could not rule efficiently without devices to retard his actions." John Plamenatz, *Man and Society*, vol. 1 (London: Longman, 1963), p. 111.

16. At one point, Bodin suggests that laws are nothing but prohibitions with penalties attached (III, 5, 325). But he subverts this claim by his lucid discussion of office-creating laws.

17. Friedrich Meinecke, *Machiavellism: The Doctrine of Raison d'Etat and its Place in Modern History* (New Haven: Yale University Press, 1957), p. 56.

18. Cf., Aquinas "On Kingship," in *The Political Ideas of Thomas Aqui-*

nas, ed. Dino Bigongiari (New York: Hafner, 1953), chap. 10, pp. 192–95.

19. Bodin himself claimed that his ideas about unlimited sovereignty were especially appropriate to democracies for there "The people make but one body, and cannot bind itself to itself" (I, 8, 99). Jefferson's thinking was perfectly analogous to Bodin's: Constitutional precommitments violate the full sovereignty of the present generation. The only solution is to hold constitutional conventions every twenty years to reaffirm or rewrite the foundational compact (Thomas Jefferson, Letter of 6 September 1789, in *Writings*, ed. Merrill Peterson [New York: Library of America, 1984], pp. 958–64).

20. Cf., "The power of the law is much greater than the power of custom; for customs are by laws abolished, but not laws by custom" (I, 10, 160–161).

21. The same passage continues, "There is nothing more difficult to handle, nor more doubtful in event, nor more dangerous to manage, than to bring in new decrees or laws" (ibid.).

22. Cf., "Publication or approbation of laws in the assembly of the Estates or parlement, is with us of great power and importance for the keeping of the laws" (I, 8, 103); "As for the names of Lords and Senators, which we oftentimes see joined unto laws, they are not thereunto set as of necessity to give thereunto force or strength, but to give unto them testimony and weight, as made by the wisdom and discretion of the chief men, so to give them the better grace, and *to make them to be the better received*, and not for any necessity at all" (I, 10, 159–160, my emphasis).

23. Montesquieu took over and refined this argument: A king who relinquished the power to punish crimes would actually increase his overall power because this arrangement would prevent involved parties from applying extortionate pressure on the crown (Montesquieu, "De l'esprit des lois," *Oeuvres complètes*, vol. 2, ed. Roger Caillois, Paris: Pléiade, 1951, Book 6, chap 5, p. 315).

24. A similar point is made by another theorist of the early modern state. In his famous essay "Of Empire" from the *Essays* of 1625, Francis Bacon wrote: "For their nobles: to keep them at a distance, it is not amiss; but to depress them may make a king more absolute, but less safe and less able to perform any thing he desires. I have noted it in my History of King Henry the Seventh of England, who depressed his nobility; whereupon it came to pass that his times were full of difficulties and troubles; for the nobility, though they continued loyal unto him, yet did they not cooperate with him in his business. So that he was fain [forced, obliged] to do all things himself." Francis Bacon, *A Selection of His*

Works, ed. Sidney Warhaft (Indianapolis: Bobbs-Merrill, 1965), p. 96.

25. Cf., "If the king should be subject unto the assemblies and decrees of the people, he should neither be king nor sovereign" (I, 8, 95).

26. Note that, like Rousseau, Bodin makes a very sharp distinction between the sovereign and the government.

27. Cf., "We see that they themselves who would have these estates and communities and societies of the people suppressed and abolished, have in time of their necessity no other refuge or stay to fly unto, but even to these estates and communities of the people: which being united together, strengthen themselves for the defense and protection, not of their prince only, but even of themselves also, and of the whole state and subjects in general" (III, 7, 384).

28. Owen Ulph, "Jean Bodin and the Estates-General of 1576," *The Journal of Modern History* 19 (December 1947): 289–96.

29. *Remonstrance au roi par le sieur de la Serre, sur les pernicieux discours contenus au livre de la République de Bodin,* Paris, 1597, cited and summarized in Weill, *Les Théories sur le pouvoir royal en France pendant les guerres de religion,* p. 170.

30. Allen, *History of Political Thought,* p. 415–16.

31. Ibid. "For we have seen the kingdom of Sweden, of Scotland, of Denmark, of England, and Cantons of the Swiss, yea and the German empire also, to have changed their religion, the estate of every of these monarchies and commonweals yet standing entire and whole" (IV, 7, 535). In all these cases, the prince unwisely abandoned his position of sovereign aloofness and participated as a party in the denominational struggle. As a result, these transformations have only been accomplished "with great violence, and bloodshed in many places."

32. In the *Heptaplomeres,* Coronaeus says: "I believe that all are convinced that it is much better to have a false religion than no religion. Thus there is no superstition so great that it cannot keep wicked men in their duty through fear of divine power and somehow preserve the law of nature, since rewards for the good and punishment for the wicked are considered part of divine judgment" (Bodin, *Colloquium of the Seven about the Secrets of the Sublime,* Princeton: Princeton University Press, 1975, p. 162).

33. "It is no marvel that the people of the south be better governed by religion than by force or reason" (V, 1, 560).

34. Cf., "Such is the nature of man, as they esteem nothing more sweet & goodly than that which is strictly forbidden them" (VI, 2, 670).

35. "The great emperor of the Turks doth with as great devotion as

any prince in the world honor and observe the religion by him received from his ancestors, and yet detesteth he not the strange religions of others; but to the contrary permitteth every man to live according to his conscience" (IV, 7, 537).

36. *Colloquium of the Seven,* p. 151.

37. This argument could have come down to Madison through, among others, Voltaire: "Si il n'y avait en Angleterre qu'une religion, le despotisme serait à craindre; s'il y en avait deux, elles se couperaient la gorge; mais il y en avait trente, et elles vivent en paix heureuses" ("Lettres philosophiques," letter six, *Mélanges,* Paris: Pléiade, 1961, p. 18).

38. Bodin is not thinking of a classical "prisoner's dilemma" here. As he sees it, the crucial problem stems not from a conflict between individual and collective rationality, but rather from an inherited code of honor which makes individuals, not just groups, behave irrationally.

39. Bodin's later adherence to the League (1589) was probably motivated by concerns for personal safety and, in any case, has no bearing on the argument of the *République.*

40. This argument is very similar to the one advanced by Arend Lijphart in discussing the crucial role of semi-detached elites in governing primordially divided societies. Arend Lijphart, *Democracy in Plural Societies: A Comparative Exploration* (New Haven: Yale University Press, 1977), p. 53.

41. *Colloquium of the Seven,* p. 163.

42. *Colloquium of the Seven,* p. 167.

43. *Colloquium of the Seven,* p. 471.

44. Cf., "The princes of the Germans at a great assembly at Augsburg, after destructive and lengthy wars, proclaimed that there would be no more discussion about religion among Catholics and priests of the Augsburg confession. When one man rashly violated this edict, he was put to death, and the uprisings in that city were quelled up to the present" *Colloquium of the Seven,* p. 167.

45. Benedict Spinoza, *A Theologico-Political Treatise,* (New York: Dover, 1951), chap. 20, p. 265.

46. "*Law,* in its true Notion, is not so much the Limitation as *the direction of a free and intelligent Agent* to his proper Interest." Locke, *Two Treatises of Government,* ed. Peter Laslett, (New York: Mentor, 1963), 2, 57, pp. 347–48.

47. According to Locke, "There is only one thing which gathers people for sedition, and that is oppression." Similarly: "It is not the diversity of opinions, which cannot be avoided, but the refusal of toleration to people of diverse opinions, which could have been granted, that has produced most of the disputes and wars that

have arisen in the Christian world on account of religion." Locke, *A Letter on Toleration,* ed. R. Klibanski and J. G. Gough (Oxford: Clarendon Press, 1968), pp. 141, 145.

48. Montesquieu, "De l'esprit des lois," *Oeuvres complètes,* Paris: Pléiade, 1951, edited by Roger Caillois, vol. 2 (8, 7), p. 356; (21, 20), p. 641.

49. Montesquieu, "Lettres persanes." *Oeuvres complètes,* vol. 1, Paris: Pléiade, 1949, edited by Roger Caillois (letters 80 and 85), pp. 252–253 and 258–260. Notice that elsewhere Montesquieu had emphasized how religious disputes are peculiarly resistant to rational resolution ("Considérations sur les causes de la grandeur des Romains et de leur décadence," *Oeuvres complètes,* vol. 2, chap. 22, p. 201).

50. Kant, "Idea for a Universal History," in *Kant's Political Writings,* ed. Hans Reiss (Cambridge: Cambridge University Press, 1970), pp. 50–51.

51. Franklin, *Jean Bodin and the Rise of Absolutism,* p. 103.

2

LIBERALISM, NEUTRALISM, AND RIGHTS

ERIC MACK

I. INTRODUCTION

In recent years the increased strength and assertiveness of socially conservative political movements have heightened public debate about the legitimate role of the state in enforcing moral prescriptions that are arguably the product of particular, sectarian, religious or moral perspectives. Social conservatives, motivated by components of their religious commitments, have not only condemned homosexual activity and abortion (to pick the two most prominent issues) but have also argued that these activities ought to be legally prohibited. In opposition to such proposals, there has been a reassertion of the liberal doctrines that political institutions must be neutral between competing moral and religious ideals, between competing conceptions of the good and that political neutrality precludes state enforcement of anyone's religious or moral program. In this essay I inquire how best to understand the doctrine of neutralism, how to assess its force against conservative proposals, e.g., legal prohibitions on abortions, and how to understand the relation between neutralism and liberalism.

Unfortunately, even at the most general level, neutralism may be construed in a variety of ways. We can distinguish between noninterventionist, equal promotionist, Benthamite, and proceduralist neutralism. Under *noninterventionist neutralism*, the state is constrained from interfering with individuals in specified ways that would characteristically diminish their abilities to pursue their own life plans or conceptions of the good even if intervention would foster acknowleged or widely affirmed values. The emphasis in noninterventionist neutralism is on constraints upon state action and on the insufficiency of the promotion of the good to override these moral-political constraints. Noninterventionism is based upon the liberal, individualist idea of private spheres of control centered on each person, which others, including state officials, may not invade except under special justifying conditions.

But, neutralism can also be conceived as requiring evenheadedness in state intervention. One such neutralism would mandate the equal promotion by the state of all or nearly all diverse life plans or conceptions of the good.[1] *Equal promotionist neutralism* may be based upon either of two distinct moral outlooks. The first is that each life plan or conception of the good is equally worthy of being fulfilled. Here the demand for a life plan's fulfillment flows from the moral stature of its content. The demand for equality in fulfillment flows from the equal stature of the content of different life plans. An alternative basis for the equal promotionist doctrine is the belief that value resides *in the satisfaction* of life plans, whatever their content, combined with an egalitarian commitment that this satisfaction be equally distributed among life planners.

The third type of neutralism, viz., *Benthamite neutralism,* demands a different sort of evenhandedness. The Benthamite rejects talk about the worth, equal or otherwise, of life plans or conceptions of the good. The good consists indiscriminately in the satisfaction of any desire, preference, or plan of life. And no egalitarian rider is imposed on the distribution of the good among desirers or life planners. Rather than fostering particular life plans or conceptions of the good, state action must be justified on the basis of its promotion of aggregate utility or aggregate preference or life plan satisfaction. Under Benthamite neutralism, any promotion or thwarting of specific life plans or conceptions of the good would be entirely incidental to the social maximization of whatever forms of satisfaction are taken to have intrinsic value.

Equal promotionism, Benthamism, and noninvervenionism are all substantive in the sense that each specifies the social states, the political-legal outcomes, that must obtain if neutrality is to prevail. Substantive versions of neutralism require that the state's activities actually yield the outcomes that this or that version of neutralism demands. For example, a pro-choice advocate of any of these substantive versions of neutralism would argue that true political morality requires that the state not prohibit abortion and that this represents neutrality because the political morality that requires nonprohibition precludes any weight being given to particular life plans or conceptions of the good. What is crucial is that, as he sees it, the pro-choice conclusion is implied by this substantivist's political morality. It is no part of his case against prohibition that anyone's actual prohibitionist beliefs, proclamations or policies in fact are the psychological or sociological products of a special weighing of particular life plans or conceptions of the good. Whether neutrality obtains is a matter of the way the legal-political world is, not of how it got that way.

In contrast, *procedural neutralism* formulates the demand for neutrality as a restriction on what types of beliefs can motivate legitimate political proposals and actions. If a political proposal is in fact the product of neutrality violating beliefs or, perhaps, is the sort of proposal that typically arises from such beliefs, it is to be accorded no weight in proper political debate. For instance, a pro-choice proceduralist will argue that the demand that the state prohibit abortion is to be dismissed as politically out-of-order on the basis of the type of beliefs that motivate this demand, e.g., particular, sectarian, religious beliefs. The pro-choice proceduralist does not rely on a conception of true political morality that requires nonprohibition. His only, or at least primary, defense of nonprohibition is that anti-abortion arguments or policies are all procedurally tainted.

Unfortunately, a fine line runs between substantive and procedural neutralism.[2] When the liberal attacks an advocate of legally mandatory church membership for his attempt to impose his religious vision on others, is the liberal's underlying complaint that mandated membership would infringe individual rights? Or is it that it would unequally promote different conceptions of the good? Or is it that its advocate is moved to his proposal by his own special conception of the good? In general, the argument is proceduralist whenever criticism is directed against the sort of reasons one's opponent offers or is moved by. The outcome of the reasoning is irrelevant. While the substantivist will deny that there are sufficient reasons for certain state actions, the proceduralist will decry the reasons why certain state actions are proposed. It is proceduralist neutralism that Joseph Raz seems to have in mind when he contrasts substantive noninterventionist liberalism that is based on "doctrines of basic liberties which limit the power of the state by declaring that certain areas of conduct are outside of its authority" with "principles of restraint [which] deny the appropriateness of certain reasons for political action, or for certain kinds of political action."[3]

The noninterventionist emphasizes constraints on the state's promotion of all valued ends. The equal promotionist emphasizes distributional requirements on the state's promotion of values. The Benthamite does not constrain state promotion of ends, even distributionally. But his restrictive theory-of-value precludes the state's favoring certain preference or life plan satisfactions over quantitatively similar preference or life plan satisfactions. The proceduralist seeks to block the state's pursuit of particular conceptions of the good by banning arguments and proposals that are motivated by those particular conceptions. All four have some claim to represent the liberal doctrine that the state is not to promote any particular and, hence, contentious conception of the good.

In this essay I shall argue in favor of the noninterventionist version of neutralism and against its three competitors. Arguments against the equal promotion and the Benthamite forms of neutralism are presented in section II. Proceduralist neutralism, which is the most common form of neutralism used against social conservatism in recent political debate, is criticized in section III. Finally, in section IV, I try to give an attractive explication of the noninterventionist view and, making this view less attractive to some, to show the extensive ties between this form of neutralism and liberal individualism.

II. Equal Promotionist and Benthamite Neutralism

The equal promotionist advocates that each conception of the good or, better, each individual's pursuit of his conception of the good ought to be promoted by the state and promoted equally. This advocacy puts *all* conceptions of the good on a par. So the sadist must receive encouragement equal to that received by his more conventionally motivated victim. This collides with bedrock moral intuitions and with all neutralists' expectations about what a regime of neutrality would look like. Can the equal promotionist escape equal respect for sadists and their intended victims?[4] To do so, he must argue that some life plans, e.g., the plans of sadists, fall outside the range of plans to which neutralism applies. Here, however, we must recall the alternative bases for equal promotionism. It may be thought to rest on the value of the *satisfaction* of life plans combined with a separate egalitarian rule that these satisfactions be equally distributed. Or it may be said to rest on the equal worthiness of life plans. If the equal promotionist turns to the first of these bases, it is hard to see how he can even begin an orderly retreat from equal respect for the sadist and his intended victim. For both the sadist and his victim precisely the same thing is at stake, viz., satisfaction, and this is supposed to be equally divided.

If, on the other hand, equal promotionism is held to rest on the relative worthiness of life plans, its proponent can at least begin to argue that some life plans are beyond the pale. The argument would have to be that some pursuits can be excluded because they are so patently *less worthy* than others. But, once comparative judgments about the worth of different life pursuits are brought into political morality, there does not seem to be any mark on the worthiness-of-pursuit continuum that would allow the equal protectionist to say, *on the basis of worthiness*, that while certain pursuits are not worthy of state encouragement, the rest should receive *equal* support. Different degrees of worthiness among those pursuits meriting support would seem to call for different degrees of encouragement. Also troublesome for the equal promotionist is the fact that some of the activities that manifest unworthiness would seem to disqualify have been protected by standard demands for political neutrality. Consider typical unworthy behavior that proponents of neutralism usually take to be protected: addictive drug use, promiscuous sexual conduct, religious cult membership, the consumption of wine coolers and so on. If disvalue or unworthiness disqualifies certain life plans from equal promotion, then the resulting pol-

icy of equal promotion will protect far less than liberals generally expect when they invoke neutralism.

Note that the equal promotionist cannot avail himself of the
strategy employed by Nozick in addressing a case parallel to
our sadist-victim example. Nozick maintains that:

> Not every enforcement of a prohibition which differentially ben-
> efits people makes the state non-neutral. Suppose some men are
> potential rapists of women, while no women are potential rapists
> of men or of each other. Would a prohibition against rape be
> non-neutral ? It would, by hypothesis, differentially benefit peo-
> ple; but for potential rapists to complain that the prohibition was
> non-neutral between the sexes, and therefore sexist, would be ab-
> surd. There is an *independent* reason for prohibiting rape.[5]

For here Nozick rejects the core of equal protectionism, viz.,
that neutrality consists in equal encouragement. How a position
like Nozick's should be construed as noninterventionism is developed in section IV.

Benthamite neutralism relies on the political theory that since
"the state is an instrument for satisfying the wants that men
happen to have rather than a means of making men good,"
only "want-regarding principles" and never "ideal-regarding
principles" should determine the proper activities of the state.
Want-regarding principles are "principles which take as given
the wants which people happen to have and concentrate attention entirely on the extent to which a certain policy will alter
the overall amount of want-satisfaction."[6] The Benthamite has
his own problems with the sadist and his victim. While the equal
promotionist appears to be committed to the equal encouragement of the sadist and his victim, the Benthamite appears to be
committed to maximizing satisfaction across the sadist and his
victim. As much sadism is to be allowed, indeed fostered, as
brings the sadist more satisfaction than it brings dissatisfaction
to the victim. Similarly, as much and only as much freedom in
pursuit of one's conception of the good is to be permitted as
will yield satisfaction for one greater than the dissatisfaction
this pursuit will yield for others, e.g., those who despise one's
conception of the good. True, Benthamism precludes any status for the *worth* of the sadist's conception of the good in making it right that he enjoy himself at the expense of his victim.

Similarly, it precludes any place for the *worth* of the teetotaler's conception of the good in making prohibition justified. The quality of the sadist's or the teetotaler's desires plays no justificatory role. Instead, everything depends on the range and intensity of the preferences expressive of the competing conceptions—on how many individuals subscribe to them and how fervently. It is clear, though, that the view that only want-regarding considerations should count, and count aggregatively, in determining political right and wrong implies nothing like what the liberal has in mind when he invokes neutralism against conservative proposals for, e.g., the suppression of immoral life plans.

Once again, the obvious alternative for the principled rejection of the demands of the sadist, the teetotaler, etc., for political support is noninterventionist neutralism. For it is not the disvalue of their plans, nor their demand for more than equal support, nor any insufficiency in the range or intensity in their desires that shows that these proposals should be rejected. Rather, what fundamentally condemns them is their invasiveness of others' privileged spheres of choice and control. And, it is interventionist neutralism that specifies state neutrality in terms of respect for private spheres of choice and the moral side-constraints defined by, or defining, them.

A final and common problem confronts equal protectionist and Benthamite neutralism. Neither is responsive to the real challenge posed by social conservatives. That challenge is to reconcile a moral realism that affirms that some life plans are morally superior and others are to be morally condemned with a refusal to permit the state to promote the valuable or to suppress the defective. The most extensive recent public debate about the state's role in promoting good and vanquishing evil occurred during the 1984 elections when the conservatives attacked Catholic political leaders who both endorsed state neutrality and condemned many of the practices that neutrality would allow. The main charge was that Catholics like Mario Cuomo and Geraldine Ferraro were inconsistent in morally condemning most abortions while maintaining that it would be wrong for the state to prohibit these evils. So, one of the key parameters of recent debate about neutrality is the presumption that important sound judgments can be made about the comparative value of different ways of life and different conceptions of the good. This presumption of moral realism sets the stage for the conservative demand that some good explanation be given why the state is not to be guided by these admittedly sound judgments. Both the equal promotionist and the Benthamite fail to address this challenge because they do not share this presumption of moral realism. Rather both equal promotionism and Benthamism put all, or almost all, conceptions of the good on a moral par. The former affirms the equal worth of each life plan (or each within a set of minimally acceptable plans). The latter affirms the moral irrelevance of what is qualitatively distinct about particular life plans.[7] In these ways both the equal promotionist and the Benthamite rely upon moral scepticism about our ability to make significant comparative judgments of different conceptions of the good. In contrast, the two remaining versions of neutralism, proceduralism and noninterventionism, do attempt to accommodate the liberal rejection of the state as moral disciplinarian with moral realism.

III. Proceduralist Neutralism

The noninterventionist reconciles moral realism and systematic restraint on the state's activity by insisting upon a fundamental distinction between two branches of morality. The first branch is the theory of the good, which specifies valuable ends and the means to those ends and allows us to evaluate life plans and conceptions of the good in terms of their worth. The second branch is the theory of rights, the theory of moral side-constraints on the means that any agent may employ in the pursuit of any end no matter (or, perhaps, almost no matter) how valuable that end be. For the noninterventionist, these rights define or at least predominantly characterize enforcible public morality. Activities that do not violate these side-constraints are not subject to prohibition even if they are strongly condemned by the theory of the good. And activities that do violate these side-constraints are to be suppressed even if they produce valuable results. It can be *consistent* to condemn abortions while denying that they are appropriately subject to state suppression. And it can be *consistent* to acknowledge the overall good of vigilante suppression of abortions while insisting that this use of coercion is morally impermissible and itself properly subject to state prohibition. Because of the noninterventionist's separation of judgments generated by the theory of the good from the dictates of political morality, no degree of realism about values, about our capacity to rank alternative life plans, seriously threatens to justify an expansion of the state's mandate for action.

Contemporary liberals are, however, understandably reluctant to accept the noninterventionist insistence that political morality is at least predominantly a matter of respecting and enforcing moral side-constraints on the pursuit of goals and the narrow role for the state that this political morality seems to imply. They do not want to surrender the vision of the state as a promoter of value. The problem, then, if moral realism is embraced, is to explain why the state should promote certain acknowledged values while not promoting other equally acknowledged values. The problem is "to find any reason for supporting politically some elements of a conception of the good and not others that are admitted to be valid and valuable."[8] Yet no explanation seems possible in terms of discrepancies in value between equally acknowledged goods. And arguments that invoke the impermissible invasiveness of certain promotions of values by the state would be to noninterventionist in spirit. The solution advanced by the liberal proceduralist is that certain sound judgments about worthy and unworthy pursuits are, nevertheless, inadmissible in political debate and in the motivation of political policy.

An address by New York Governor Mario Cuomo, given at the University of Notre Dame during the 1984 campaign, is a characteristic statement of the proceduralist position.[9] As one would expect, the central illustrative issue is abortion—more specifically, the compatibility of Cuomo's moral condemnation of most abortion with his rejection of its prohibition by the state. Cuomo makes two suggestions, which he wisely does not pursue. The first is that his oath of office requires him to uphold "the Constitution that guarantees this [abortion] freedom."[10] But this basically proceduralist argument needs the premise that the Supreme Court is currently *correct* about what the Constitution requires (perhaps, because the Supreme Court *must* be correct about the Constitution). Yet this premise will be dis-puted by almost anyone who sees many or most abortions as instances of morally unjustified manslaughter, a perspective that Cuomo himself presumably shares! Moreover, even if sound, this argument in no way indicates that either Cuomo or anyone else should hestitate to bring about an anti-aboration constitutional amendment. Cuomo next proposes the "truth" that "to assure our freedom we must allow others the same freedom, even if occasionally it produces conduct by them which we hold to be sinful."[11] But this is an argument for noninterventionism, not for proceduralism; and it is an argument with a crucial unstated premise about who is to be included among the others who must be granted equal freedom.

In contrast to these preliminary suggestions, Cuomo's central argument cites both the religious origins of anti-abortion judgments and the absence of consensus about the prohibition of abortion. Usually it seems that the argument is supposed to turn on the absence of consensus, which is to be *accounted for* by the influence of diverse religious perspectives. The key passage declares that:

> Our public morality, then, the moral standards we maintain for everyone, not just the ones we insist on in our private lives, depends on a consensus view of right and wrong. The values derived from religious belief will not, and should not, be accepted as part of the public morality unless they are shared by the pluralistic community at large, by consensus.[12]

Yet why should correct, enforcible public morality depend on consensus? Is it only right, e.g., to prohibit slavery when there is a consensus in favor of this prohibition? And is *anything* politicially right if there is a consensus in its favor? Cuomo replies to this objection by identifying the rightness of a political program with its political feasibility. According to Cuomo, since the "legal interdicting of abortion . . . is not a plausible possibility and even if it could be obtained, it would not work,"[13] it is contrary to political morality to interdict abortion. In parallel fashion, Cuomo maintains that the failure of the American Catholic bishops to condemn slavery in the pre-Civil War period was justified because such a condemnation would have been ineffective or counterproductive.[14] But, clearly, even if these factual claims are correct, they do not establish that an anti-abortion crusade now is wrong or that an antislavery crusade then would have been wrong. And even less do these facts establish the rightness of allowing and protecting abortion or allowing and protecting slavery.[15] By identifying political virtue with political pragmatism, Cuomo's argument disarms the liberal who wants to argue and campaign against legal enforcement of any item of the current moral consensus.

Cuomo might have placed more emphasis on the specifically religious sources of anti-abortion sentiment. And he does seem implicitly to appeal to these sources when he repeatedly condemns the imposition of some people's "religious values" on others, even while he acknowledges that these values may also have a fully secular basis.[16] Indeed, liberal opponents of the conservative program commonly invoke the specifically *religious* coloration or source of anti-aboration sentiment and try to argue that these judgments should not be part of anyone's public morality. Yet there seems to be a simple dilemma facing this downgrading of political arguments that rely upon religious premises. Either the use of religious premises should be rejected because of their falsity, or their use should be rejected independently of their truth or falsity. No doubt the proposed exclusion of religious or religiously based propositions from legitimate political debate is often based on the substantive idea, implicitly endorsed by those notorious "secular humanists," that no religious or religiously based beliefs are true or worthy of being acted upon. Yet, however true this judgment about religious propositions, it is not a judgment that the opponents of conservatism are willing to assert as part of their political argument. Nor would even a blanket and valid dismissal of all religious routes to pro-prohibition conclusions justify the dismissal of those conclusions. Moreover, this denial of the truth value of religious premises would not be a proceduralist maneuver. It would not be an instance of showing why certain ordinarily good reasons for action were not good or admissible reasons in political discourse.

On the other hand, how can one downgrade the significance of conclusions arrived at by means of religious premises if one does not discount the verity of those premises? Why should the adherent to, e.g., an anti-abortion argument that employs some religious premise, find it plausible that this argument and its conclusion has any less political validity than an argument he equally endorses that arrives without the aid of religious premises at the conclusion that killing burdensome cripples should be forbidden? It is difficult to see what quality might be thought to inhere especially in the religious premises, other than falsity, that would justify this discounting.

However, perhaps a type of contractarian argument can be formulated that relies upon a contingent fact about such religious premises, viz., their contentiousness within religiously and culturally pluralistic societies. The argument goes something like this: Even advocates of religiously based prescriptions must acknowledge that each of many conflicting religiously based views will, from the inside, seem so vitally correct that no compromise with any conflicting view will, from the inside, seem tolerable. Moreover, any person, including any participant in such religiously based views, can recognize the intransigence with which such views are held. So there is little prospect of noncoerced conversion of religiously based disputants. This intransigence, insofar as it is not merely pathological, is due to the lack of any common authority for people's diverse religiously based norms. One person appeals to his holy text, another to his church tradition, and a third to his revelatory experience. In addition, it follows from the fact of conflict among these religiously based beliefs that, from the outside, any one of them is quite likely to be false. Given this, the argument proceeds, it seems reasonable for anyone recognizing these general facts, including individuals who themselves participate in such religiously based beliefs, mutually to accept a ban on appeals to private authorities in their common debate about public policy. It is rational for each to agree to put forward only contentions that appeal to public, objective, and secular arguments and, hence, to bracket as inappropriate to the political realm prescriptions that proceed upon religious commitment.

This argument is not at all loony. But major problems arise with its application. For one thing, it presumes a line between idiosyncratic, subjective, religious bases for moral belief and public, objective, secular bases. The line must be bright, and perception of it must not depend upon the observer's substantive position on the issue under debate. But whether or not the basis for someone's beliefs is perceived to be idiosyncratic or subjective will very much depend upon who is scrutinizing that basis. And, of course, the rational theologist and ethicist will argue that he has perfectly public and objective, if not secular, grounds for his theological commitments and their associated ethical precepts. Worse yet, in many cases of hot dispute about public policy—abortion is a perfect example—disputants on the allegedly religious based side can easily be found who argue in unquestionably public, objective, and secular terms. The contractarian argument will not banish *these* anti-abortion arguments. And, of course, even if all actually offered arguments for a given prohibition are banished, this hardly establishes that the prohibition would be improper. One need only recall the example of a prohibition on slavery in a society where all anti-slavery opinion is significantly colored by religious conviction.

If the proceduralist wants to avoid the objection that it is hard to discriminate between religious and some nonreligious premises within policy arguments and that many avowedly nonreligious supporters can be found for supposedly religiously inspired conclusions, he must broaden his characterization of the premises that are, because they are deeply contentious, to be banished from legitimate political dialogue in pluralistic societies. If the ban is sufficiently broadened it will, perhaps, become plausible to hold that every argument any sane person might actually use in defending certain conservative prohibitions utilizes at least one tainted premise. The argument for this broader ban would run something like this: Commitments expressive of people's personal moralities are intransigent and beyond the scope of objective public debate. Moreover, insofar as anyone can step outside these personal commitments, anyone can see that his own most cherished values are quite likely to be objectively mistaken or without truth value.[17] So it is rational for people to agree to exclude personal commitments from political debate. Exclusion may take the form of a procedural principle to the effect that when there is some fundamental division among the members of the political community expressive of divergent personal moral commitments—with, perhaps, the divergence itself being the evidence of the merely "personal" status of the commitments—those commitments should have no weight in the determination of public policy.

Unfortunately, this argument for a more encompassing ban on personal commitments is in danger of being either self-destructive or question-begging. It is self-destructive if it impartially includes all moral premises—and aren't they all contentious?—within the tainted personal commitment category. For then, in general, no premises will be left to justify any public morality and, in particular, there will be no available non-tainted arguments against the conservative's political demands. It will be question-begging if only the premises needed to justify the conservative's favored prohibitions turn out to be matters of intransigent personal commitment while the liberal's political morality, perhaps including the premises needed for his favored prohibitions, survive this screen. Certainly it is conceivable that the proceduralist's proposal be neither self-destructive nor question-begging; some principled reasons might be found for identifying certain premises and, perhaps, all the relevant possible premises for certain conclusions, as personal commitments of the sort that it is reasonable for us mutually to agree to ban from political debate. However, it is not even clear how one would go about developing such principled reasons.[18]

These two contractarian arguments, formulated in terms of what contentious beliefs it is reasonable for individuals mutually to agree should have no political significance, involve a nonstrategic sense of rationality. Each person is thought to recognize that it would be unreasonable to expect others to convert; albeit each also insists that others recognize that it would be unreasonable to expect him to convert. The threat these reasonable people seek to avoid is the threat of their making unreasonble demands upon others, given others' moral perceptions, and of others' making unreasonable demands upon them, given their moral perceptions. However, one can also construct contractarian arguments that employ a more strategic sense of rationality. On this construction, an individual does not really care about what is reasonable for himself or for others to expect or believe. Rather, each individual is worried about the ways in which clashing and intransigent views threaten social peace. It is strategically rational for each to give up any chance for the enforcement of his contentious views, if, by doing so, he can secure similar concessions from others. The proceduralist version of this argument's conclusion is that it is strategically rational for individuals in a pluralistic society to agree to a set of "gag rules" for political debate that prohibit invocation of religious or all personal commitments in arguments for public policy. The substantive version of this argument's conclusion is that it is strategically rational for individuals to agree to "privatize" the areas of choice over which intransigent dispute exists by declaring these areas within the protected private spheres of individuals.[19] By excluding these areas from the state's legitimate purview, battles over who will capture and use the state's authority are avoided. The substantive version of the strategic argument is, then, an argument for noninterventionist neutralism.

The procedural version of the strategic argument will face the same problems already noted for proceduralism:

> What beliefs are to be subject to the gags?; How can these beliefs be specified in a non-self-defeating and non-question-begging way?; and Why believe that a non-self-defeating and non-question-begging specification of beliefs to be subject to gag rules will guarantee that all arguments for conservative prohibitions will include some banned premises?

But, the strategic argument has one advantage over the nonstrategic. If I genuinely believe that God will punish any society that allows homosexuality, it is difficult to see how it can be reasonable for me to bracket this belief simply because others reject it along with many other of my cherished beliefs. But it is not difficult to see how it might be strategically rational for me to agree not to invoke this belief in exchange for others' not invoking their belief that God only smiles on those societies that require everyone to engage in some homosexual activities. This example, however, employs a highly contrived countervailing belief. In reality, if I have this belief about God's hatred for even tolerance of homosexuality, it is very likely that, as I see it, I have more to lose by agreeing not to invoke this belief in debate than I have to gain by others' agreeing not to invoke certain of their religious or personally moral beliefs. In most cases, the strategic contractarian argument will give the religious prohibitionist *some* reason, but not at all a decisive reason, for abandoning his prohibitionist program. The example of the crusading homophobe brings out another weakness in the strategic contractarian argument. Mutually agreed to gag rules or privatizations of areas of choice that heighten the prospects of social peace are only strategically, mutually attractive to those who, because their worldviews are already sufficiently alike, prefer peace partially on their opponents' terms to going to war for their own terms.

Finally, in this critique of proceduralist neutralism, we should note that part of the attractiveness of proceduralist restraint derives from the intuition that restraints of some sort must be valid if a pluralistic social order is to thrive. But the proceduralist as proceduralist has no right to draw support for his position from the independent attractiveness of pluralism. The proceduralist can associate himself with pluralism only insofar as he establishes the rationality of restraints on what may properly motivate political discourse and policy and these restraints would foster pluralism. The noninterventionist has a far stronger claim to invoke the pluralist image of individuals and associations of individuals freely pursuing their diverse conceptions of the good—whatever their ultimate true worth—and restricted only by the enforcement of social rules that support the freedoms needed for these varied pursuits.

IV. NONINTERVENTIONIST NEUTRALISM

The proceduralist wants to affirm a rich theory of value and he wants to maintain that considerations of value determine political right and wrong. But he does not want to give political effect to all of his favored theory of value. Unhappily, it is difficult for him to find a principled basis for reserving political significance for only that part of his theory of value that he wants to give political effect, and it is difficult to argue for the political nonsignificance of the other part while still genuinely affirming it as part of his full theory of value. The noninterventionist avoids this problem by denying that political right or wrong is a matter of the state's promoting or thwarting even what the most correct and rich theory of value identifies as the good or the bad. The noninterventionist need not hold that there is no theoretical connection between his theory of value and his basic principles of political morality. But the connection will be sufficiently indirect that the principles of politics will be structurally unlike the principles of value theory. In particular, the principles of politics will contain, or entirely consist in, moral side-constraints that apply both to how individuals may treat one another and how the state may treat those under its sway. These side-constraints define, or are defined by, private spheres' interference with which is impermissible, absent, extraordinary, justifying conditions; and the basic role of the state is to prevent such interference.[20]

Connected to the dual affirmation of a theory about what life pursuits are valuable, worthy, etc., and a side-constraint conception of political morality is the idea that actions or ways of life can be wrong in two radically different ways. An action can be wrong by virtue of being invasive of the sphere rightfully inhabited or controlled by another, and this type of wrong is not, or not simply, a matter of the disvalue associated with that action or the way of life that gave rise to it. State actions to suppress such wrongs are entirely compatible with neutrality, since what justifies these actions is the prevention, or nullification, of side-constraint violations, not the value of the suppression or the disvalue of the actions suppressed. In light of the distinction between value and side-constraint reasons for moral condemnation, Nozick speaks far too generally when he says that the suppression of rape is consistent with neutrality because "There is an *independent* reason for prohibiting rape." The more precise point for the noninterventionist is that there is a side-constraint reason for condemning the rape that is quite separate from any view about the value or disvalue of the prohibited action's particular consequences. The prohibition is compatible with neutrality because it does not need to be vindicated by any conception of the good.

In contrast, actions can be wrong solely because in their performance agents diverge from valuable or rational goals or ways of life. If actions are wrong only in this second fashion, their political suppression would itself violate side-constraints. And suppression of merely disvaluable or unworthy actions would violate neutrality because it would not be justified by the contra-value, side-constraint, dimension of morality. It is liberal individualism of this sort that best accommodates an idea crucial to moral realists who also demand state neutrality, viz., the idea that one can have a right to do wrong. One can both be doing wrong and have every right to do what one does.

At least implicit in the liberal individualist structure of private rights is the belief that an agent's failure, even his knowing failure, to prevent another's loss of a rightfully held object or condition does not constitute that agent's violating the other's right to that object or condition. Of course, if this agent has a special obligation to the other to prevent this loss, his failure to act violates the other's right to that prevention. We may sometimes think poorly of an agent for standing aside when he could prevent another's loss, but standing aside remains significantly morally different from invading the other's rights, from *imposing* the loss upon the other. This liberal individualist belief in a significant distinction between *allowing* and *producing* is essential to any coherent doctrine of neutralism. For, if state neutrality is to be possible, it must be possible for the state to *stand aside* even when it can intervene and determine a given outcome. State neutrality when the state cannot, in any case, determine the outcome does not merit demanding. Consider state neutrality with regard to Pushkin versus pushpin. Suppose that if the state does not impose severe penalties on the playing of pushpin the craze for this game will result in the complete cessation of Pushkin reading while rather severe penalties on pushpin playing will lead to a resurgence in Pushkin reading. The state's decision not to intervene to prevent the demise of Pushkin reading cannot be described as neutrality if this non-intervention itself is thought of as being morally on a par with causing the demise of Pushkin appreciation.

The state can be described as neutral vis-à-vis competing social alternatives only if its allowing one of the alternatives to triumph, or gain an edge, is not thought of as being the moral, equivalent of its intervening to cause the other alternative to triumph, or gain an edge. In short, and on reflection not surprisingly, the demand for neutrality presupposes that significant nonintervention is possible. And this means that it must be possible knowingly to allow an outcome, even an undersirable one, without being to blame for that outcome in the way one would be, had one straightforwardly brought it about. Those who wish to advocate state neutrality and to maintain coher-

ence of their arguments will have to eschew the many arguments in current political philosophy that morally equate knowingly allowing some disvaluable outcome with causing that
outcome and, hence, morally equate the state's forcing individuals to prevent untoward outcomes with the state's forcing individuals not to cause those outcomes. The neutralist will have
to avoid, e.g., the many variations on the argument that the
able should be forced to aid the needy because to allow the able
to escape this responsibility would be to allow them to be responsible for the suffering of the needy. A careful avoidance
of such arguments will tend to make the neutralist more classically, and less contemporarily, liberal.

Of course, the fact that it must be possible for the state to
stand aside if the demand for neutrality is to be coherent does
not mean that the state displays neutrality whenever it stands
aside. The state does *not* display neutrality when it stands aside
and allows the rapist to proceed with his crime if the rapist's
victim has a right to protection from that state. Given that right,
the state would be violating moral side-constraints in failing to
protect the victim. Given that right to protection, the state's
nonintervention would at least approach moral parity with the
assailant's intervention. But if victims do not have rights to protection by a given state as, for example the Spanish Loyalist's
did not have rights to protection by the United States government, then it is neutrality when that government merely stands
aside neither aiding the criminal aggressors nor the victims.

What about actions by the state that do not involve the use
of force, at least in a comparably direct way, but which predictably influence the outcome of some social competition? For instance, what of the choice of the state to include knowledge of
Pushkin, but not skill in the game of pushpin, on state employment exams or within the curriculum of state schools? Or what
of the curricular choice of evolutionary theory over creationism, or "values clarification" over good old biblical ethics, in
public schools? The noninterventionist answer continues to be
that neutrality is violated whenever the state's influence on contested social issues is a product of moral side-constraint violation. So, for example, religious and social conservatives are correct in charging that often state education violates neutrality by
fostering "secular humanism" over this or that religious vision

if, but only if, it is correct to judge the state's coercive funding of this education, its compulsory attendance laws and the like as illegitimate infringements upon moral side-constraints. What about the inclusion of Pushkin but not pushpin on state employment exams, which predictably fosters Pushkin over pushpin? In such a case, one would have to reach further to argue for non-neutrality. One possible line of argument might focus on whether or not illegitimate state restrictions on non-governmental employment improperly forced people to turn to the state for employment. Another, quite different, possible line of argument would introduce an additional sort of neutrality that could especially be demanded of the state. This would be the neutrality of not fostering particular values except as the by-product of efficiently carrying out its legitimate functions. If testing aspiring bureaucrats on their knowledge of Pushkin is a good way of enhancing the efficient legitimate functioning of the state, the inclusion of Pushkin does not violate this neutrality. Otherwise it does.

Coherent advocacy of state neutrality is tied to the type of substantive political theory that I have labeled "individualistic liberalism," which adheres to a basic structure of private rights that plays at least a very prominent role in the definition of enforcible political morality. Neutrality is a matter of action and policy in accordance with this sort of political morality, in contrast with action and policy justifiable only on the basis of the promotion of particular values. But I have also tried to indicate how specific judgments about whether or not neutrality is violated depends upon particular judgments about what people's rights are—about what moral side-constraints exist. Thus, the coherent advocacy of neutrality is not tied, or not at all tightly tied, to any specific version of individualistic liberalism. Individualistic liberals may differ about the precise definition of persons' private rights, about the boundaries of persons' private spheres, and even about who possesses such rights. There may be disputes about who has what sort of private rights over natural resources or over ideas, or about whether the imposition of certain psychic costs counts as an illicit invasion of others' private spheres. Thus, it is helpful to distinguish between the noninterventionist *concept* of neutrality and specific noninterventionist *conceptions* of neutrality which result from adherence to the concept and also to a set of particular judgments about who has precisely what private rights.

This distinction is important for understanding the inadequacy of another common liberal response to conservative proposals in the recent abortion debate. This inadequacy reflects a final attempt at pulling the substantive rabbit, the illegitimacy of prohibitions on abortion, out of a procedural or, in any case, formal hat. The liberal argument that is put to the anti-abortion conservative is: Surely even you prohibitionists acknowledge that there is a distinction between private and political morality; surely you are not prepared to hold that the state should force people to be virtuous. All we are saying, as pro-choice advocates, is that choices about private morality ought not to be determined by the state.

This sort of argument is rhetorically effective to the extent that it fosters the impression that the anti-abortionist is commited to challenging the private morality/public morality distinction and to rejecting the ideal of the neutral state in favor of a state that presses a particular conception of the good upon its populace. The liberal hopes to appeal to all those who are not willing to entrust the state with the task of "soulcraft"—and this includes most of those favoring the prohibition of abortion. His method is to claim a monopoly on neutralism for the pro-choice position. But this confuses a claim to represent a particular conception of neutrality with a claim to represent neutrality as such. The liberal's particular conception of neutrality is a function of his judgment about what particular rights pregnant women have and fetuses lack. But the anti-abortionist may lay claim to another particular conception of neutrality which is a function of his different judgment about what particular rights the parties to abortions have. On the anti-abortionist's view, there are side-constraint reasons against abortion, perhaps absent special countervailing conditions. So, on his view, abortion and the protection of it violates neutrality—as much as state's sanctioning of other forms of unjustified manslaughter.

This is a substantive dispute between this prohibitionist and the pro-choice advocate, and no appeal to the ideal of state neutrality or to the beauty of the private morality/public morality distinction can settle this dispute. What matters is who is right—and right about where the rights lie. Only a sound appeal to specific rights can supply the state with justifications for its coercive activity that neither depend upon comparative evaluations of life plans or their components, which would render the state's activity non-neutral, nor depend upon justifications that make it difficult to sustain moral realism and to arrive at the specific restraints on the state's activity that the invocation of neutralism normally connotes.

What happens if there is no sound appeal to specific rights? What happens if, as is sometimes suggested about the abortion controversy, the moral arguments by the prohibitionist and the pro-choice advocate, which center on rights asserted and denied, are comparably plausible?[21] This moral indeterminacy would favor neither side. The common argument that, given moral uncertainty, one should opt for tolerance and against state prohibition works no better on behalf of those seeking abortions than on behalf of those engaged in the vigilante suppression of them. If there is no sound appeal to specific rights, state neutrality would consist in standing aside and letting the prohibitionists and the pro-choice advocates fight it out in the streets and in the back alleys. Or state neutrality would consist in enforcing the terms of the armistice these contending parties would enter into, should there be armistic terms that they both prefer over the fortunes of social warfare.[22]

NOTES

1. Equal promotionist neutralism is exemplified in the second and third principles of neutralist restraint formulated by Joseph Raz. Joseph Raz, "Liberalism, Autonomy, and the Politics of Neutral Concern", in *Midwest Studies in Philosophy VII* (1982) ed. Peter A. French et al. pp. 92–93.
2. An alternative mapping would describe both substantive and procedural interpretations of noninterventionist, equal protectionist and Benthamite neutralism. But it would not be fruitful to spell out procedural interpretations of these three types of neutralism since what would be most significant about those three interpretations would be what they had in common, viz., proceduralism.
3. Raz, "Liberalism, Autonomy," pp. 89–90. Subsequently, in specifying variants on the principles of restraint route, he uses the formula, "No political action may be undertaken or justified on the ground that . . ." This, again, seems to be a proceduralist restric-

tion to the effect that political action or argument is invalidated insofar as it proceeds from certain beliefs—insofar as it has a certain causal history. Raz is not himself an advocate of "the doctrine of neutral political concern." See p. 116.

4. We leave aside all the obvious, but very vexing, questions about what would constitute equal promotion, e.g., does equal promotion require that everyone's "expected life plan fulfillment" be equalized?; or is it a matter of equal additions to each person's "expected life plan fulfillment" given some inegalitarian baseline?; how can equality in life-plan fulfillment be characterized or measured across qualitatively different life plans? And, of course, any program for equal promotion of life pursuits has to take account of scarcity of resources that require constant choices between the promotion of this or that pursuit.

5. Robert Nozick, *Anarchy, State and Utopia* (New York: Basic Books, 1974), pp. 272–73. Interestingly, Nozick then heads in the direction of a proceduralist interpretation of his noninterventionist neutralism. "That a prohibition thus independently justifiable works out to affect different persons differently is no reason to condemn it as nonneutral, *provided it was instituted or continues for (something like) the reasons which justify it, and not in order to yield differential benefits.*" (Emphasis added.) However, he then seems to recognize and be dubious of the idea that a policy's neutrality is a matter of its causal history. For he adds, "(How should it be viewed if it *is* independently justifiable, but actually is supported and maintained because of its differential benefits?)"

6. Brain Barry, *Political Argument* (London: Routledge and Kegan Paul, 1965); quoted by Raz, "Liberalism, Autonomy," p. 98. Barry's characterization of want-regarding principles continues so as to allow a distributional component, viz., "or in the way in which the policy will affect the distribution among people of opportunities for satisfying wants." In the text I have omitted this last clause in order, among other reasons, to maintain a strong contrast between the distributionally oriented equal promotionist and the aggregation oriented Benthamite.

7. More precisely, one route to equal promotionism affirms the equal worth of all, or nearly all, life plans while the other route to equal promotionism joins Benthamism in denying the moral significance of the content of life plans.

8. Raz, "Liberalism, Autonomy," p. 100.

9. Mario Cuomo, "Religious Belief and Public Morality: A Catholic Governor's Perspective," *Notre Dame Journal of Law, Ethics and Public Policy* 1 (1984).

10. Ibid., 16.

11. Ibid., 16.
12. Ibid., 18.
13. Ibid., 24–25.
14. Ibid., 23.
15. While from the absence of consensus against abortion Cuomo in-
    fers both that a crusade to prohibition abortion would be wrong
    and that it is right for abortion to be allowed and protected, he
    does not infer from the previous absence of a consensus against
    slavery that slavery ought to have been allowed and protected. But
    he should be making this inference.
16. Cuomo, "Religious Belief," 17.
17. Here we see the tension between this contractarian argument and
    moral realism. The case for its being reasonable not to favor im-
    position of one's moral judgment consists in downgrading the truth
    value of that judgment. This is nicely illustrated in Geraldine Fer-
    raro's book. See Geraldine Ferraro, *Ferraro, My Story* (New York:
    Bantam Books, 1985), p. 215ff. She begins by asserting her belief
    in the wrongness of abortion but explains her defense of allowing
    abortion by unwittingly recounting how her anti-abortion views
    came to be downgraded to the status of a personal (dis)taste con-
    ditioned by her religious background. She does not merely reject
    prohibitions on abortion. She does not expect those with different
    conditioning backgrounds to share her "moral" distaste. She re-
    jects abortion in the way in which I reject frog legs.
18. Ronald Dworkin, "Neutrality, Equality and Liberalism" in *Liberal-
    ism Reconsidered,* eds., Douglas MacLean and Claudia Mills. (To-
    towa, N.J.: Rowman and Allanheld, 1983), p. 3. Ronald Dworkin
    formulates procedural neutralism upon an egalitarian base—or,
    more specifically, upon a right of people to be treated with equal
    concern and respect. In proceduralist fashion, Dworkin maintains
    that the government, "must impose no sacrifice or constraint on
    any citizen *in virtue of an argument* that the citizen could not accept
    without abandoning his sense of equal worth." But his neutralism
    provides the citizen with no protection against systematic interfer-
    ence with his private choices based upon other arguments, e.g.,
    arguments about the great benefits these inroads allow others to
    enjoy, or against gratuitous interference motivated by no argu-
    ments at all. In addition, Dworkin's neutralism provides no pro-
    tection at all for the citizen who already lacks a sense of his own
    worth. The self-esteeming prostitute receives more immunity than
    the self-condemning prostitute.
19. Stephen Holmes discusses what I call the strategic argument in his
    historical essay, "Jean Bodin: the Paradox of Sovereignty and the
    Privatization of Religion" (this volume). He does not distinguish

between a proceduralist version with its emphasis on the idea of a "gag rule" and a substantivist version with its emphasis on "rights [that] define a nonpolitical sphere withdrawn from the jurisdiction of public authorities."

20. I presume throughout the legitimacy of some set of institutions that use coercion to enforce certain social rules. This legitimate "state" may or may not fit standard definitions of the state.

21. Joan Callahan, "Religion, Abortion, and Public Policy" in typescript, portions of which appear as idem, "The Fetus and Fundamental Rights," *Commonweal* 11 (April 1986).

22. This essay was written during the tenure of a summer research grant from the Murphy Institute for Political Economy of Tulane University.

3

COMMENT ON HOLMES, "JEAN BODIN: THE PARADOX OF SOVEREIGNTY AND THE PRIVATIZATION OF RELIGION"

JOHN H. MANSFIELD

In 1641, a group of courageous or foolhardy persons set forth from the wintry, intolerant shores of Massachusetts to establish a tolerating state in the gentler clime of Providence Isle off the coast of Nicaragua. They probably had become fired up by events in England and talk of religious liberty coming from there, but having no opportunity to put their new beliefs into practice in Massachusetts, they looked elsewhere to establish them. To their libertarian beliefs, however, there was one limit: anyone who spoke against another's religion would be put to death.[1] Thus like Jean Bodin, they agreed with the provision of the Peace of Augsburg mentioned by Professor Holmes and embraced what he calls a "gag rule."[2] They were intolerant in the cause of toleration.

On arriving at Providence Isle, the people from Massachusetts found it already occupied by Spaniards and so were forced to sail on to another place. Here conditions were hard and soon they were reduced to eating rats. But by the provident hand of God, as a contemporary account puts it, a ship came to that place and rescued them. Some of the lovers of liberty and warm climate returned to New England and, as the same account says,

71

"[T]he Winters discourse [in Massachusetts] ceased, and projects for a warmer Country were husht and done."[3]

There is an echo of the intolerant tolerance of these people from Massachusetts and the Peace of Augsburg in contemporary United Nations documents regarding religious freedom. In the *International Covenant on Civil and Political Rights,* adopted by the General Assembly in 1966, it is laid down that states subscribing to the Covenant must prohibit advocacy of religious hatred that constitutes incitement to discrimination,[4] and in the more recent *Declaration on the Elimination of All Forms of Intolerance and of the Discrimination Based on Religion or Belief,* adopted by the General Assembly in 1981, it is specified that states shall enact laws prohibiting discrimination on grounds of religion or belief and shall combat intolerance.[5] The United States is criticized for not adhering to documents of this sort. But the provisions referred to could conflict with the First Amendment.[6] The situation is ironic, for the United States has surely played an important role in spreading ideas about religious freedom around the globe. Evidently two different notions of religious freedom are involved.

One reason for punishing attacks on the religion of others and assertions that government should be based upon the doctrines of a particular religion is that such talk imperils civil peace. This was Bodin's reason, Professor Holmes tells us. Civil peace was the highest good for political authority according to Bodin, Professor Holmes seems to say,[7] and whatever was necessary to maintain that peace and avoid its opposite, civil war, was justified. Bodin advocated the absolute sovereignty of the king as a means for achieving and maintaining civil peace.

Perhaps Bodin did truly believe that civil peace was the highest good. What he had seen of civil war might well have convinced him of that. On the other hand, perhaps he thought simply that civil peace was a very great good, and civil war a very great evil, but feared that unless these conditions were treated as absolutes, the value of peace would not be adequately appreciated. The tendency of passions furiously to break forth has been sufficiently demonstrated in sixteenth-century France. Whether or not the passions that broke forth are properly characterized as religious passions is a difficult question.

Are the conflicts in Northern Ireland and Lebanon religious conflicts?

Other examples of particular experiences leading to the absolutizing of certain values come readily to mind. Some abolitionists saw slavery as such a great evil that almost anything was justified to eliminate it. But after the Civil War, the terrible evil of that war having been experienced, it seemed permissible for the sake of ending tension between North and South to leave blacks under the burden of discrimination for another hundred years. Nazism, with its genocide and enslavement of whole nations, seemed such a great evil that a world war, involving the loss of tens of millions of lives, many of them innocent, seemed justified. The destruction and suffering of World War II having been experienced, the ultimate evil became the repetition of such a war or a nuclear war, for the avoidance of which many believe all measures are warranted, including, perhaps, the creation of an absolute international sovereign along Bodin's lines. Nuclear war threatens human existence, and without human beings there can be nothing good, it is argued. Thus we see in regard to the world the attitude Bodin had toward the nation: it is better to have an evil commonwealth than none at all and even the worst form of political oppression is better than universal destruction. Of course, the belief that peace is the highest good rests upon some philosophical or perhaps religious basis.

According to Professor Holmes, Bodin thought the only means for avoiding the absolute evil of civil war was the absolute sovereignty of the king. Holmes's account of Bodin's thought is unclear as to whether sovereignty is simply a fact—a certain kind of power—or whether it implies rights and duties: rights in the king and duties in the subject. It is clear that Bodin would not consider a person to be sovereign unless he had some capacity for being effective, but he may have intended to go beyond this and, in speaking of sovereignty, assert a value: because of the advantages that flow from obedience to a certain person, he ought to be obeyed.

Bodin, Professor Holmes tells us, thought that his proposals for maintaining sovereignty would be as attractive to a self-interested, unvirtuous king as to a selfless, virtuous one. Of course, the self-interested, unvirtuous king has a philosophy: he acts for purposes and is not driven simply by instinct. But Bodin evidently thought he had devised a way of linking up the morality of the self-interested, unvirtuous king with the morality of peace to which Bodin adhered, so that if the self-interested, unvirtuous king intelligently pursued his self-interested, unvirtuous ends, the morality of peace would be served as well.

That civil peace was the highest goal for political authority, Bodin evidently thought indisputable. At least from Professor Holmes's account it seems that Bodin believed that the value of peace rested upon grounds entirely different from those that supported the programs of the warring religious parties of his time. Professor Holmes describes the justifications for Bodin's civil peace as "secular."[8] Secular is not defined. If the sovereign withdraws from religious disputes, eliminates religious questions from the state's agenda and confines himself to promoting civil peace and the goods that flow from it, there is a chance of attaining that peace and achieving those goods.

Here I think we see the fundamental question raised by Professor Holmes's paper. Has Bodin really discovered in civil peace based on secular values an unassailable foundation for the state? If it was unassailable in sixteenth-century France, will it be unassailable at other times and in other places? Professor Holmes says that by removing certain questions from the state's agenda and by "staying clear of the religious thicket,"[9] and by not identifying too closely with the moral aspirations of the citizens, the state can augment its power so as to deal effectively with those items that remain on its agenda. However, the questions claimed to have been removed from the state's agenda by accepting civil peace as the highest good have not, in fact, been removed. Instead, certain answers to these questions—religious answers— have been ruled out. The misdescription of what has been done may explain the guilty conscience that Professor Holmes discerns in liberal democracies. Religious answers have been privatized, but not the questions to which they have been proposed. For those who think that heaven and earth should be connected up in some way—in what particular way was the preoccupation of the Middle Ages and the Reformation and most premodern cultures—the decision to base the state on secular values is neither neutral nor indisputably correct. If the

Shah supposed that by concentrating on secular values he would necessarily win the approval of his people and provide an indisputable ground for civil peace, he was in for a rude awakening. Even if political rulers confine themselves to disputing among secular values, who can be certain that peace will be given the importance that Bodin attached to it. Are not Marxism and fascism, and perhaps even liberal constitutionalism, as capable as Calvinism and Catholicism of laying waste the earth?

Professor Holmes recognizes that restricting government to secular considerations may in some instances exacerbate social tensions and even lead to revolutionary explosions. Perhaps the establishment of government on a secular basis tends to peace only under certain cultural and historical circumstances—those of sixteenth-century France and twentieth-century America, for instance—whereas under other circumstances such a program may lead to disorder and war. And these other circumstances may not represent simply a primitive stage in social and political development.

At the beginning of his paper, Professor Holmes declares that by examining Bodin's argument for religious toleration—that it will augment state power and help bring about civil peace—we can shed a good deal of light on "our own constitutionally mandated separation of the political and religious spheres."[10] No doubt it sheds some light, but how much? I have already noted that a readiness to stifle religious controversy is not part of our constitutional tradition. The free speech and free exercise clauses of the First Amendment provide generous room for religious controversy and cannot plausibly be interpreted to mean that it is an evil to be stamped out. Furthermore, if it is the case that under the First Amendment legislation must be capable of justification on some "secular" ground, it is not definitely settled that the subjective motivation of legislators,[11] much less of voters, must be secular. The idea that government action must rest upon values beyond dispute is not supported by American judicial decisions: legislation is often upheld though its value is far from indisputable.[12] The notion that government must not identify itself with the moral aspirations of the people is refuted by numerous decisions of which only *Brown v. Board of Education*[13] need be mentioned.

The point that Bodin taught to which Professor Holmes gives

greatest attention is that the sovereign can increase his power by observing limitations on his own actions, and, in particular, by granting a measure of religious toleration. This is a point that certainly has received recognition in our constitutional development,[14] but by no means has it been the only theme in this complex process. Although Roger Williams believed that the peace of the city would be better assured if the magistrate did not seek to bring about the kingdom of God, his main concern was with religion, not with government. Government involvement in religion, in his view, tended to degrade religion. This view was picked up by Baptists and other pietists in late eighteenth-century America, groups without whose advocacy the First Amendment probably would not have been adopted.[15] Madison's Remonstrance Against Religious Assessments to support the teaching of Christianity in Virginia skillfully interwove the themes of the rights of religion and the strengthening of government. Since the religion clauses of the First Amendment embody judgments regarding both the rights of religion and the best way to maintain government, they probably should be understood as accepting greater risks to civil peace than would be tolerable to those who concentrate exclusively on the importance of such peace and the power of government. Thus, I conclude that although Bodin's political philosophy sheds some light on our constitutional tradition, it neglects a perspective that is an important part of that tradition.

NOTES

1. Edward Johnson, *Wonder-Working Providence of Sions Saviour in New England* (Andover: Draper, 1867), pp. 171–72, quoted in Larzer Ziff, *Puritanism in America* (New York: Viking, 1973), p. 126.
2. Stephen Holmes, "Jean Bodin: The Paradox of Sovereignty and the Privatization of Religion," in this volume.
3. Johnson, *Wonder-Working Providence*, p. 172.
4. United Nations General Assembly, *International Covenant on Civil and Political Rights*, G.A. Res. 2200, 21 U.N. GAOR Supp. (no. 16) U.N. Doc. A/6316 1966, p. 55.
5. United Nations General Assembly, *Declaration on the Elimination of All Forms of Intolerance and of Discrimination Based on Religion or Belief*, G.A. Res. 36/55, 36 U.N. GAOR Supp. (no. 51) U.N. Doc. A/36/51 1982, 171–72.

6. Louis Henkin, "Rights: American and Human," *Colum. L. Rev.* 79 (1979): 405, 415, 423.
7. Holmes, *"Jean Bodin."* "Preventing subjects from slaughtering one another is the immediate purpose of all political authority—that is what we learn throughout the *République.* This negative goal takes precedence of all rival objectives, including more inspiring religious ones." This statement may or may not be qualified by Professor Holmes's later statement: "[For Bodin] peace was not an end-in-itself, to be sure, any more than food and shelter; but it was the essential precondition for every worthwhile goal." This volume.
8. Ibid.
9. Ibid.
10. Ibid.
11. Although the recent Supreme Court decision in *Wallace v. Jaffree,* 105 S. Ct. 2479 (1985), goes far in this direction.
12. See the recent Supreme Court decision upholding a state sodomy law as applied to homosexual conduct. *Bowers v. Hardwick,* 106 S. Ct. 2841 (1986). "The law, however, is constantly based on notions of morality, and if all laws representing essentially moral choices are to be invalidated under the Due Process Clause, the courts will be very busy indeed. Even respondent makes no such claim, but insists that majority sentiments about the morality of homosexuality should be declared inadequate. We do not agree, and are unpersuaded that the sodomy laws of some 25 States should be invalidated on this basis." Idem. at 2846.
13. 347 U. S. 483 (1954).
14. See, e.g., Illinois ex rel. *McCollum v. Bd. of Ed.,* 333 U. S. 203, 212 (1948).
15. For a discussion of the difference between the views of Roger Williams and Jefferson regarding religion and government and the contribution each made to the First Amendment, see Mark DeWolfe Howe, *The Garden and the Wilderness* (Chicago: University of Chicago Press, 1965).

4

BAYLE'S COMMONWEALTH OF ATHEISTS REVISITED

GEORGE A. KELLY*

". . . it cannot be said that the world is atheist, that the human world is atheist. There are still too many people who believe."—Jean-Paul Sartre. Simone de Beauvoir, *Adieux: A Farewell to Sartre,* p. 444.

I

In the triad law, morality, religion, it is distinctively the third term with which modern political theory feels least comfortable. Despite fierce debates over their nature, genesis, and relation, law and morality are the *sine quibus non* of the social experiment, unless one is an anarchist or an antinomian. It is broadly recognized that law is the central feature of the territorial state and its matrix of authority—*nulla iustitia, hulla iniuria.* Somewhat more imaginatively, we have "moral territories" as well, spaces of intention and action where we cooperate in ways that the laws do not prescribe and where, by common consent, we assign the verdicts "good" and "bad," "right" and "wrong," "fitting" and "improper."

Religion, for us, is somewhat different. Undeniably, it, too, has its "territories"; and at least some of these are more impregnable than legal boundaries. But the prevailing tendency in Western civilization has been to deterritorialize and depoliticize religion, regardless of numerous and well-publicized re-

*Professor Kelly, a former Vice President of our Society, died while this volume was in press.

sistances or counter currents. Religion—which most archaeo-logical and sociological research shows to have been once, in virtually all societies, the fountainhead of social control, the inspiration of morality and the ultimate sanction of legal observance—has been increasingly regarded as a privilege or a snare of private choice: a matter between person and conscience, "ego" and "superego." Fundamentalism and liberal religion alike stress this matter of choice: "Choose ye this day!"

That, of course, is a phenomenon with very deep roots. In our culture, it goes back at least as far as Christ's call to his disciples and to the formation of the so-called primitive church. From the standpoint of the modern political theorist, it may be traced at least as far back as the French *politiques* of the sixteenth century, and it is doubly anchored in state-building (where political theory sought to reduce *sacerdotium* to a contingent particularism) and in social resistances to the new centralizing state (where religion first appeared lastingly as *sola fide,* an act of the private believer, his faith posited against all works in the world). Through these influences—Erastian or Protestant—religion has slowly but surely tended to become "religiosity" or "religious experience" detached from formal theology, the theory of belief, and from ecclesiology, the "political culture" of beliefs. Both these trends have made religion otiose to the political order, despite passing ideologies of the "secular city" or "civil religion," or have provided politics with transient perspectives on its own order that are necessarily as fluid as the types of religion that sponsor them.[1] Thus, religion and "creeds," religion and "churches" have become unravelled. Immanuel Kant wrote, almost two hundred years ago: "We must carefully distinguish the church from religion, which is an inner attitude of mind."[2] That *Innerlichkeit* might be regarded as a radical separation of the Aristotelian conjunction of form and material, the thesis on which an earlier Christianity had been based. By 1978, according to George Gallup's report, 80 percent of Americans—allegedly "the most religious people in the Western world"—agreed with the statement "An individual should arrive at his or her religious beliefs independent of any churches or synagogues."[3] Or as John Dewey in his late acknowledgment of the value of a "religious attitude" (1934), put it: "The very idea that was central in religions has more and more oozed

away, so to speak, from the guardianship and care of any particular social institution. . . . What has been gained is that religion has been placed upon its only real and solid foundation:
direct relationship of conscience and will to God."[4] On such a
view, in an earlier writing by Dewey, religion was a kind of
science accompanied by awe, intended "to create an intelligence
pregnant with belief in the possibility of the direction of human
affairs by itself."[5] That indeed makes religion direct democracy—*vox populi, vox Dei*—and it is perhaps here that enthusias-
tic theorists of that elusive form of legitimacy might look, rather
than at Vermont town meetings or New York cooperative
apartment management. Human beings, as William James virtually suggested, elect their gods.[6] Yet the electing of a god by
secret ballot in the private soul is mostly bereft of participatory
rewards. It is more like Tocqueville's democratic individualism,
which "throws [every man] back forever upon himself alone
and threatens in the end to confine him entirely within the sol-
itude of his own heart."[7]

The political implications of such an attitude, the ultimate
privatized consequence of *sola fide,* are clear. For better or worse,
religion gradually ceases to be a bond of common action—or
common self-restraint—in a life framed by other institutions.
Religion is then protest or resignation, neither of them close to
the fulness of life. It can no longer mediate coherently for the
two cities it acknowledges. Unless it is becomingly mute, it will
tend to get in the way of the *civitas terrena* and will most certainly prove irksome and vulnerable to the preferences of nonbelievers. On the one hand, for those who care to practice it,
religion will be too holy to be encumbered by political compromise and too personal to be constrained by ancestral creeds or
the custodial authority of churches. On the other hand, it will
be too speculative, too detached from the order of *things visible,*
to do much more than interfere with statesmanship or ordinary
social practices. Like the ideal family or the legendary Swiss
bank account, it had best be made a private affair. Its precepts,
such as "love thy neighbor" or "turn the other cheek" or "judge
not, lest ye be judged," are no doubt admirable, but they are
hardly prudent in this world. The full panoply of religion—
going beyond such maxims to an entire view of the universe—
is rarely useful: It is a complication and an embarrassment in a

world struggling as hard as it does for another kind of certainty.

Would it not, therefore, be a blessing if we could live in a "commonwealth of atheists"—of rational persons who, it may be argued, would be law-abiding and, if not compassionate, at least trustworthy, because they would see clearly and calculate accurately the things at stake in this world, instead of confusing its values with supernatural and improbable priorities? Couldn't some such institution as the "market," construed as a comprehensive system of human action (cf., Hayek's "catallaxy"),[8] not only rid the economy of irrational planning and misinformed "commands," but also exorcise the very notion of a higher will from the demonology of the Great Society?

The commonwealth of atheists is, of course, a thought-experiment. The rationale of libertarianism, although hostile to religion, is compelled to tolerate it in all its forms by its own premises; it could only hope to master religion by making each one "his own church," thus neutralizing its collective proportions. Yet it is possible to conceive, especially in a society of plenty, that human beings, absorbed in their own desires and interests, might bring such a commonwealth into existence, making the credentials of religion, in Popper's terms, "falsifiable," and hence scientific. But the fact is that, up to now, we have no historical report of such a society, not even—or especially—in lands where political authority represses religion. Expert opinion divides on the significance of this fact. Some argue that it is impossible for a society to cohere without religious underpinnings, whether divinity is ontologically true and necessary or whether it is merely a projection of psychological or social needs. Others hold that it is the progressive human mission to replace religion with a divinization of humanity or with a "disenchantment," a desirable or reluctant avowal that there is no meaning in the cosmos outside of mankind's own transient and conflicting meanings. A third group would contend that divinity does not depend on what earthlings decide to believe, that a commonwealth of atheists is conceivable, if not likely, and that this result would be impoverishing and probably fatal to human society.[9]

But before construing and commenting on the thought-experiment made famous by Pierre Bayle in very different circumstances at the end of the seventeenth century, some remarks should be devoted to law and morality. The social functions of religion cannot be adequately explored without reference to these complementary, and sometimes adversarial, features of human control and conduct.

II

Man is not an angel. As Kant says, "He is an animal who requires a master."[10] His most obvious immediate constraint is law, a body of coercive rules that he has come to accept, but often violates. Law issues out of custom, and it may be regarded at its base as a necessary minimum of enforced custom (*consuetudo, mores*) made possible by the creation of the state, itself a consequence of society's need for authoritative coercion and regular justice. It is probably quite anachronistic or idealistic to regard law as a rationalistic substitute for, or challenge to, custom (even Rousseau does not quite go so far as to say this in *Contrat social,* II, vii). It is better regarded as a rationalizing of custom: The heroic lawgiver is rationalized custom incarnate.[11] However, classical or classically inspired texts (Plato, Machiavelli, Rousseau) insist unsparingly that laws, as opposed to customs or folkways, are not palatable to peoples without auxiliary conviction, and that this conviction is provided by the belief that laws are given by divine ordinance (by an oracle or prophet, or by the direct revelation of a god). The law is, to that extent, believed, accepted, and sacralized, as well as "discovered," in the practices of the tribe. Ultimately, in more "civilized" and cosmopolitan times, a third appeal is made: Laws are held to derive not from custom or will, but, in the nature of things, from a higher power, "reason," which logically entails the premises of the laws, so that good laws cannot be in obvious conflict with right reason, a faculty shared by God, human legislators, and, eventually, all men of discernment and morality.

The history of Western legal philosophy is a rich and complicated mixture of these three themes: custom, higher will or "revelation," and reason. Each theme has a quite ancient lineage; and their mélange in theoretical practice is as remarkable as their competition in pure theory (where, however, two of three often combine). Each of these types of legal theory seems to be ever renewed (custom in Hume, higher will in Austin, reason in Kant), no matter whether the formula is religion-laden or distinctively secular.

Seen from this perspective, law and morality appear to have quite similar origins or modes of justification: in the *mores maiorum*, in sovereign command (originally divine), or in obedience to right reason. That is indeed true. But law departs from morality in several salient respects, since it is produced and prosecuted by a territorial state, is generally defined by a narrower range of prohibitions, and is centered in external coercion rather than in self-management. Morality has, in a certain sense, come to be connected with the right or power of personal choice (often with the tautological hope that this choice will be "moral"). One can of course choose to obey or not obey the law, but those circumstances are not the same. Law might include some of the properties of personal choice in being either the fiat of a tyrant, to which all others must conform, or in approaching a bargaining situation where several wills or choices receive satisfaction (as implied in Rousseau's concept of *"volonté de tous"*). Generally, law has a higher and a lower errand. It is both a translation into human conduct of "what is right" ("the interpreter of equity," as John of Salisbury put it) and an armature of enforceable, imperfect rules with which society girds itself for its survival and well-being. Law is also commonly perceived as a composite force and institution beyond the sum of specific actionable events; when one "breaks the law," one not only commits an injustice against a person or the community; one also transgresses a dense system of security known as "the law."

The performance of law in a legal territory (typically the state) is *lawfulness*, which means essentially a persisting obedience to public statutes as interpreted by courts of law (their separation from executive power has been one of the hallmarks of modern liberal civilization). It is obligatory to be lawful; and one has, under ordinary circumstances, the duty to know what the law is (hence the laws should be published and understandable). Since law is invariably associated with a physical power to compel and since most (though not all) laws involve prohibitions on conduct, the lawful individual will need to be prudent (not necessarily moral, even a member of Kant's "race of devils") as a matter of course. Lawabidingness will surely be encouraged if people accept the law's propriety and fairness and grasp its rationale. But people cannot be, and are not expected to be, enamored of the law: Love and law are not easily reconciled, whether it is self-love or love of others. At most, one will refrain from lawbreaking because of the penalties attached (some of which will be moral, in the realm of "opinion"). One's respect for the law will of course vary according to its correspondence to one's beliefs and values and one's confidence that bad laws might be changed. And one's hesitation from crime will depend not only on the likelihood of detection and prosecution but on a surrounding civil morale that condemns lawbreakers and "free riders." There are even elements of social altruism and sacrifice that affect lawfulness, especially in times of emergency.

It has been said that the laws should be as mild as possible.[12] That they should be as just as possible is indubitable (although a Draconian fairness would be resisted); but the ideal of "mildness" either assumes an improvement of civilization demanding ever more lenient penalties (much cast in doubt by the events of our century); or a notion that mankind, now more sensitive to pain, requires less of it for adequate chastisement; or that where the laws are more lenient or more silent, other forms of social control will take up the slack (i.e., morality, religion). The first two arguments seem dubious; the third seems the most correct. But it comes down to a question of institutions. If morality, religion, the school, the family, etc., do less than their share of promoting peace, civility, and honest behavior, can milder laws then be in order?

The advantage of law—mild or severe, provided that it is coherent, non-arbitrary, and felt to be just—is that it is enunciated in public statutes *("gesetze")*. As so promulgated, it provides a clarity of expectation and conduct not so easily discerned in morality and religion. Because of this clarity it also helps to illuminate the boundaries and resources of those other institutions. In the best of cases, its spirit is renewed from them. Its adversarial form—a long refinement and mitigation of private war—is well designed to explore the vicissitudes of uncertain truth.

The inadequacies of law in the general range of social control are these:

(1) Because of its formalism and professionalism in complex societies, it tends to favor the strong, the rich, and the clever over the weak and unresourceful.

(2) It deals almost completely with externals and outward behavior, leaving the disposition to virtue basically unaffected; indeed, at worst, it can be counter-ethical.

(3) It is predominantly expressed in the form of prohibitions, making few, and usually mediated, claims on positive performance.

(4) It is only territorially enforceable and thus, whatever its refinements, it speaks with the language of the tribe.

The emergence of law, that is, of political society, would, as we have noted, have been impossible without a pre-existing substrate of regulated group behavior called custom or, as one might say, proto-morality. Since time out of mind, moral philosophers have debated the mystery of how moral judgment and action came to be implanted in homo sapiens, using such notions as instinct for survival, sociability, pity, sympathy, desire for approval, law of duty, and so forth. We may be forgiven for not entering that quagmire. We will just express the view that conflict over scarce goods (inanimate and human property) or values (dignity, reputation, power) has always been a central problem of human conduct. Rules of cooperation, however developed, fine-tuned, and internalized, are always fragile, needing social and political sanctions behind them. What ordinary language calls morality has developed in parallel with those sanctions, internalizing itself in the conscience, to pattern conflict into acceptable channels and, the need arising, to season it with compromise or even altruism. In counterpart, however, morality partakes naturally of certain traits of aggressiveness that might, at first glance, seem foreign to it, rotating around questions of honor, reputation, just reward, and compensation. They do not vanish in the effort to bring conduct under moral rules, for they are a part of the same impetus. Common morality is not the Sermon on the Mount. What is held "fitting" or "good" is not always sublime. "He got his comeuppance" is a moral remark.

Yet this does not mean—and here ordinary language once again comes to our rescue—that morality might simply consist in following precepts of self-interest, avoiding pain and seeking pleasure, unless these terms are understood in some lofty Socratic sense. A morality is not simply an "individual life style" that one has chosen for better or worse. It cannot be the mere pursuit of one's selfish goals, but must frequently involve the pain of choice, the deferral of reward, and even submission to harsh sacrifice. On the other hand, saintly conduct is not to be expected, or desired, from the mass of persons. "Self-interest rightly understood" appears to mean, in the last analysis, a patterning of action where the self and the social milieu stand in healthy balance and where the criteria of merit and demerit are mutually recognized. As I have written elsewhere: "The most moral society is not that which has the greatest number of moral options or moral experiences but that which most properly understands itself in moral terms."[13] It might be true, in some technical sense, that a truly moral action takes place only when the agent obeys duty and not interest. But such an explanation tells us no more about the anthropological functioning of a moral system than the thesis "private vices, public virtues." The rules of a moral system are considerably beneath Kant's formula, considerably above Mandeville's paradox. Of the two, we should prefer Kant, not only because he recognized the "crooked wood" of legality but also because a moral system is not simply an ironical description of what might seem to be the case. Language still possesses the powerful word "immoral" to separate what is reprehensible from what is commendable or neutral.

Moral behavior is not purely "situational," for the agent always brings rules, habits, and maxims to the situation; neither is it an absolute matter of "thou shalt" or "thou shalt not" (there is always the possibility of extenuation or pardon) because absolute commands and prohibitions bear on the general principle or maxim, not directly on the situation (hence the proper role of casuistry). Morality is rightly called "practical" as opposed to "cognitive" or "deductive," although its experimentalism is limited by stern social injunctions. Assessable and subject to judgment in action, it is never accurately measurable at rest. The supremely good and the supremely true are no doubt one; but, short of that climax, there is room for dispute. Hence morality is typically analyzed in terms of virtues and vices (rather abstract) into which persons or nations step, colors which they take on in terms of character or character-building, and thus of education in the full sense: evaluatively, not propositionally. Morality depends on the assumption that it can be inculcated. But it also depends on the axiom that the will is free and that it has the capacity to choose the better over the worse. When this is done, the agent is being moral.

Moralities are not, in the last analysis, "relative," to be judged only for their coherence of practice within closed and equivalent social systems. Morality is never "closed." Here again ordinary language helps us: for we must ask: "relative to what?"— and the only answer can be: "relative to a higher morality." Montaigne's celebrated essay on the cannibals does not teach us that eating people is nice; it merely instructs us that savages have traits of natural candor that more sophisticated peoples might well admire, if not exactly imitate. Ethnocentrism cannot be the point; there are no obvious links between intelligence and moral life. There is no group on the planet that fails to distinguish between better and worse. But in complex societies, with their information and propensity to curiosity and inspiration, criteria of value are regularly imported from the outside, giving moral judgment a cosmopolitan flavor.

Neither is morality, in essence, subjective. Moral qualities are, of course, always imputed to individual acts and choices and their agents; but they are brought to persons from the outside. Morality is not what each individual believes in his heart to be right. The right that the individual chooses is pre-established by the common consent of his peers or by some code of ethics that he has not made, but to which he adheres. He applies this to his situation, his duties, and his desires. He chooses, but he conforms his will and his deed to possibilities always available in the repertory of his culture and by dint of previous moral experience. This is why teaching a child to be moral means to teach it both the ways of the community and some latitude for independence within, and sometimes against, common standards.

Moral practices are the dispositions of persons toward each other or things rightfully assigned to them that are unregulated by law or, if so regulated, not influenced in the last resort by the law's power to punish. Morality has a wider range than law, since it is not subject to political obligation, if we take this to mean that people act morally under many circumstances where they are not beholden to the writ of the sovereign. However, despite the alleged "internality" of the one and the "external-ity" of the other, law is sometimes regarded as a "minimum morality" of social cohesion, since, like morality, it has its roots in custom and—more problematically—since strict observance of law might, by itself, permit society to function. But when it comes to be widely believed that morality is, or should be, more lenient than the law in its demands, the society holding that view is in danger of breakdown.

Using terms taken from Oakeshott, we could argue that in modern societies two distinct forms of morality operate: the morality of individualism (MI) and the morality of communal ties (MCT).[14] The first of these stresses the right of the individual to conceive and project a personal moral life; the second constrains this practice by the traditional or consensual feelings of the community. The advantage of MI is that it privileges autonomous choice and responsibility (in this form, it is Kant's ethic); its deficit is that, seen another way, it can lead to flagrant egoism or caprice (as Hegel suggested), or place intolerable burdens on the willing self (the evidence of much recent psy-chiatry). Conversely, MCT can be seen as robustly cooperative, as an ethic of "pitching in," or even "my station and my duties," but it may also be the seed-plot of narrow bigotry and igno-rance (cf. the plays of Ibsen). Though these models seem to be in conflict, aspects of each are in conflict, too. Also, and more significantly, most moral agents in modern settings make semi-reflective compromises between them in practice. MI asserts the priority of the person; but it would be fatiguing and fatal if each person had to *think through* each moral choice. MCT stresses the connection between *mores* and morals, the role of social dis-position and milieu in the insensible formation of moral char-acter. In the best practices, each is an ethic of education (the child is not, as the poet said, "the father of the man"); but MCT features an education of *habitus*, while MI stresses individuality, curiosity, and "enlightenment."

There is the further point that MI creates in us not only "self-awareness," but the complementary capacity to extend it to all other human beings (in this sense, cosmopolitanism begins with self and leaps across the tribe).[15] But MCT produces a concrete sense of moral bondedness, at first consanguinous, then extended to a wider horizon, without which individualism is vaporous.

It is mistaken to think that people can live in the suspension of moral judgments. However morality came about in the human race, its destiny does not seem to be its elimination in a chaos of personal whim where "what you do is none of my business, and what I do is none of yours." The decision to refrain from critical moral expression, the practice of the most neutral and benign tolerance toward others, may veil a hidden arrogance, a grudging accommodation, or a saintly humility. It cannot entail a renunciation of moral priorities or a suppression of moral feelings.

As the matter has been proposed here, there can be no precise settlement of the boundaries or content of a doctrine of duties or of what is virtuous. Morality is always an adjudication of claims that arise, first of all within each of us, the goal being to find and act on what is right under the aegis of self-governance, which is the true task of morals, not of politics. Outside the self, there can be only an adjudication of the claims of the "moral territories." This does not release any agent, personal or collective, from framing a proper sense of what is right and wrong, nor does it require anyone to condone a perceived wrong for the sake of some other value, e.g., freedom. If there were not these pleas and pleaders bearing convictions, how could there be adjudication? The burden is not really on the forcefulness of the plea, but on the nature of the adjudicator. In modern societies, judgments about virtue are usually referenced to the self; but it is always a self in the presence of others.[16] No individual can, by whatever act of will, make an integral moral lifeworld for himself or herself: even if God is dead, society lives on. While today's freedom of moral choice makes the "good" far more problematic than the "right" supplied by many theories of justice, the number of plausible moralities remains quite finite, diversified by MI, but held in check by MCT.

Morality supplies what law cannot achieve in bending human beings to their task, because, as we believe, it is an inner resource, prescribed by ourselves and by those who influence us with their approval or friendship, but not by the law. As such, it seems more of our choosing and it is so hallowed. It deals with a wider circle of appropriate conduct than the law; it faces us with genuine choices of self-legislation. Whether or not it arose in the *mores maiorum*, it now reserves a retreat in our consciousness protected from external legislation.

Is this enough for civility and social order: Certainly in a commonwealth of atheists, it would seem that, joined to the law, morality would be sufficient to operate the good, if not the "best," society. But can its flaws—the uncertainty and divisiveness of multiple moralities, their boundary questions with other forms of social control, their preemptive attitudes toward the law and their occasional negligence of or terrorism against it—meet the specifications? Might it not be true that the social order was like a three-legged stool and that religion was one of the supports of that inelegant piece of furniture where the human race sits or has been seated?

III

Bayle's remarks about atheism, and the commonwealth of atheists in particular, are mostly found in his *Pensées diverses sur les comètes* (1682).[17] His major point is negative: Study a code of religious precepts (especially the Christian, Bayle intimates) and then look around at life; or imagine yourself a visitor from another planet. What will you observe? You will see that "theory does not square with the findings of experience."[18] The Martians "would not have lived two weeks among us without declaring that in this world people do not conduct themselves according to the light of conscience."[19] It is not that religion does not teach men what they ought to do (Bayle is far from saying that the morality of the Decalogue and the Sermon on the Mount is ignoble); it is that the ideal of duty derived from religion is woefully ineffective. In general, "Man does not decide between two possible actions by his abstract idea of duty [or, as Kant would later say, his 'pure practical reason'], but by the particular judgment he makes of each one as he is on the point of acting." Thus, "He very seldom adopts false principles and almost never abandons the ideas of natural equity in his conscience, and yet he almost always concludes in favor of his dissolute desires."[20] Bayle sees the destructive passions "reigning constantly in all countries and in all ages"[21]—in truth he sees a mitigated "war of all against all," although his philosophy is not at all that of Hobbes.

Thus, the commonwealth of atheists is not exactly presented by Bayle as an exemplary solution to man's moral affliction; but rather as a retort to those who hold that a belief in the efficacy of divine punishment is required to control our reckless ways or, so to speak, "civilize us." Since "We have no annals informing us of the customs of a nation completely immersed in atheism, . . . We cannot . . . refute that atheists . . . are ferocious beasts more to be feared than lions and tigers."[22] But since evidence shows "that the inclination to do evil does not come from the ignorance of God's existence and that it is not corrected by acquiring the knowledge of a God who punishes and rewards," we may at least surmise that atheists could form as lawful a society as do Christians, Jews, Mohammedans, or Tartars.

Before proceeding further with Bayle's argument, a few observations are in order. The first of these is that while the notion of atheism implicates both the inner disposition of the social member (his conception of how to act and his source of motives) and the outer—we might say structural—properties of a legal and moral community, it is explicitly the latter aspect that Bayle is stressing. Bayle is not asking whether such a thing as salvation exists or should be sought; he is nibbling at the famous question: "How is society possible?" Still, his assumptions about atheism are highly intellectualized. Atheism is a cultivated state of mind supported by some such philosophical stance as Epicureanism or scepticism: not a putative common inclination. This is not some kind of imaginary primitivism. Even Montaigne's thought-experiment with the cannibals was not quite rid of superstition: that society had prophets, and a grim requirement for the constancy of favorable results from them.[23]

In the second place, Bayle's bold paradox cuts in several directions. It not only cuts against Christianity, regarding which Montaigne had already declared bitterly: "We willingly accord to piety only the services that flatter our passions. There is no hostility that exceeds Christian hostility. . . . Our religion is made to extirpate vices; it covers them, fosters them, incites them."[24] It equally undermines the resolute paganism of Machiavelli, who argued that "There never was any remarkable lawgiver amongst any people who did not resort to divine authority, as otherwise his laws would not have been accepted by the people. . . . Where the fear of God is wanting, there the country will come to ruin, unless it be sustained by the fear of the prince, which may temporarily supply the want of religion."[25] Religious fear or awe—as expressed in portents, preaching, and oaths—was, according to Machiavelli, universally potent, "For all men . . . are born and live and die in the same way, and therefore resemble each other."[26] In his own time, Savonarola's religious charisma had made the case. Bayle's attitude toward the *virtù* inspired by Roman religion is clear: "The ancient pagan, who had an unbelievable baggage of superstitions . . . still did not fail to commit every crime imaginable."[27] Yet, with an inconsistency from which Bayle is not always exempt, he slides to the more defensible position: "I will not hesitate to say that with regard to morals and civic affairs, [a society of atheists] would be just like a society of pagans."[28] This nevertheless remains at the antipodes of Machiavelli, for whom the belief in religious sanctions is paramount to civic prosperity.

In the third place, Bayle rebuffs the philosophically popular solution of "natural religion," according to which (1) all higher religions are, more or less, when relieved of their superstitions, branches of the same stock, variations or corruptions of a single human faith that features a minimum but necessary belief structure; and (2) it is not so much the fear of divine punishment or retribution that moralizes conduct as a positive disposition of benevolence or sociality that the Creator has placed in all human beings. Rather, Bayle suggests, it is neither the religion nor the moral disposition that we share, but the acquisitive, prideful, and vengeful passions that we vent on one another.[29]

Bayle's position thus manages to offend or agitate Christians, civic humanists, and "enlighteners" alike—and we are not astonished to find the commonwealth of atheists briskly attacked from a number of angles.

Bayle's argument is both sceptical and empirical. The weapons of scepticism are turned against both reason and revelation, both natural-law and will-of-the-Creator arguments. Bayle's thesis makes room neither for teleology nor progress nor *Bildung*. At most it maintains a hedonistic presumption that human beings might be socially managed by calculations of pain and pleasure, profit and loss, reputation and scandal. While it would be doing Bayle an injustice to claim that in his scattered and fertile thoughts this is his last or only word on the subject, it comes close to the mark in this specific text. Bayle ambiguously grants that motives of opinion and reputation may join the physical sanctions of the law in enforcing conduct among atheists (here anticipating Hume). But his entire argument is from the standpoint of prudence and self-interest. In this sense, Bayle is not so much the continuer of Montaigne as the forerunner of Helvétius. Yet that too, is subject to caution: Helvétius believed in the "science" of every word he wrote, while in Bayle's case the preoccupations of the satirist and moralist also mingle. Bayle conveys shame; Helvétius is never ashamed of the "facts of the case." Bayle's moral or literary strategy is not, however, central to our treatment of his thought-experiment.

The empirical surface covering his sceptical depth is not terribly impressive as a matter of logic or proof. As examples of the powerlessness of religious precepts, Bayle appeals to generalities, to worst cases, and to a presumed impotence of God's design. As evidence for the saliency of atheism, he canvasses a number of familiar instances: the exemplary life of Epicurus; the Saducees, who, despite denial of an afterlife, probably lived as well as any of the Jews; Vanini; Jean l'Hôpital.[30] At most, Bayle seems able to show only a striking incongruity between religious practice and the good life. But he nowhere shows that the existence of a nonreligious society would foster any improvement. As Kolakowski puts it:

> When Pierre Bayle argued that morality does not depend on religion, he was speaking mainly of psychological independence; he pointed out that atheists are capable of achieving the highest moral standards (Spinoza was to him an eminent example; occasionally Vanini) and of putting to shame most of the faithful Christians. That is obviously true as far as it goes, but this matter-of-fact argument leaves the question of validity intact; neither does it solve the question of the effective sources of the moral strength and moral convictions of those 'virtuous pagans.'[31]

What exactly did Bayle claim for his commonwealth of atheists? We have already seen that he claimed for them a parity with a "society of pagans" and that, following Montaigne and others, he contrasted them favorably with Christian hypocrisy. The pagans were cruel and riddled with superstition; there was an ugly gulf between Christian teaching and Christian conduct. Having dispensed with or quieted the calumny that atheists are "wild beasts," Bayle proceeds to assert that religion counts for nothing, except possibly confusion, in civil life. Human beings really act as if they had never heard of divine rewards and punishments. The hope of a felicitous immortality does not sway them; at best they desire a glorious reputation among the living. They caress this pleasant image in their mind, as Diderot would do so passionately in his *Lettres à Falconet.*[32] This is true of atheists and believers alike. Hence, "It is not any stranger for an atheist to live virtuously than for a Christian to commit all sorts of crimes."[33]

In the last analysis, Bayle asserts that the state's justice "is the cause of the virtue of most people, for as soon as it fails to punish the sinner, few people keep themselves from the sin."[34] In this, he aligns himself with the later materialists (Helvétius, Diderot, d'Holbach, etc.) who place the entire burden of crime prevention on the resources of positive law. Yet he vacillates here. After claiming that "A society of atheists would practice both civic and moral actions just as other societies practice them, provided that crimes were severely punished and that honor and shame were associated with certain acts," he goes on to "expect to see people who would be honest in their business dealings, who would help the poor, who would oppose injustice, who would be faithful to their friends, who would scorn insults addressed to them [meaning here that they would refuse the duel], who would restrain their carnal appetites, and who would do no harm to anyone."[35] To be sure, Bayle imputes the motives of such conduct to external pressures, but a good part of the conduct he cites is what we would call internally or morally motivated (honesty, charity, loyalty), things that the law rarely enjoins. He argues from a basic standpoint of physical prudence, but illustrates his text with samples of exemplary moral courage. Here we must ask how he distinguishes the wise from the *vulgus;* and he is not too clear about that. Still, Bayle is no utopian, for he does not doubt "that there would be crimes committed of every kind."[36] But these would be no worse than in any other society; and, elliptically, Bayle hints that with religion removed, the real patterning of conduct would not be obscured.

Bayle's main point is not that religion fanatically persecutes good people (although he anticipates Voltaire in preferring atheism to fanaticism), but that its impact on conduct is nugatory. His society of atheists, which is like utopia in the respect that it has never existed and probably never will, cannot describe a general possibility for human nature (any more than Rousseau's Sparta) because it would need to be populated with Spinozas and Vaninis, not ordinary men and women.

One can, for the moment, imagine what lines of argument a religious response to Bayle might pursue: That will be reserved for fuller treatment in the last section of the essay. But there is also a range of arguments that, while not "devout," carry some weight against the commonwealth of atheists. I shall examine a few.

In his *Dictionnaire philosophique*, Voltaire, no friend of organized religion, gives Bayle rather short shrift.[37] While he fully concedes that Bayle's paradoxical view of the society of atheists is not ill-taken, he deplores its consequences. According to Voltaire, Bayle could have made a more powerful case if he had gotten his facts in order: For example, Vanini was not an atheist. However, "In Caesar's and Cicero's time the Roman senate was really an assembly of atheists" and "they were the conquerors and legislators of the known world."[38] Voltaire—like Bayle—was part wit, part philosopher. He admired Bayle's irreverence and supported his positions where he could: but both his political theory and philosophy of history deviated from what one may take to have been Bayle's intentions. Despite his scepticism and ahistoricity, Bayle seemed to think that his society of atheists was more conceivable among the moderns than the ancients. Voltaire demurs: The Gentile intellectuals of antiquity were riddled with atheism; but, in modernity, science gives atheism the lie, "since philosophers have perceived that there is no vegetative being without germ, no germ without design."[39] Teleology rushes to the support of deism and a creation, denying the beliefs of those ancients for whom the world was eternal and without purpose. In the second place, Voltaire thinks that society cannot cohere without the power of a sacred oath (here following Locke); and he concludes, *contra* Bayle, "that it is infinitely more useful in a civilized city to have even a bad religion than none at all."[40]

Nonetheless, Voltaire concedes to Bayle that religious fanaticism is worse than atheism: "Atheism does not discountenance crime, but fanaticism causes crimes to be committed."[41] Voltiare's emphasis is on "purifying" religion; Bayle raises objections to its social utility. Voltaire does not say that there could not be a commonwealth of atheists, but he does not care for the consequences of such a state. He would not wish to be a sovereign surrounded by atheist courtiers.[42] Although the God of the Christians, and especially the Jews, is absurd and a major cause of atheism among otherwise "firm and wise minds," a necessary notion of divinity that rulers should possess still exists.[43] Since "atheism" is a monstrous evil in those who govern" (for it will make political authority tyrannous and untrustworthy), it is also an evil in the minds of learned men, "even if their lives are innocent," for "their studies . . . can affect those who hold office."[44] "True philosophers accept [final causes] . . . a catechist announces God to children, and Newton demonstrates him to wise men."[45] Newton and political prudence separate Bayle and Voltaire.

Montesquieu's approach to the problem is somewhat different. While writing not as a *"théologien"* but as an *"écrivain politique,"* Montesquieu is not as concerned as Voltaire with the speculative properties of religion. He agrees with Voltaire that it is better to be an idolator than an atheist.[46] But he is not playful in tone. He finds Bayle lacking in rigor and fairness: "To say that religion is not a controlling element *(un motif réprimant)* because it doesn't always control is the same as saying that civil laws are not a controlling element either. It is a bad argument against religion to collect, within a large work, a long enumeration of evils it has caused, if the good it has accomplished is not also brought out."[47] Montesquieu will have no society of Vaninis. According to him, "He who has no religion is that terrible animal who senses his freedom only when he is tearing and devouring [his prey]."[48] This is an obvious rejoinder to Bayle's "lions and tigers." Montesquieu then goes on to compliment the Christian religion, which "in making princes less timid, makes them less cruel. The prince counts on his subjects, and the subjects on the prince. How admirable! The

Christian religion, which seems to have no other object than felicity in the other life, creates our happiness in this one."[49] So much for Machiavelli. And Montesquieu praises—rather seditiously—the Protestant forms of Christianity.[50] The main point, he says, is not to know whether an individual or a people would be better off without religion than in abusing the one they have; it is to know whether sporadic abuses of religion are worse than having none at all.[51] On this subject Montesquieu is both clear and positive: "[Bayle] dares to claim that true Christians could not form a durable state. Why not? They would be citizens infinitely enlightened about their duties, with a great zeal for fulfilling them; they would closely feel the rights of natural defense; the more they believed they owed the religion, the more they would feel they owed to the fatherland as well."[52] The principles of "true Christianity" in fact rise above the deficiencies of all political regimes. Yet Montesquieu is fundamentally speaking of utility, not truth-value: "In a land where one is unfortunate to have a religion that is not given by God, it must always be suited to morality; because even a false religion is the best guarantee men can have of honest dealings by their fellows."[53]

Montesquieu, a connoisseur of civilizations and modeler of political regimes, is convinced, like Voltaire, that Bayle's thought-experiment would fail. Perhaps Bayle was the boldest "enlightener" of all; but we have seen evidence that his successors saw the needs of society differently. Probably the most acute contribution of Montesquieu to the commonwealth of atheists debate was this: "Since both religion and the civil laws should principally contribute to making men good citizens, we can see that when one of the two strays from its goal, the other should be firmly fastened on it: the less religion disciplines (*sera réprimante*), the more the civil laws ought to."[54] This notion of a sharing of control (and we might add morality as a third element, between, because it emerged as an independently construed force in Montesquieu's time) is infinitely suggestive about how we might study and diagnose societies.

I shall conclude this section by making a few comments on a work little read today but nonetheless significant because of its placement in the intellectual history of social change: Jacques Necker's *De l'importance des opinions religieuses*, published in the

year before the French Revolution. As one knows, Necker was
a Genevan Protestant who was three times called to the minis-
try of finance by Louis XVI. As the political crisis of France
worsened, and for years after during his retirement at Coppet,
Necker was possessed by the idea that political society required
religious stabilization. He was a mild Calvinist, not a Gallican
Catholic—a proponent of toleration and latitudinarian doctrine; nevertheless, he attempted to fit his views to the matter
at hand. He did not assert, with Montesquieu, that a false religion was better than none at all. But he was well aware, in 1788,
that in France the old religion was losing its savor, failing to
command belief and govern conduct in high places. He felt
that experiments in a "civil religion" were brewing, based on a
secularized philosophy of rights and legitimacy that touched the
mind more than the heart, and he wished to refute that solution. So he wrote his windy work, which still contains some passages of great interest.

According to Necker, it had always been religious ideas that,
through the power of the sworn oath, created loyalty, reciprocity, and understanding between peoples and their rulers,
and tied the rules to their promises.[55] But, especially in the
eighteenth century, a rival mediator had come on the scene,
"political philosophy," whose injunctions professed to teach rights
and duties, while attacking religion to its roots.[56] Religious trust
is, according to Necker, broadly social. This is not true of the
new claimant, for its rationale is the work of subtle intellectuals,
or, as we would now say, "ideologists." "Already," he writes, "it
is very hard to gain influence for political morality, since its
necessary basis is a love of order, which is an abstract and complicated idea." But political philosophy only worsens the situation by agitating the minds of the ignorant with its vision of a
"scientific harmony of the whole," which can only tempt them
to overreact on all the numerous occasions of injustice and in-
equality.[57]

Government is the "only natural defender of the civil order,"
of the "whole." It reposes on a trust akin to faith. The morality
of public trust and public action cannot be founded on some
mere theory of how particular interests could combine in a
general interest, nor can the effectiveness of social laws dispense with the support of religion (Necker is not stressing the

sanction of eternal rewards and punishments, but the mercy of religion).[58] The public is not best instructed by some political catechism of rights and duties; religious morality operates more swiftly and surely to this end in the *"situation singulière du plus grand nombre d'hommes."*[59] Irreligion debases persons in both their private and public settings.[60] Religious ideas make the task of government less onerous; a political morality deprived of religion would "open up a whole new scene."[61] The ascendancy of "public opinion" is not to be compared with, and cannot compensate for, "the general influence of religious morality."[62] And so forth, for another four hundred pages, most of them devoted to the private virtues that a liberal, charitable religion enjoins, with an insistence at the end that "The Christian religion alone [clearly in its Genevan version] has, by dispensing with superstitious ceremonies and opinions, constantly kept us close to nature."[63]

Necker hovered on the brink of a new dispensation or new dawning. After a century of complex transactions and advancement in the minds of intellectual elites, an entity called "society" was about to take over many of the lapsed functions of religious belief and control. Coincident with this, but hardly accidentally, a great political revolution was about to burst forth. For today's readers, Necker will seem like a testy, lumbering dinosaur, far less exciting than a Joseph de Maistre. But Necker very accurately saw an important feature of the modern political dilemma: If God or religion is banished from the public realm, how can society reasonably be the judge in its own case? We do not take this position in our law courts: in that respect, they conserve vestiges of a more ancient practice. But we tend in our moral and political reasoning to confuse judge, plaintiff, and accused *(Rousseau juge de Jean-Jacques)*; and we have created exotic solutions in the separation of powers, persons, moods, and faculties to be able to do this. Necker's tedious, and often obtuse, treatise is a kind of last answer to Bayle from the perspective of the old ideology of God and His people, worth reviewing for that reason. Today's problems are different; and that is why we "revisit" Bayle with a sense of distance, a curiosity for what he might tell us, and the possible need of an interpreter.

IV

It will be granted that, in its highest sense, religion is not a mere form of social control. Religion implies an access of creature to creator, of the visible to the invisible, and of the perishable earth to the eternal. Geertz calls it "a system of symbols . . . formulating conceptions of a general order of existence and clothing these conceptions with such an aura of factuality that the moods and motivations seem uniquely realistic."[64] Kolakowski calls it "the realm of worship wherein understanding, knowledge, the feeling of participation in the ultimate reality (whether or not a personal god is meant) and moral commitment appear as a single act."[65] Dozens of roughly parallel definitions could be given, each, to be sure, with its own nuance. But it is not of direct concern to political theory or political sociology to deal with the whole scope of religion (the provinces of theology and ecclesiology). We are here concerned with its role in a certain broad enough, but worldly, perspective: solidarity, reciprocity, views on history and institutions, public piety, oaths, legitimation, and the like. And yet, if a power is to be conceded to religion in the identification and stabilization of rules of order in this world, its transcendental features cannot be totally ignored. Religion's utility is not confined to its being "useful"; it has positive and disturbing features that are not. In providing secular life with meaning and consequently with incentive, as a prelude to order, religion explains and consoles, but it never simply reduplicates other resources of the social system. If it did that, Bayle would be right: it would be superfluous as a social agent.

Bayle proposed the notion that secular society was rational enough in its calculations to cohere without religious suasion. Pain and pleasure would be its guides to "ultimate meaning." In Bayle's time, "nature" was supposed to provide this kind of guarantee. Religion was an irrational scaffolding that would be taken down as mankind learned to follow nature. But, as Voltaire perceived, Bayle's nature really had no plan, no capacity to give life meaning. A few trenchant Epicureans might be able to live by such rules, but mankind at large could not. Montesquieu keenly observed not only that calumnies against Christian societies were blown out of all proportion by enemies of that religion, but that society, needing discipline from several quarters, ought to balance its controls as best it could. Of course Montesquieu also knew, as well as anyone, that what seemed evident in theory was often quite impossible in practice, that the political diagnostician hadn't the same kind of control over his patient as the private doctor. Necker raised the point—and he was not alone in this—that religious morality, aside from being, as he believed, "true," was far more easily and effectively communicable to members of a commonwealth than "political philosophy," a dangerously intellectualized way of teaching rights and duties, of persuading peoples to allegiance and sovereigns to honesty.

A number of things have changed since then. These changes perhaps do not refute the answers made to Bayle; but they situate his paradox of the commonwealth of atheists somewhat differently. In the first place, nature has ceased to be our great standard and protector: We are now charged with protecting it—even by prayers said in churches. And, more generally, we have entered the age of the "artificial." The ideology of nature—in whichever of the numerous forms it was grasped by social thought—ceded in the nineteenth century to the ideologies of "progress" and "history." Now, they also appear transient. Today, it is increasingly said in the intellectual community—which is not, of course, a fair sample of the human race—that man, in his forfeiture of higher meaning, is summoned "to form and re-form the infinite potentialities which are truly his. . . . The individual person is expected to make his own truth, thereby satisfying his own diverse needs."[66] Now, individualism is nothing new (witness Thoreau or Kierkegaard); but this self-referential world of private meaning and plastic capacity is really the strange sunny side of Sisyphean existentialism. It will seem a scarecrow to many readers; but it will be secretly pleasing to others—and, in a debased version, it even makes contact with a certain politics that uses a religious façade. The advance from "nature" to history to "self" has been a profound feature of Western thought, not least in America. As Peter Berger has brilliantly put it: "The *realissimum* to which religion refers is transposed from the cosmos or from history to individual consciousness. Cosmology becomes psychology. History becomes biography."[67] If the deification of the self—which appears to

follow dethronement of "society," whose coronation was mentioned in the previous section—is the outcome of the "education of the human race," with conquests to show in law, morality, and religion alike, one might take atheism and its ideal
commonwealth to be right on the mark: For there is nothing
less godly imaginable than the frail self with its "infinite potentialities," in conditions where *ars* remains *longa*, and *vita brevis*.

Secondly, the extraordinary rise of a morality of self (where,
to be sure, the self is sometimes disguised as "human nature,"
sometimes as "world-historical agent," sometimes even as "religious prophecy") suggests another feature of our landscape that
would have been occluded to Bayle. Earlier Christian civilization (here somewhat in debt to pagan antecedents) had harshly
dualized the world: truth/opinion; form/material; city of God/
city of man; *sacerdotium/regnum;* spirit/body; mind/matter. The
arousal of an independent third force called "morality" (as the
title of this volume reflects) disturbed the binary relationship. I
do not mean that the notion of morality was suddenly invented
(see the second section of the essay), but that it was taken to
have autonomous standing. If one reads at all deeply in Bayle,
one begins to doubt that he is a consequent metaphysical ma-
terialist, despite the emphasis he appears to place in his commonwealth of atheists on *sola lege*, prudential and physical rewards and penalties. But his available language is a kind of
Cartesianism in which the essence of social control must be either
assigned to the reasons of the body or those of the mind or
soul. Since Bayle finds spiritual incentives more or less nugatory, his instinct is to opt for the physical or natural.

But, at the same time, another powerful current of belief—
not alien to this Protestant exile—was arising out of the premise of *sola fide*: Religious in origin, and directed first against
abuses of ecclesiology, it would, in time, lead to setting morality
apart from both positive law and revealed religion as an arbiter
of social control and human choice. Bayle has sensed this, but
he does not exactly grasp its full implications. Even Montesquieu, half a century later, will typically speak of a human progress from *moeurs* to *lois*, although his more important dualism
between *"le physique"* and *"le moral,"* outer and inner, identifies
him transitionally with modern usage.[68]

The fact seems to be that Western man is more comfortable

with duality than triplicity. The triad "law, morality, religion" causes him apprehension. "Either/or" and "both" are more to his liking. The positive law of the state, then and even now, grounded in certain rituals of sacralization, has been indispensable to society as its *minima moralia*. That reserves an ambiguous, often fierce, competition over the spiritual dimension to morality (first liberated as a "morality of society or opinion," then as a "morality of the self") and religion (a transcendent source of being and right conduct). The tendency has been to live with the triad but to find it mildly disconcerting and unstable. Above all, the trend has been to replace religion by morality—by taking religion out of the social and into the private sphere, by effectively reducing it to an ethic competing with secular ethics, or by claiming for it essential properties unconnected with human conduct.

What does this make of our three-legged stool image? Man walks on two legs but sits better on three. On the whole, he needs to walk, not sit. But since he experiences fatigue—not least, historical fatigue—he is doomed to sit down for long stretches. The duality achieved in his characteristic either/or posture ("God-beast") is unstable and returns him to sedentary repose as a "creature of the middle span."

Although many milestones had already been placed, the full consequence of the debate between morality and religion was only fully clear in Kant's philosophy. Kant certainly did not recommend atheism as a social practice. Yet if he did not exactly say it boldly, he suggested to his followers that morality was more sanctified than anything typically called religion. For Kant, God (with the reverence appropriate to him) was a postulate created by the moral freedom endemic in human beings and inseparable from their reason. The traditional premises of religion were reversed in order to save freedom: God did not command morality; the existence of a "moral metaphysics" in man demanded the idea of God. It demanded also the idea of personal immortality—but not (or at least Kant, like so many deist and theist contemporaries, is mute on this) so as to punish wickedness, but to promise felicity to those who have proved worthy of it. The proper dignity of man's capacity for virtue was a matter of *sola fide*—rational faith in himself.

The rest is not silence. In Wilhelm von Humboldt's essay on

the limits of the state, we read that "Religion is wholly subjective, and depends solely on each individual's unique conception of it."[69] Moreover, "Neither what morality prescribes as a duty, nor what enforces its dictates and recommends them to the will, is dependent on religious ideas."[70] Humboldt's self-generating morality and exemplary *Bildung* would, of course, be democratized, first by J. S. Mill, and later by John Dewey. At the same time, cultural and intellectual shocks too legion to record (especially science, war, and industrialism) worked either to free conscience entirely from religious scruple or to cause it to protect its domain against other doctrines, notably positivism, by shedding the support of an embarrassing ally.

A third issue is that the modern denial of an impulse, sentiment, or faculty that is indigenously religious (*à la* Dewey)—the equation of "religiosity" with aesthetic wonder or satisfaction in scientific problem-solving—has appeared to render otiose the specific institutions, vocabularies, rituals, and ways of thought that religion had generated over the centuries. They were not just "differentiated," but called into question as fossilized relics, bereft of any value that did not come from "public opinion" or certain aggregated needs of "selves." Theories of belief and of organized worship have been, as I have suggested, the principal casualties of this trend—no longer dangerous nests of intolerance but simply Baylian superfluities.

However, the gravest problem of religion, as could be guessed, is the widespread suspicion that it might not be true and that its falsehood is not innocent. It might be a delusion of mankind's coming of age; or it might be a deceit visited on ordinary persons by unscrupulous power-holders anxious to legitimate their privileges and mask their injustices. The metaphysical implications and the political ones are not quite of the same order, although they combine in the control of conduct. As regards the first—which is chiefly a post-Darwinian, post-Nietzschean development—in the words of Hannah Arendt, "The important historical fact is that an overwhelming majority has ceased to believe in a Last Judgment at the end of time."[71] Bayle of course thought that this feature was centrally important to the impact of religion on conduct: But he did not argue that a majority of persons had lost the belief; he said (as did many after him) that God's judgment was such a distant and exotic event that it made little difference in moral choice. Aside from intellectual *angst* in a world where "God is dead," Arendt's argument is not terribly more powerful than Bayle's: We would have to examine deathbeds to see where the distinction might lie. There is, however, a mood abroad in modern society, despite well-documented religious resistances, that distinguishes our time from Bayle's. This is expressed well in a quotation from Alasdair MacIntyre: "The survey of contemporary attitudes among the readers of *New Society* (1963) showed a majority both for the belief that Christian morality is moribund and for the belief that this is a sad thing."[72] Perhaps, twenty years later, a similar population of respondents, less exposed to Christian morality, would find this not quite so sad. On the other hand, they might still regret the diminishment of a perennial resource for controlling the terror of history.

The more strictly political problem—which might be named the *Polybian problem* after the writer who first brought it forward—has been with us a very long time. Its "exposure should have ceased to shock us. Despite the madness of our century and certain remarkable practices in the Third World, we might judge that the resources of civilization still allow for quite substantial guarantees against the cynical political manipulation of religious dogma. Neither is it true that religion lends itself to this practice as a matter of course. Religion tends in the main to support order; but it is not automatically the partner of any regime that solicits it.

At this writing religion remains a part of the three-legged stool, while morality, for reasons I have tried to show, may be the most vulnerable. While some today, I think, would find a commonwealth of atheists congenial (more than in Bayle's time), I doubt if they would sit comfortably. Simone Weil said profoundly: "I have to be atheistic with the part of myself which is not made for God."[73] She did not say that she had made that part herself; she did not wish that she had. Perhaps nonbelief seems easier and more tempting to try to make than belief; but it is not clear that either is ours to make or to legislate.

NOTES

1. Clearly, in order to make this claim, I am mostly rejecting the functionalist argument that secularist or, in the words of some writers, "Gnostic" ideologies take the place of religion in reinforc-

ing the sacred controls of society. Although I most certainly grant
that secular ideologies (nationalism, cosmopolitan liberal humanism, international socialism, and fascism) make salvationary claims
and may, by a distortion of understanding, be held "sacred," I
take religion to imply a condition of belief where perspectives from
a realm that cannot be specified as world-immanent inspire worship and motivate conduct. So-called "civil religions" scarcely meet
this standard, although they may do duty for it for a time and
characteristically present relics, shrines, sacred days, and legends
for public edification. My main argument, however, is not over
religion-substitutes, but is directed toward the incompleteness of
a religion measured, defined, and stabilized by the individual consciousness. Erastianism leads in the first direction; radical Protestantism in the second: but there seems to be an ineradicable dialectic between these two positions. When the prince declares the
sacred, the subject sooner or later exclaims: *"Qui t'a fait roi?"*

2. Immanual Kant, *The Metaphysical Elements of Justice*, trans. John
   Ladd (Indianapolis: Bobbs Merrill, 1964), p. 34.
3. Cited by Robert Bellah, Introduction to *Religion and America*, eds.
   Mary Douglas and Steven M. Tipton (Boston: Beacon Press, 1983),
   p. 9.
4. John Dewey, *A Common Faith* (New Haven: Yale University Press,
   1934), pp. 65, 68.
5. John Dewey, *Democracy and Education* (New York: Macmillan, 1924),
   p. 263.
6. See William A. Clebsch, *American Religious Thought* (Chicago: Chicago University Press, 1973), p. 150.
7. Alexis de Tocqueville, *Democracy in America*, 2 vols. trans. Henry
   Reeve (New York: Harvest Books, 1945), vol. 2, 106.
8. See Friedrich von Hayek, "The Principles of a Liberal Social Order," in *Studies in Philosophy, Politics and Economics* (London: Routledge & Kegan Paul, 1967), pp. 164–65.
9. My own position is stated in George A. Kelly, *Politics and Religious
   Consciousness in America* (New Brunswick: Transaction Books, 1984),
   chap. 8.
10. "Idea for a Universal History from a Cosmopolitan Point of View,"
    in *Kant's Political Writings*, ed. H. Reiss (Cambridge: Cambridge
    University Press, 1970), p. 46.
11. See, on this, Werner Stark, *Safeguards of the Social Bond: Custom
    and Law*, vol. 3 of *The Social Bond*, 4 vols. (New York: Fordham
    University Press), (1980), pp. 227–28.
12. E.g., Wilhelm von Humboldt, *The Limits of State Action*, ed. J. W.
    Burrow (Cambridge: Cambridge University Press, 1969), p. 108.
13. Kelly, *Politics and Religious Consciousness*, p. 249.

14. Michael Oakeshott, *Hobbes on Civil Association* (Oxford: Basil Blackwell, 1975), pp. 76–77.

15. Recall Rousseau's famous sentence from *Emile:* "Tel philosophe aime les Tatares, pour être dispensé d'aimer ses voisins." *Emile,* eds. François and Pierre Richard (Paris: Garnier, 1961), bk. 1, p. 9.

16. See Gabriel Marcel, *Creative Fidelity,* trans. Robert Rosthal (New York: Farrar, Straus, 1964).

17. My discussion of Bayle does not refer to any fine points of text and interpretation, so I cite the most easily available source for English-language readers, *The Great Contest of Faith and Reason: Selections from the Writings of Pierre Bayle,* ed. Karl C. Sandberg (New York: Ungar, 1963).

18. Bayle, *Great Contest,* p. 11.

19. Ibid.

20. Ibid., pp. 12, 13.

21. Ibid., p. 13.

22. Ibid., p. 15.

23. "Of Cannibals," in *Essays and Selected Writings of Montaigne,* ed. Donald M. Frame (New York: St. Martin's Press, 1963), pp. 97–99.

24. *Selected Writings of Montaigne,* "Apology for Raymond Sebond," p. 210.

25. Niccolò Machiavelli, *Discourses,* in *The Prince and the Discourses* (New York: Modern Library, 1950), chap. 10, p. 147.

26. Ibid., p. 149.

27. Bayle, *Great Contest,* p. 13.

28. Ibid., p. 15

29. Ibid., p. 13.

30. Ibid., pp. 20–21.

31. Leszek Kolakowski, *Religion* (New York: Oxford University Press, 1982), p. 191.

32. Bayle, *Great Contest,* p. 18. In Diderot's literary letters to the sculptor Falconet, he emotionally defended the remembrance of great men—especially from the arts and literature—by the living.

33. Bayle, *Great Contest,* p. 19.

34. Ibid., p. 16

35. Ibid.

36. Ibid., p. 17.

37. Voltaire, article "athée, athéisme," *Philosophical Dictionary,* trans. Theodore Besterman (Harmondsworth: Penguin Books, 1983), p. 54–55.

38. Ibid., p. 55.

39. Ibid., p. 57.

40. Ibid., p. 56.
41. Ibid.
42. Ibid., p. 57.
43. Ibid.
44. Ibid.
45. Ibid., p. 58.
46. Charles-Louis de Secondat, baron de Montesquieu, *De l'esprit des lois*, ed. Gonzague Truc, 2 vols. (Paris: Garnier, 1956). There is no first-rate translation of this classic in English, although Melvin Richter has done well with an abridged version in Melvin Richter, *The Political Theory of Montesquieu* (Cambridge: Cambridge University Press, 1977). I translate here from the Truc edition, and hereafter cite only book and chapter to facilitate reference to other editions. Here, *EL*, 24, 2.
47. Ibid.
48. Ibid.
49. Ibid., 24, 3.
50. Ibid., 24, 1.
51. Ibid., 24, 2.
52. Ibid., 25, 6.
53. Ibid., 24, 15.
54. Ibid., 24, 14.
55. Jacques Necker, *De l'importance des idées religieuses* (London, Paris: Hôtel de Thou, 1788), p. 30.
56. Ibid., p. 30.
57. Ibid., p. 34.
58. Ibid., pp. 39–40.
59. Ibid., p. 54.
60. Ibid., p. 71.
61. Ibid., p. 94.
62. Ibid., p. 110.
63. Ibid., p. 516.
64. Clifford Geertz, "Religion as a Cultural System," in *The Religious Situation*, ed. Donald R. Cutler (Boston: Beacon Press, 1968), p. 643.
65. Kolakowski, *Religion*, p. 174.
66. Henry Kariel, *In Search of Authority* (Glencoe: The Free Press, 1964), p. 5.
67. Peter L. Berger, *The Sacred Canopy: Elements of a Sociological Theory of Religion* (Garden City: Doubleday, 1967), p. 166.
68. In at least one instance, and an important one, Montesquieu displays the triadic separation. Man has "laws of religion" to remind him of his creator; "laws of morality" to remind him of himself; and "political and civil laws" to remind him of his duties to his

fellows. But this is not exactly the same separation we commonly make today (or that Kant or J. S. Mill made) between law and morality. *EL,* I, i. On the adjacent point, see Sergio Moravia, " 'Moral—physique'—genesis and evolution of a 'rapport,' " in *Enlightenment Studies in Honour of Lester G. Crocker,* eds. Alfred J. Bingham and Virgil W. Topazio (Oxford: The Voltaire Foundation, 1979), pp. 163–74.

69. Humboldt, *Limits of State Action,* p. 58.

70. Ibid., p. 60.

71. Hannah Arendt, in "Religion and the Intellectuals: A Symposium," *Partisan Review,* no. 2 (1950):115.

72. Alasdair MacIntyre, *Against the Self-Images of the Age* (London: Duckworth, 1971), p. 21.

73. Simone Weil, *Gravity and Grace* (New York: Putnam, 1952), p. 168.

5

A CHRISTIAN CRITIQUE OF CHRISTIAN AMERICA

STANLEY HAUERWAS

I. Setting the Agenda: A Report on a Conversation

At a conference on narrative and virtue I had an encounter
with a philosopher that raises the problem with which I wish to
deal. My philosophical counterpart is a Piercian who is also a
committed Jew. In his paper he had argued that most of the
rational paradigms accepted by contemporary philosophy cannot make sense of Judaism. We began by exchanging views about
why current ethical theory seems so committed to foundation-
alist epistemological assumptions. We shared in general a sympathy with antifoundationalist arguments though neither of us
wanted to give up any possibility of some more modest realist
epistemology. We also found we were equally critical of liberal
political theory and in particular the ahistorical character of its
methodology. Then our conversation suddenly took a turn for
which I was completely unprepared. It went something like this:

Philosopher: Do you support prayer in the public schools?
Theologian: No, I do not because I do not want the state spon-
soring my faith.
Philosopher: That is not the real reason. You are just afraid to
be for anything that Jerry Falwell is for. You really are a
liberal in spite of your doubts about liberalism's philosophical
adequacy.

Theologian: That is not fair. I did not say I was against school
prayer because I think such prayer is coercive, though I think
such considerations are not unimportant, but because state
sponsored prayer cannot help but give the impression that
the state is friendly toward religion. Moreover prayers, insofar as they can pass muster in a religiously pluralistic context,
are so anemic that they cannot help but give a distorted view
of God. So I am against school prayer not because it is against
the tenets of liberalism but because it is theologically a scandal.

Philosopher: That is not good enough. As a Christian you typically do not give a damn about the Jews. You want to create
a civilization and society and then walk away from it when
the going gets a little tough. Of course the prayers sponsored
by public authorities are degraded but they still remind people that they are creatures. A vague god prayed to vaguely is
better than no god or prayer at all. Otherwise we face the
possibility of a neo-pagan culture for which liberal procedural rules of fair play will be no match.

Theologian: I am a bit surprised to hear you argue this way.
After all, Christians have persecuted and killed Jews with as
much enthusiasm as anyone. I would think you would feel
safer in a secular culture than one that is quasi-Christian. Indeed has that not been the dominant social strategy of Jews
since the Enlightenment? The way to secure protection from
the Christians is to create and support liberal societies where
religion is relegated to the private sphere and thus becomes
unavailable for public policy directed against the Jews or those
of any other religious faith.

Philosopher: I do not deny that is the strategy of many Jews,
but I think this century has shown it to be a decisive failure.
Pagan societies kill us with an abandon that Christians can
never muster. Christianity even in a degraded form at least
has material convictions that can make the persecution and
killing of Jews problematic. Paganism has no such convictions
so I will take my chances with the Christians and their societies. After all, we Jews do not ask for much. We just do not
want you to kill our children. Living in quasi-Christian societies means we have to put up with a lot of inconvenience
and prejudice—i.e., Christmas as a school holiday—but we

Jews have long known how to handle that. We flourish under
a little prejudice. What we cannot stand is the false tolerance
of liberalism that relegates us to the arena of being just one
religion among others.

Theologian: So if I understand you rightly, you are suggesting
that you want me as a Christian to support school prayer,
even if such prayers are but forms of degraded Christian religiosity, because at least that continues to underwrite the assumption we are a "religious" society. Such an assumption
allows an appeal to a higher standard of justice that makes
the survival of the Jewish people more likely.

Philosopher: That is about right. You Christians have to take
responsibility for what you have done. You created a civilization based on belief in God and it is your responsibility to
continue to support that civilization.

Theologian: But you know yourself that such a social strategy
cannot help but lead to the continued degradation of Christianity. The more Christians try to make Christianity a philosophy sufficient to sustain a society, especially a liberal society, the more we must distort or explain away our
fundamental beliefs. Therefore in the name of sustaining a
civilization Christians increasingly undercut the ability of the
church to take a critical stance toward this society. Even when
the church acts as a critic in such a context, it cannot be more
than a friendly critic since it has a stake in maintaining the
basic structure of society.

Philosopher: Why should that bother me? Christians have always been willing to degrade their convictions in the past to
attain social and political power (of course, always in order
that they might "do good"). Why should they start worrying
about being degraded now? On that score it seems a little
late. For the church to start to worry about being pure is
about as realistic as Madonna to worry about being a virgin.
It is just too late. So if you care anything about the Jews you
ought to support school prayer.

Our conversation did not end at this point but it is enough
for my purposes. Even though I think most of what my philosopher friend has to say is right, for theological reasons I still
cannot support school prayer. That I cannot puts me at odds

with the social strategy of most Christians, both liberal and conservative, in America. In the next section I will try to explain why this is the case. Then the ground will be prepared for me to suggest what a more radical Christian critique of America entails both in terms of its logic as well as a political strategy.

II. Liberal Christianity and American Democracy, or Why Jerry Falwell Is Such a Pain

Since the turn of the century, one of the dominant themes in Christian social ethics has been the Christian's responsibility for societal affairs. Time and time again it is argued faith and action cannot be separated. Our religious convictions cannot be relegated to one sphere of our lives and our social and political activities to another. Since the faith of Christians is a faith that does justice there is no way we can avoid political activity. Whether the political realm is viewed Lutheran-like as a realm of lesser evil or more Calvinistically as the arena of the mediocre good, Christians cannot avoid involvement in the political process. That is especially the case in a democratic society in which the actions of individual citizens can make a difference.

Armed with this set of presuppositions, Christians in the "mainstream" denominations attacked those Christians who accepted no particular social or political responsibilities. This position, they argued, pietistically relegates salvation to the individual's relation to God and thus betrays the essential Christian claim that God is Lord of all creation. What must be remembered is that Jesus came preaching a kingdom that makes it impossible for his followers to be indifferent to the injustices in their surrounding social orders. On these grounds mainstream churches, such as those that constitute the National Council of Churches, urged Baptist and other pietistic Christians to join them in the political struggle to make this a more just society. As is often pointed out, not to take a political stand in the name of being Christian in fact is to take a political stand.

Pietists, in defense of their position, sometimes responded by appealing not to their theological convictions but instead to what they considered the normative commitments of the American society—namely that our constitution has erected a "wall of separation between church and state." In the name of maintaining the freedom of religion the church claims no competency in matters political. The difficulty with this position, however, is that it attributes a perspective to the Constitution that simply is not there. Neither the free exercise clause nor the non-establishment clause prohibits Christians, either as organized in churches or as individuals, from seeking to influence their society or government. Just to the extent the free church tradition allows itself to be so excluded from the public arena, moreover, it underwrites an individualistic account of Christianity that is antithetical to its very nature.

Such was the state of the debate among Christians until recently. But now suddenly everything has changed because the message finally got across to the pietistic Baptists. They have become politically active seeking to influence our society and government to support causes in the name of making this a better society. Jerry Falwell represents the triumph of mainstream Christianity in America as he is convinced, just like Martin Luther King, Jr., that Christians cannot abandon the political realm in their desire for justice. They must seek through the constitutionally guaranteed means to influence our political representatives to prevent abortion, to support democratic regimes around the world, to support Israel, to provide support for the family, and so on.

Therefore the mainstream won, but it is not a victory they are celebrating. For it turns out that once politically inactive Christians became active, the causes they supported were not those the mainstream wanted supported. The temptation is to try to defeat this new political activism by using the slogans of the past—religion and politics do not mix or you should not try to force your religious views on anyone through public policy— but to do so is to go against the position the mainstream has been arguing for years.

In order to understand how we have reached this point in American Protestantism I need to call your attention to some aspects of the history of Christianity in America. I do not mean I am going to give you a rendition of Puritan America or engage in the debate about how "Christian" America has been.[1] While such studies and questions are interesting and may still have some normative importance, they are not crucial for helping us understand why Falwell presents such a challenge to mainstream Christianity. To understand that we need to appreciate why Christian thinkers about ethics in America, especially since the nineteenth century, have assumed that Christianity and democracy are integrally related.

That they have done so is because America stands as the great experiment in what Max Stackhouse has identified as "constructive Protestantism." Stackhouse notes that in *Social Teaching of the Christian Churches*, Ernst Troeltsch argues that only two major Christian social philosophies have ever been developed—the Catholic and the Calvinist. Yet each of these as social philosophies no longer seems viable. "The vision of an organic, hierarchical order sanctified by objectified means of grace, and that of an established theocracy of elect saints who are justified by grace through faith, must both be judged as no longer live options for social reconstruction. This is not to suggest that these visions do not still hold power. . . . But this *is* to suggest that these two forms of 'Christendom' have ended—or rather, have played their part and now must yield the stage after their immeasurable contribution to the drama of Christianity in modern culture."[2]

According to Stackhouse, the crucial question is whether Christianity can develop another "social philosophy." If it cannot it would then seem the social ethical power of Christianity is at an end. Stackhouse argues that American Christianity has in fact developed a third option that he calls "conciliar denominationalism."[3] The character of this new social philosophy Stackhouse sees prefigured in Walter Rauschenbusch who held together two conflicting motifs, sectarianism and Christendom, that constitute the unique blend of conciliar denominationalism. "On the one hand, Rauschenbusch comes from an evangelical background from which he gained a sense of intense and explicit faith that could only be held by fully committed members. On the other hand, Rauschenbusch lived in the age of lingering hope for a catholic 'Christian culture' and in an age that, especially through the developing social sciences, saw the legitimacy of secular realms. He, like the developing 'conciliar denominations,' saw the necessity of the select body of believers anticipating the kingdom in word and deed in good sectarian fashion, and of taking the world seriously on its own terms, as did all visions of Christendom. These motifs conspire in his thought to produce a vision of a revolutionized responsible society for which a socially understood gospel is the catalyst."[4]

Rauschenbusch as the champion of liberal Christianity could speak straightforwardly of the need to "Christianize" social orders. "It is not enough to christianize individuals; we must christianize societies, organizations, nations, for they too have a life of their own which may be made better or worse."[5] On that basis he thought it quite possible to speak of saved and unsaved organizations. "The one is under the law of Christ, the other under the law of mammon. The one is democratic and the other autocratic. Whenever capitalism has invaded a new country or industry, there has been a speeding up in labor and in the production of wealth, but always with a trail of human misery, discontent, bitterness, and demoralization. When cooperation has invaded a country there has been increased thrift, education, and neighborly feeling, and there has been no trail of concomitant evil and no cries of protest."[6]

The difference between saved and unsaved social orders from Rauschenbusch's perspective is quite simple—saved social orders and institutions are democratic. As he says, "Social sciences confirm the correctness of Christ's protest against the stratification of society in ranks and classes. What is the general tendency toward democracy and the gradual abolition of hereditary privileges but history's assent to the revolutionary dogmas of Christ?"[7] The kingdom of God is not a concept or ideal for Rauschenbusch; it is a historical force at work in humanity. The way it ultimately works its way out, moreover, is in the form of democracy. As he puts it, "Where religion and intellect combine, the foundation is laid for political democracy."[8]

If, as Stackhouse suggests, America is the great experiment in "constructive Protestantism," it seems what is Christian about that construction is democracy.[9] For Rauschenbusch is hardly an isolated figure who claimed a close interrelation between Christianity and democracy. As Jan Dawson has recently argued, at the turn of this century there developed a "faith in the spiritual oneness of Christianity and democracy, based on the democratic theology of Christianity and concerned primarily with the survival of Christianity in troubled modern democracies."[10]

To support democracy became a means of supporting Christianity and vice versa.

Dawson quotes Lyman Abbott, successor to Henry Ward Beecher, in the liberal Christian paper *Outlook* to the effect that "Democracy is not merely a political theory, it is not merely a social opinion; it is a profound religious faith. . . . To him who holds it, this one fundamental faith in the Fatherhood of God and in the universal brotherhood of man is the essence of democracy."[11] If democracy was seen as the institutionalized form of Christianity it was no less true that democracy was dependent on religion to survive. Thus in 1907, the year following the article by Abbott, Robert Ashworth wrote in the *Chicago Divinity School Journal* that "The fate of the democratic movement rests ultimately upon religion. Religion is essential to democracy, and is, indeed, its foundation. It is based upon the New Testament principle of the equal value of every soul in the sight of the Divine Father."[12]

This kind of direct theological appeals in support of democracy becomes more muted as Christian thinkers become increasingly aware of the religious and social pluralism of America, but that does not lessen their enthusiasm for democracy as that form of society and government that best institutionalize Christian social philosophy. Reinhold Niebuhr is certainly a case in point. Vicious in his critique of the theological and social optimism of the "social gospelers" defense of democracy, he never questioned the assumption that democracy was the most appropriate form of society and government for Christians. What was needed, according to Niebuhr, was to provide a more adequate basis for democracy in a realistic account of human nature. Such an account he thought was to be found primarily in the "Christian view of human nature [that] is more adequate for the development of a democratic society than either the optimism with which democracy has become historically associated or the moral cynicism which inclines human communities to tyrannical political strategies."[13]

In effect, from Rauschenbusch to the present, Christian social ethics has had one agenda—to show why American democracy possesses distinctive religious status. The primary subject of Christian ethics in America has been America.[14] This has now even become the project for Roman Catholic social ethics as exemplified in the work of John Courtney Murray. It was Murray's task at once to make America amenable to Catholic social theory by interpreting the separation of church and state as a confession by the state of its incompetence in matters of religion [15] and to make Catholics amenable to America by showing that Catholics can enthusiastically support democracy as an imaginative solution to the problem of religious pluralism.[16] Murray argued even a stronger case by suggesting that American democracy, whose political substance consists in an order of antecedent rights to the state,[17] can only be sustained by the kind of natural law theory carried by Catholicism in contrast to the individualism of Locke and Hobbes.[18]

It is only against this background that one can understand and/or appreciate the work of Richard Neuhaus. In his much publicized book, *The Naked Public Square: Religion and Democracy in America,* Neuhaus argues that we are facing a crisis in our society. Because religious discourse has increasingly been excluded from our public life he fears a moral vacuum has been created. This vacuum threatens constantly to be filled by totalitarianism as the isolation of the individual from mediating structures gives us little power to stand against the omnivorous appetite of the bureaucratic state.[19] The only way out of this predicament is to mend the "rupture between public policy and moral sentiment. But the only moral sentiment of public effect is the sentiment that is embodied in and reinforced by living tradition. There are no a-religious moral traditions of public, or at least of democratic, force in American life. This is not to say that morality must be embodied in religion nor that the whole of religion is morality. It is to say that among the American people, religion and morality are conjoined. Religion in our popular life is the morality-bearing part of culture, and in that sense the heart of culture."[20]

From this perspective Neuhaus is appreciative of the Moral Majority. For in spite of the crudeness with which they often put their position they have at least raised the issue of the public value of religion that at one time was the agenda of political liberals. Rather than condeming the Moral Majority, Neuhaus seeks to help them enter the public debate by basing their appeals on principles that are accessible to the public. "Publicly assertive religious forces will have to learn that the remedy for the naked public square is not naked religion in public. They will have to develop a mediating language by which ultimate truths can be related to the penultimate and prepenultimate questions of political and legal content. In our several traditions there are rich conceptual resources for the development of such mediating language—whether concepts be called natural law, common grace, general revelation, or the order of creation. Such a civil engagement of secular and religious forces could produce a new public philosophy to sustain this American experiment in liberal democracy. The result may not be that we would agree with one another. Indeed there may be more disagreement. But at least we would know what we are disagreeing about, namely, different accounts of the transcendent good by which we might order our life together. Contra Justice Blackmun and legions of others, democracy is not served by evading the question of the good. Democracy becomes a political community worthy of moral actors only when we engage the question of the good."[21]

Neuhaus challenges mainline Protestant liberalism to live up to its rightful commitment to sustaining democracy as the socially specific form that Christianity should take.[22] As he puts it "The main line of the mainline story was confidence and hope regarding the Americanizing of Christianity and the Christianizing of America."[23] Indeed he argues that in spite of their fervor for disestablishing Christianity in America most liberals remain committed to "Christianizing" the social order. Only the synonyms for "Christianize" today "include terms such as justice, equality, and sustainability."[24]

That such is the case helps explain the enthusiasm for the work of John Rawls among those working in Christian ethics. Harlan Beckley puts the matter well as he notes that the emergence of a politically powerful Christian right has made vivid a dilemma that Christian ethics has still to resolve. "The dilemma is: How can an evaluation of the distribution of rights, duties, benefits, and burdens which society necessarily imposes upon all of its citizens be faithful to Christian beliefs without forcing others to accept the distinctive moral implications of beliefs they do not and should not be required to share?"[25] According to Beckley, "This dilemma can only be resolved if the justification for principles of justice is founded upon general beliefs and values that others hold, or can be reasonably expected to hold, and which Christians can affirm on the basis of their distinctive beliefs."[26] In order to accomplish this resolution Beckley argues "that the distinctively Christian moral ideal of love obligates those who adhere to it to embrace the beliefs which undergird John Rawls's idea of justice as fairness."[27] Rawls thus becomes the language of common grace that continues the project of Christianizing America.

Of course there are disagreements among Christian ethicists on this score. Neuhaus, for example, thinks Rawls's theory threatens to destroy "the individual by depriving him of all those personal particularities that are the essence of being an individual."[28] As a result, Rawls's account is ahistorical in contradistinction to the "Judeo-Christian tradition" which is "premised upon the concept of real history, real change, happening in an incomplete universe that is still awaiting its promised fulfillment."[29] What is needed, according to Neuhaus, is a recovery of some substantive account of the goods that make a good society possible through attending to the concrete desires of real people who are not required to leave their religious convictions behind when they participate in the public arena.

This same set of issues is at the center of the much discussed and praised book *Habits of the Heart: Individualism and Commitment in American Life.* For the critique of "individalism" that is the hallmark of that book is but part of a larger agenda that is in essential continuity with the hope to Christianize America. For as the authors suggest, in spite of our individualism, "We have never been, and still are not, a collection of private individuals who, except for a conscious contract to create a minimal government, have nothing in common. Our lives make sense in a thousand ways, most of which we are unaware of, because of traditions that are centuries, if not millennia, old. It is these traditions that help us to know that it does not make a difference who we are and how we treat one another. But if we owe the meaning of our lives to biblical and republican traditions of which we seldom consciously think, is there not the danger that the erosion of these traditions may eventually deprive us of that meaning altogether? We would argue that if we are ever to enter that new world that so far has been powerless to be born, it will be through reversing modernity's tendency to obliterate all previous culture. We need to learn again from the cultural riches so that they can speak to our condition today."[30] Which sounds very much like a calling for reconstituting Christian America.

I have no interest in trying to resolve the many disagreements between Neuhaus, Beckley, Bellah, and Falwell. Rather what I have attempted to do is to show that the reason Falwell is such a challenge to the Christian mainstream in America is not because he is so different from them, but because he has basically accepted their agenda.[31] The Christian right and the Christian left do not disagree about the religious status of the American experiment. They just disagree about what language and/or political theory will allow them to accomplish their common goal of making American democracy as close as possible to a manifestation of God's kingdom.

III. WHAT A CHRISTIAN CRITIQUE OF CHRISTIAN AMERICA SHOULD LOOK LIKE

For most Christians in America, from the nominal Christian, the committed social activist, to the theologian, it is simply unthinkable to theorize outside the tradition I have just tried to sketch. I refuse to support prayer in school because I find myself outside that tradition. I do so because I do not believe that the universalism that is intrinsic to the Christian faith is carried by the culture of the West, but instead is to be found first and foremost in the church.[32] From this perspective something has already gone wrong when Christians think they can ask, "What is the best form of society or government?"[33] This question assumes that Christians should or do have social and political power so they can determine the ethos of society. That this assumption has long been with us does nothing to confirm its truth.

That assumption in short is the heritage of what John Howard Yoder has called "The Constantinian Sources of Western Social Ethics." It is an assumption shared by Christians and non-Christians alike for the very logic of most contemporary philosophical accounts of ethics and social theory accept its essential rightness only in secular terms. By calling our attention to Constantine, Yoder has no stake in determining the sincerity of

Constantine's conversion or whether it was exactly at that time that a decisive shift in Christian assumptions took place. Rather Constantine is the symbol of the decisive shift in the logic of moral argument when Christians ceased being a minority and accepted Caesar as a member of the church. It is that logic we must understand if a genuine Christian critique of Christian America is to be made.

The most obvious consequence of the change occasioned by Constantine, according to Yoder, is the composition of the church. Prior to that time Christians had been a minority that at least required some degree of adherence. After that time everyone is a member. It now takes conviction to be a pagan. As a result, Christians are now forced to develop a doctrine of the "true church" that remains invisible. (136).[34]

This shift is of crucial importance for how ethics is not understood. Prior to the time of Constantine, Christian belief in God's rule of the world was a matter of faith. However with Constantine, providence is no longer an object of faith for God's governance of the world is now thought to be empirically evident in the person of the Christian ruler. With this changed eschatology ethics had to change "because one must aim one's behavior at strengthening the regime, and because the ruler himself must have very soon some approbation and perhaps some guidance as he does things the earlier church would have perhaps disapproved" (137). As a result, the distinctive character of Christian life is now primarily identified with inwardness since everyone by definition is already Christian.

Once Christianity becomes dominant, moreover, it is now thought that moral discourse must be that which can direct the behavior of anyone. Servanthood and love of enemy, contentment and monogamy, cannot be expected of everyone. So a duality develops in ethics between "evangelical counsels" for the motivated and "precepts" for everyone else. Perhaps even a more significant change is the assumption that the decisive ethical question becomes "What would happen if everyone did it? If everyone gave their wealth away what would we do for capital? If everyone loved their enemies who would ward off the communists? This argument could be met on other levels, but here the only point is to observe that such reasoning would have been preposterous in the early church and remains ludicrous wherever committed Christians accept realistically their minority status. Far more fitting than 'What if everybody did it?' would be its inverse, 'What if nobody else acted like a Christian and we did?' " (139)?[35]

With this new universalism comes an increasing need to test moral discourse by its effectiveness. Once the course of history is thought to be empirically discernible, and the prosperity of our regime is the measure of the good, efficacy becomes a decisive test for the moral rightness of our action. Self-sacrifice that is not tied to some long-term account of result becomes irrational. This is particularly important in assessing the validity of violence and the Christian's participation in war.

What is important about Yoder's depiction of the change in moral logic occasioned by the Constantinian turn is that the effects he describes are still with us. With the Renaissance and Reformation "Christendom" is replaced by the nation-state. Christians, however, did not respond to this change by maintaining the cosmopolitanism of the Holy Roman Empire, but rather now maintained Christian societies could wage war on one another in the name of preserving their Christian culture. With the Enlightenment, the link between church and state is broken, but the moral identification of Christians with the state remains strong. This is especially the case in America where "once the separation of church and state is seen as theologically desirable, a society where this separation is achieved is not a pagan society but a nation structured according to the will of God. For nearly two centuries, in fact, the language of American public discourse was not only religious, not only Christian, but specifically Protestant. Moral identification of church with nation remains despite institutional separation. In fact, forms of institutional interlocking develop which partly deny the theory of separation (chaplaincies, tax exemptions)" (142).

If there is to be a genuine Christian critique of Christian America, I am convinced that this habit of thought, which Yoder calls "Constantinianism," must be given up. Otherwise we Christians remain caught in the same habits of thought and behavior that implicitly or explicitly assume that insofar as America is a democracy she is Christian. As a result Christians lose exactly the skills necessary to see how deeply they have been compromised by the assumption that their task is to rule, if not the government, at least the ethos of America. That is why Christian social strategy in America continues to be caught in a fateful ambiguity—namely, Christians claim that Christianity, or at least religion, should be more present in public life, yet they want to make government itself religiously neutral. The history of the Supreme Court decisions on church-state issues should be enough to convince anyone that there is no easy way to resolve this tension in the American legal, much less the social and political system.[36]

Am I therefore suggesting that Christians must "withdraw" from the social, political, and legal life of America? I am certainly not arguing that, but rather I am trying to suggest that in order to answer questions of "why" or "how" Christians participate in the life of this country we do not need a theory about the Christian character of democracy. Rather I am suggesting, with Yoder, that as Christians we would "be more relaxed and less compulsive about running the world if we made our peace with our minority situation, seeing this neither as a dirty trick of destiny nor as some great new progress but simply as the unmasking of the myth of Christendom, which wasn't true even when it was believed" (158).

As Yoder argues, since almost all rulers claim to be our benefactors in order to justify their rule there is no reason that Christians cannot use that very language to call the rulers to be more humane in their ways of governing. Moreover, if we are lucky enough to be in a situation where the ruler's language of justification claims to have the consent of the governed we can use the machinery of democracy for our own and our neighbor's advantage. But we should not, thereby, be lulled into believing that "we the people" are thereby governing ourselves. Democracy is still government by elite though it may be less oppressive since it uses language in its justification that provides ways to mitigate oppressiveness. But that does not make democracy, from a Christian point of view, different in kind from states of another form (158–159).

Perhaps the hardest habit of thought deriving from our Constantinianism is the assumption if we do not govern then surely society and/or government will fall into anarchy or totalitarianism, but I notice no shortage of people willing to rule or any absence of ideologies for rule. The problem is not Christians' disavowing ruling, but rather that when Christians rule they tend to create international and national disorder because they have such a calling to make things right. To quote Yoder for the last time, if Christians "claim for democracy the status of a social institution *sui generis,* we shall inflate ourselves and destroy our neighbors through the demonic demands of the claims we make for our system and we shall pollute our Christian faith by making of it a civil religion. If, on the other hand, we protect ourselves from the Constantinianism of that view of democracy, we may find the realistic liberty to foster and celebrate relative democratization as one of the prophetic ministries of a servant people in a world we do not control" (165–166).

I am aware that the position I have taken will be a surprise to most Christians schooled on the assumption that Christianity is intrinsically related to America. Yet I suspect the position will be as unwelcome by many who dislike calls like that of Neuhaus for a recovery of the role of religion in American life. They want people who still use their private time to entertain religious convictions to be willing to work to create a social order and corresponding government that relegates those convictions to the private sphere. That is done, of course, in the name of creating a democratic society that is based on universal claims justified by *reason qua reason.*[37] Constantinianism is a hard habit to break even for those who no longer understand themselves to be religious.

From this perspective the problem with Yoder (and Falwell) is their refusal to find a neutral or at least nonconfrontational way to state the social implications of their religious convictions.[38] That is not playing the game fairly as it makes religion more public than is healthy for an allegedly pluralistic society. After all there have to be some limits to our pluralism.

Of course Yoder might well respond that he is willing on a case-by-case basis pragmatically to use the allegedly more universal language of our society. But for many I suspect such a pragmatic approach would be insufficient. It is not enough to be willing to play the game of the putative neutral or objective language and procedures of pluralist democracy, you must be willing to believe that such a language and procedures are truly the form of society any people anywhere would choose if they had the material means, institutional creativity, and philosoph-

ical acumen. To challenge that presumption, as Yoder has, I
think is the necessary starting point for any genuine Christian
critique of Christian America.

IV. On Being Christian in America

But where does this leave us? If America is not the "new Jerusalem" does that mean Christians must seek to make America
live consistently with secular presuppositions? In order to make
the line between being Christian and American clear must we
side with those who wish to force any religious phenomenon
out of the public arena? Should we rejoice in the destructive
kind of individualism that is so graphically displayed in *Habits
of the Heart*? Do we not have a stake in sustaining a public ethos
that might make the rise of paganism, which might well use the
language of Christianity, less likely?

I see no reason that the position I have taken would make
me give an affirmative answer to these questions. I believe that
Christians should not will that secular society be more unjust
than it already has a tendency to be. Therefore we have a stake
in fostering those forms of human association that ensure that
the virtues can be sustained. Virtues make it possible to sustain
a society committed to working out differences short of violence. What I fear, however, is that in the absence of those
associations we will seek to solve the moral anomie of the
American people through state action or by a coercive reclaim-
ing of Christian America.

Therefore if I refuse to support prayer in the public school
it becomes all the more important that I urge Christians to learn
to pray authentically as Christians. For if Christians reclaim
prayer as an end in itself rather than a way to confirm the
"Christian nature" of our society, we will perform our most important civic responsibility. For as Origen argued, what more
important public service can we render than to pray that the
emperor recognize his or her status as a creature of God. Such
a prayer is no less significant in a society that believes "the people" have in fact become the emperor.

NOTES

1. For an extremely interesting approach to this latter question see Mark Noll, Nathan Hatch, and George Marsden, *The Search for Christian America* (Westchester, Illinois: Crossway Books, 1983), p. 17. In summary, their position is "A careful study of the facts of history shows that early America does not deserve to be considered uniquely, distinctively or even predominantly Christian, if we mean by the word 'Christian' a state of society reflecting the ideals presented in Scripture. There is no lost golden age to which American Christians may return. In addition, a careful study of history will also show that evangelicals themselves were often partly to blame for the spread of secularism in contemporary American life. We feel also that careful examination of Christian teaching on government, the state, and the nature of culture shows that the idea of a 'Christian nation' is a very ambiguous concept which is usually harmful to effective Christian action in society."

2. Max Stackhouse, Introduction to *The Righteousness of the Kingdom* by Walter Rauschenbusch (Nashville: Abingdon Press, 1968), p. 21.

3. Ibid., p. 22.

4. Ibid., pp. 22–23.

5. Rauschenbusch, *Righteousness of the Kingdom*, p. 102.

6. Walter Rauschenbusch, *Theology for the Social Gospel* (Nashville: Abingdon Press, 1917), pp. 112–13.

7. Rauschenbusch, *Righteousness of the Kingdom*, p. 199.

8. Rauschenbusch, *Theology for the Social Gospel*, p. 165.

9. For Stackhouse's own constructive efforts to extend Rauschenbusch's program, only now in terms of human rights see Max Stackhouse, *Creeds, Society, and Human Rights* (Grand Rapids: Eerdmans, 1984), p. 103. In defense of his position, Stackhouse provides a history of the joining of Puritanism and liberalism to create the universalistic creed of rights that culminated in the United Nations Declaration on Human Rights. He notes these "principles could not be articulated in the particular language of Christian piety which had shaped both the Christian and secular liberal philosophers who had first developed them. Representatives from many cultures and religions would have resisted overt theological formulations in christological or deist terms. The principles had to be stated in 'confessionally neutral' terms. But even at this point we see the triumph of the basic assumptions of the Liberal-Puritan synthesis. The state itself should not be 'religious.' In this view the theologically and morally valid state is not limited by righteous principles and one that allows other organizations to define what

is religiously valid. In brief, the 'godly state' is a secular state."
Stackhouse's account seems far too sanguine about how the obvious tensions between the Puritan sense of community can be
reconciled with the individualism of liberalism. But even if that
were not a problem one cannot help but wonder what has happened that a "secular state" by definition can be called "godly."

10. Jan Dawson, "The Religion of Democracy in Early Twentieth-
Century America," *Journal of Church and State* 27 (Winter, 1985):
47.

11. Ibid., p. 48.

12. Ibid.

13. Reinhold Niebuhr, *The Children of Light and the Children of Darkness*
(New York: Scribner, 1944), p. xiii. In fairness to Niebuhr, it should
be pointed out that he wrote *The Children of Light* at the end of
WWII in the interest of trying to deflate some of the more enthu-
siastic celebrations of democracy the war had occasioned. Yet Niebuhr remained throughout his life a firm supporter of democracy
as that social system which best embodies the Christian understanding of man.

14. For a more complete development of this claim see Stanley
Hauerwas, *Against the Nations: War and Survival in a Liberal Society*
(Minneapolis: Winston-Seabury Press, 1985), pp. 23–50.

15. This part of Murray's work is often unfortunately ignored. One
of the reasons for this may be because these were articles published in *Theological Studies* 13 (1953). John Courtney Murray, "The
Church and Totalitarian Democracy," and idem, "Leo XIII: Separation of Church and State," *Theological Studies* 14 (1953). They
are still worth reading.

16. This is, of course, the main argument of John Courtney Murray,
We Hold These Truths (Garden City, N.Y.: Image Books, 1964).

17. Ibid., p. 308.

18. John Coleman, *An American Strategic Theology* (Ramsey, N.J: Paulist
Press, 1982). Coleman provides the best Roman Catholic attempt
to continue Murray's project. Coleman, however, is much more
interested in how Catholicism can act to renew the ethos or civil
religion of America than the more strictly constitutional issues with
which Murray was concerned.

19. Richard Neuhaus, *The Naked Public Square: Religion and Democracy
in America* (Grand Rapids: Eerdmans, 1984), pp. 83–86. Richard
Taylor rightly argues that no one saw this problem clearer than
Hegel—namely that "Absolute freedom required homogeneity. It
cannot brook differences which would prevent everyone partici-
pating totally in the decisions of the society. And what is even
more, it requires some near unanimity of will to emerge from this

deliberation, for otherwise the majority would just be imposing its will on the minority and freedom would not be universal. But differentiation of some fairly essential kinds are ineradicable. Moreover they are recognized in our post-Romantic climate as essential to human identity. Men cannot simply identify themselves as men, but they define themselves more immediately by their partial community, cultural, linguistic, confessional and so on. Modern democracy is therefore in a bind. I think the dilemma of this kind can be seen in contemporary society. Modern societies have moved towards much greater homogeneity and greater interdependence, so that partial communities lost their autonomy, and to some extent, their identity. But great differences remain; only because of the ideology of homogeneity these differential characteristics no longer have meaning and value for those who have them. Thus the rural population is taught by the mass media to see itself as just lacking in some of the advantages of a more advanced life style. Homogenization thus increases minority alienation and resentment and the first response of liberal society is to try even more of the same: programs to eliminate poverty, or assimilate Indians, move populations out of declining regions, bring an urban way of life to the countryside. But the radical response is to convert this sense of alienation into a demand for 'absolute freedom.' The idea is to overcome alienation by creating a society in which everyone, including the present 'out' groups, participate fully in the decisions. But both these solutions would simply aggravate the problem, which is the homogenization has undermined the communities or characteristics by which people formerly identified themselves and put nothing in their place. What does step into the gap almost everywhere is ethnic or national identity. Nationalism has become the most powerful focus of identity in modern society. The demand for radical freedom can and frequently does join up with nationalism and is given a definite impetus and direction from this." Richard Taylor, *Hegel and Modern Society* (Cambridge: Cambridge University Press, 1979), pp. 114–15. Neuhaus's point is profound but I do not see how he provides an adequate response since he continues to support the political and economic presumptions that are the source of difficulty.

20. Neuhaus, *Naked Public Square*, p. 154.

21. Richard Neuhaus, "Nihilism Without the Abyss: Law, Rights, and Transcendent Good" (Paper delivered at 1985 conference on Religion and Law at Catholic University Law School), 14–15. For a similar claim see Neuhaus, *Naked Public Square*, p. 36. While agreeing with Neuhaus that religion needs to help our society discover or create a moral discourse for the public sphere, John

Coleman rightly raises questions about the assumed neutrality or objectivity of that discourse. Thus he criticizes Brian Hehir for requiring Christians to come to the public arena shorn of their particularistic commitments. As Coleman says, he does not think it possible to escape "the 'permanent hermeneutical predicament' of particular languages and community traditions in a conflict of interpretive schemes through the emergence of a common universal language. I fear that this proposal could court the risk of a continuation of the pernicious intertwining of an ethics of deep concern with an ethic of looking out for number one. But finally, and most persuasive for me, I simply do not know anywhere else to look in American culture besides to our religious ethical resources to find the social wisdom and ethical orientation we would seem to need if we are to face as Americans our new context of increasing interdependence at the national and international level." Coleman, *An American Strategic Theology*, pp. 197–98. Thus Coleman, like many Protestant thinkers, calls us to renew the biblical and republican-virtue tradition against contemporary liberalism. [This is, of course, the main theme of William Sullivan, *Reconstructing Public Philosophy* (Berkeley: University of California Press, 1982).] It is a strange social order indeed that makes Catholics so committed to making America work they accept the project of constructive Protestantism. For a provocative article on the destructive results this process has had on orthodoxy see Vigen Guroian, "The Americanization of Orthodoxy: Crisis and Challenge," *The Greek Orthodox Theological Review* 29, no. 3:255–67.

22. Neuhaus, *Naked Public Square*, p. 121.
23. Ibid., p. 220.
24. Ibid., p. 230. For one of the ablest critiques of Neuhaus see George Marsden, "Secularism and the Public Square," *This World*, 11 (Spring-Summer, 1985): 48–62. Marsden challenges Neuhaus's contention that religion is the morality bearing part of our culture thus denying Neuhaus's statement of the problem. As Marsden says, "Non-theistic secularism also promotes a morality. The problem regarding public philosophy is not simply that of whether or not we have morality in public life. More basically, it is a problem of having competing moral systems and hence less of a consensus in public philosophy than we might like. Putting more religion into public life would not resolve this problem unless we decide first whose religion it would be. In fact, there is even less consensus regarding religion than there is on public philosophy; it is difficult to see how adding more religion would increase the needed consensus." p. 59.
25. Harlan Beckley, "A Christian Affirmation of Rawls' Idea of Justice

as Fairness—Part I," *Journal of Religious Ethics* 13 (Fall 1985): 210–11.

26. Ibid., 212.
27. Ibid.
28. Neuhaus, *Naked Public Square*, p. 257.
29. Ibid., p. 258. Neuhaus's criticisms are broad strokes of the much more detailed and refined criticism of Rawls offered by Michael Sandel. Michael Sandel, *Liberalism and the Limits of Justice* (Cambridge: Cambridge University Press, 1982). Yet Neuhaus does not explain how he can at once criticize Rawls on such grounds and yet continue to underwrite America as the exemplification of what a Christian social order should look like. For whether Neuhaus likes it or not, the public philosophy of America is liberal and Rawls in many ways is its most eloquent spokesman.

    The very fact that many Christian theologians such as Beckley feel the need to adapt Rawls in order to have a comprehensive theory of justice may mean something has already gone wrong in Christians' understanding of the social and political role of the church. Put overly simply, you need a theory of justice when you no longer assume that the very existence of the church is a social stance. Christian thinkers obviously must and can test various accounts of justice offered by different societies in order to find areas of common cause. But it is quite another matter to assume that in order for Christians to act politically they need a theory of justice such as Rawls's that claims to order the basic structure of society. In that respect Beckley's contention that Rawls's theory does not pretend to comprehend all of morality fails to adequately denote the tendency of Rawls's account to render some goods, such as the family, problematic. See, for example, John Rawls, *A Theory of Justice* (Cambridge: Harvard University Press, 1971), pp. 511–12. I am indebted to Mr. Greg Jones for helping me see this.
30. Robert Bellah et al., *Habits of the Heart: Individualism and Commitment in American Life* (Berkeley: University of California Press, 1985), pp. 282–83. For Bellah's more explicit views see Robert Bellah, "The Revolution and the Civil Religion," in *Religion and the American Revolution*, ed. Jerald Brauer (Philadelphia: Fortress, 1976), pp. 55–73. There Bellah observes that when his original article on civil religion was published (1967), it came just as the existence of civil religion was becoming questionable. He observes, "Only the biblical religions can provide the energy and vision for a new turn in American history, perhaps a new understanding of convent, which may be necessary not only to save ourselves but to keep us from destroying the rest of the world." p. 73.
31. Falwell is particularly interesting when he wanders into questions

of international relations. For suddenly he no longer makes direct
biblical appeals but sounds like any good American realist accepting consequential calculations for determining the right moral
policy.

32. For an attempt to develop this position see Stanley Hauerwas, *A
Community of Character: Toward a Constructive Christian Social Ethic*
(Notre Dame: University of Notre Dame, 1981) and idem, *The
Peaceable Kingdom: A Primer in Christian Ethics* (Notre Dame: Uni-
versity of Notre Dame, 1983).

33. John Howard Yoder, *The Priestly Kingdom: Social Ethics as Gospel*
(Notre Dame: University of Notre Dame, 1984), p. 154. When
Christians ask such a question they assume a majority status. In
contrast, Yoder's view, as well as my own, is that Christians cannot
help but be a minority if they are being faithful to their basic
convictions.

34. All references to Yoder will appear in the text. It should not be
thought that Yoder is committing the genetic fallacy by his appeal
to the early Christian community. He is not saying that because
the early church was a minority it should always be a minority,
but rather in this context he is working descriptively to show the
change in the logic of moral argument when this occurred. Of
course he will argue that the form of the early church is normative for Christians not because it was the early church but because
what the early Christians believed is true and results in Christians
taking a critical attitude toward the state. I share that view but I
cannot here adequately defend it.

35. Connected with this reversal is what happens once the ruler is let
into the church, for then the ruler, not the average or weak person, is the model for ethical reason. Thus the rightness of truth-
telling or the wrongness of killing is tested first by whether a ruler
can meet such standards. Yoder, however, does not mean to exclude rulers from the church but rather he expects them to act
like Christians. Thus "Caesar would be perfectly free (for a while)
to bring to bear upon the exercise of his office the ordinary meaning of the Christian faith. It might happen that the result would
be that his enemies triumph over him, but that often happens to
rulers anyway. It might happen that he would have to suffer, or
not stay in office all his life, but that too often happens to rulers
anyway, and it is something that Christians are supposed to ready
for. It might happen that he would be killed; but most Caesars
are killed anyway. It might happen that some of his followers would
have to suffer. But emperors and kings are accustomed to asking
people to suffer for them. Especially if the view were still authentically alive, which the earlier Christians undeniably had held to

and which the theologians in the age of Constantine were still repeating that God blesses those who serve him, it might also have been possible that, together with all of the risks just described, most of which a ruler accepts anyway, there could have been in some times and some places the possibility that good could be done, that creative social alternatives could be discovered, that problems could be solved, enemies loved and justice fostered." Yoder, *Priestly Kingdom,* p. 146.

36. For a romp through church-state issues see George Goldberg, *Reconsecrating America* (Grand Rapids: Eerdmans, 1984).

37. It is interesting to observe that most Americans, whether religious or secular, continue to take a missionary posture for democracy. Americans criticize our government's support for nondemocratic regimes around the world to the point of sometimes advocating intervention against nondemocratic regimes. As Yoder observes, "After the 'Christian west' has lost the naive righteousness with which it thought it should export its religion around the world, we still seem to have a good conscience about exporting our politics." Yoder, *Priestly Kingdom,* p. 151.

38. By associating Yoder and Falwell at this point, I do not mean to deny their obvious differences. Yet they both use primary religious language in the public arena without apology. The problem with Falwell isn't that he uses Christian appeals but that his understanding of Christianity is so attenuated.

6

COMMENT ON "A CHRISTIAN CRITIQUE OF CHRISTIAN AMERICA"

DAVID G. SMITH

Professor Hauerwas takes as his theme "why Jerry Falwell is such a pain." The answer is that Falwell (and Pat Robertson et al.), unlike earlier twentieth-century fundamentalists, has gone "political" in a big way and set about "Christianizing" America according to his own lights. But Falwell is really not so different. He is only doing what the "mainstream" churches have done all along: seeking to bring into closer harmony *his* version of American democracy and *his* religious views. This assimilation of religion and the political system Hauerwas calls "Constantinianism," following John Howard Yoder.[1] Most of us are frankly horrified at the thought that the Reverend Falwell's sectarian and populistic version of Christianity might be translated directly into politics, even worse, into constitutional amendments. But Professor Hauerwas points out that the "social gospel" of liberal Christianity and even Reinhold Niebuhr's "neo-liberalism" are really only "country club" versions of the same tendency to identify Christianity with American democracy. Right and Left disagree about language or political theory, not about substantive aim.

Hauerwas notes that contemporary sociological and theological alarms about growing materialism[2] and *anomie* do provide evidence of an unhealthy secularism.[3] But he argues that

Christianizing politics is not the answer. That way lies a kind of political madness. As he says, quoting Yoder with approval, we would "inflate ourselves and destroy our neighbors through the demonic demands . . . we make for our system and pollute our Christian faith by making of it a civil religion."[4] That does not mean that we can no longer be political liberals. But being Christian and being American is different. We should, therefore, say "no" to Jerry Falwell and to school prayer. We should equally reject the soft and insidious Constantinianism that identifies American democracy and liberal, mainstream Christianity, for example, of the Walter Rauschenbusch variety.[5] Only in this way can Christianity be reclaimed for itself and continue to serve as an authentic critic of society and an independent spiritual force.

In essence, Professor Hauerwas says that mixing religion and politics isn't good for either and that a disengagement would be especially healthy for Christianity. What is new and provocative about this message is, of course, that he doesn't just criticize the Christian Right. He attacks equally the political activities of mainstream, liberal Christians: for instance, the Methodist Council of Bishops or the National Council of Churches. Here, he hits not only a good many Christians, but mainstream, liberal academics as well, most of whom have been scandalized by Jerry Falwell but thought of liberal Christianity as theologically acceptable and, on balance, politically desirable.

My comments are those of a theologically innocent political scientist. While I am attracted by the austere theology of the essay, especially in the aftermath of the Great Society and the Vietnam War, I am neither competent to assess it nor to take issue with it. But as a political scientist, I am troubled by a discussion that appears to equate the threats of Christian Right and Christian liberals. For a political scientist, the differences are greater than those of "mediating language" or political theory.[6] They differ especially in the threats posed to constitutional and political values cherished by many independently of their theology. It is this difference that I would like to explore, taking as my own text: "So Jerry Falwell is a pain; but what about Reinhold Niebuhr?"[7] In other words, I would like to argue that Jerry Falwell and the new Christian Right are menaces to constitutional and democratic values of a sort *not* posed by liberal Christianity and the social gospel, especially of a self-critical variety. Indeed, I should like to argue, further, that the latter, a "chastened social gospel," may be important to the continuing health of the American polity.

Alexis de Tocqueville's notion of a "civil religion" is a good point at which to begin, for Tocqueville especially observed the importance that religion had and would continue to have in American politics.[8] His observations reflect a special historical context, for he was writing about a "developing nation" during the second "Great Awakening," a time when collective aspiration and uplift would have naturally played a large role. But he also perceived that, absent either an aristocracy or explicit political or class ideologies, religion tended to substitute as a political force communicating and giving support to domestic and civic values.

American history provides a wealth of examples to support Tocqueville's thesis. In the eighteenth and nineteenth centuries there were several great awakenings, notable both for their meliorating force and their broad appeal. In the sphere of individual manners and morality, religion contributed powerfully to gentling the frontier, to improving the status of women, and to promoting temperance (later Prohibition). In the public sphere, the impact of religion can be seen in the antislavery and civil rights movements, in political reform, and in the causes of world peace and disarmament. Especially to the point, religion in America has been a *part of* the great reform movements, not *apart from* them.

Tocqueville was particularly concerned with democracy for large numbers of people, working across a whole nation. In this context, he attributed a central importance to religion and especially to that nicely balanced mix of religion and politics he called the "Civil Religion."[9] The civil religion provided a foundation for personal and family morality needed to support honesty, sobriety, and a lawful temper. It served also as a stimulus to benevolence. As such, inspiriting the associations that mediated between the public and private spheres, the civil religion provided a great counterforce to the materialism and individualism that, in his view, might lead to despotism. Therefore, civil religion contributed vitally to the health of American democracy. At the same time, and Tocqueville stressed this point, essential to its strength and leavening influence was a common forbearance from carrying sectarian disputes into politics—restraints of the sort that we have institutionalized especially in the religion clauses of the First Amendment.

In his emphasis upon individual and family manners and upon other-directed benevolence, Tocqueville nicely captured a dualism of great and continuing importance in American politics. On the one hand there is a concern with personal morality, with being "saved" or redeemed—frequently ignoring or even eschewing "politics"—that has been historically associated with a number of fundamentalist sects or movements. On the other hand, there is a pursuit of social justice and benevolence, usually working through or mediated by institutions, or "associations," in Tocqueville's language. The first seeks individual righteousness and personal salvation not mediated by political instrumentalities, though occasionally erupting into politics. The second is civic and often political, concentrated on the social budget rather than personal morality and, perforce, mediated by "association," by social and political institutions.

These distinctions of Tocqueville's convey only roughly the political tendencies historically associated with Fundamentalism and with mainstream Christianity, but they help me, as a political scientist, to say why I find Jerry Falwell to be such a pain. They also lead me to take issue with Professor Hauerwas, especially when he says that Jerry Falwell "represents the triumph of mainstream Christianity" or that their differences, following Neuhaus,[10] are merely or mainly a matter of "mediating language." For a political scientist, the difference is important. It is that between a politics of benevolence, mediated by associations, the public and private corporations, the market, and the interest group universe, a politics of salvation and personal virtue, now turned political with a vengeance, and largely unmediated by these intermediate bodies. Moreover, much of the effectiveness of the new Christian Right and of Jerry Falwell, as well as the reason they are such a pain (and a danger) lies in their success in negating or by-passing these traditional mediating institutions.

Between 1965 and 1980, the Christian Right was both radicalized and politically mobilized. Important in accounting for these developments were such disillusioning and embittering national experiences as the Great Society, the Vietnam War, and President Nixon's "Watergate" crisis. These events both discredited traditional political institutions and raised new, divisive issues. They brought to the fore disputes about moral right and wrong in such political issues as abortion, womens' rights and E.R.A., drugs and draft resistance.[11] This development is illustrated by the contrast between the slogan of right-wing Republicans in 1952, "Communism, Corruption, and Korea", with that of the right-wingers of 1972, "Acid, Abortion, and Amnesty." Notable in the contrast is an increase in scope and intensity of ideological conflict as well as a shift in emphasis from ordinary political issues to those dealing with personal and social morality.

At the same time that these political issues stirred many individuals, the conditions and technology for political mobilization of the Christian Right were also available. The growth of T.V. evangelism and the "electric church," of computerized mail solicitation, and of political action committees facilitated the mobilization of opinion. The increased importance of issue-politics in primaries and elections and of "subcommittee government" in Congress provided opportunities to exert pressure. Together, these developments helped to create an extra-churchly church and an alternative to the party system that provided unprecedented opportunities and resources for politically minded evangelists.

Jerry Falwell and his ilk mark an important historic shift in our politics. For the first time since Franklin D. Roosevelt, the new right and the Evangelical Christians have been important in creating a winning coalition. But the reason that Jerry Falwell is so painful is not that he is successful in politics, so much as the kind of politics he practices. For it is a politics that lacks the usual pluralistic checks of mediating institutions that help to produce a moderate majority.[12] Fundamentalist religious beliefs, translated directly into political expression, foster an ideology that is socially reactionary, populistic, and dogmatic. Jerry Falwell's politics, moreover, concerns itself with personal virtue, life style, and moral beliefs with a zealotry and a venom that invite constitutional excess, particularly with respect to the First Amendment and other parts of the Bill of Rights. In time, the result will surely be to divide politics and pollute religion: even more drastically, as Tocqueville would observe, because we are less agreed, nowadays, about the central tenets of our morality.

Tocqueville's characterization of the civil religion and especially his identification of the two components of personal morality and social benevolence help me to say, furthermore, why I am not comfortable with the description of mainstream Christianity as "Constantinian" and why I continue to like Reinhold Niebuhr even though I can't abide Jerry Falwell. Reinhold Niebuhr I take as representative of a "chastened" social gospel, a version that understands the limited nature of politics and of secular victories.[13] Concerning itself with the social budget, with hunger and with human rights, the politics of benevolence is inescapably subject to institutional and pluralistic checks on policy. Knowing at least some of the limits of politics, most mainstream Christians also accept a truce on the First Amendment. For this reason, I dissent from the author's characterization of "Constantinian," for unlike Falwell or other politicized Evangelicals, the mainstream Christians—at least the chastened ones—would not seek an establishment nor an enforced conformity such as school prayer.

A question that remains is whether we need in America a political influence like the social gospel, in a moderated form. Professor Hauerwas says "No": that we can and should support social justice without Christianizing it, without an active role for mainstream Christians.[14] No doubt, if "Christian" is understood as narrowly sectarian, most of us would agree. But I should like to argue, with Tocqueville, that the civil religion can exert a beneficial influence in fostering social benevolence and in nourishing American democracy.

First, a negative argument: that the civil religion is needed to ward off a greater evil. We are, as Justice Douglas has remarked, "a religious people, whose institutions presuppose a Supreme Being."[15] A "callous indifference" to this heritage would leave a void, impelling those like Jerry Falwell to fill it. This seems to me one kind of plausible fulfillment for the dire prophesies advanced by Richard Neuhaus in *The Naked Public Square: Religion and Democracy in America*[16] and one that our recent history has taught us is more than a fantasy. There are many reasons why Jerry Falwell pains us but one of them is that he reminds us of some of our derelictions.

Mainstream Christianity and the churches also continue to be vitally important for social benevolence. Their historic importance, as Tocqueville observed, was especially great for a country like the United States, which lacked either an aristocracy or a plausible socialist movement. No doubt, their importance has declined proportionately with the development of social security, public assistance, and various publicly administered health and welfare programs.[17] Yet nothing is more distinctively American in charitable and benevolent endeavor than the mix of public and private contribution, including that of the churches along with the foundations and other private institutions. Perhaps this collaboration could continue without the social gospel or a collective force similar to it, but almost certainly it would serve with a diminished vitality, with less warmth and humanity, and lacking an important element of critical tension. This loss would be a grievous one, both for the polity and for those who live within it.

Without valuing religion less, a political scientist can agree with Tocqueville on its benefits for American democracy as a form of government. Religion has served in part as a substitute for political ideologies espoused in other countries by nationalist and revolutionary movements. Part of the "American Creed,"[18] religion has been mostly on the side of democracy. Though dogmatic and sectarian at times, the mainstream religions have generally accepted the First Amendment. Because they have been, for the most part, adaptive, tolerant, and inclusive, proponents of reform and collective uplift have been able to work with the organized religions, not constrained to fight against them. Religion has, in turn, leavened our politics and corrected it with transcendent vision. American democracy benefits from an underlying ideology, a "political creed" that gives perspective, that lifts aspiration, that recalls to core values, and that occasionally justifies resistance to tyranny. For good and ill—but mostly to our good—that mythic force is historically and powerfully religious in this country. Given these pragmatic considerations, I believe that a moderated or chastened social gospel is still a good bet and better than either Jerry Falwell or secularism.

These comments should be taken as those of a political scientist, not a theologian. They do not, nor are they meant to, deal with the theological arguments presented by Professor Hauerwas. My thesis as a political scientist is only that the social gospel, as modified by theologians such as Reinhold Niebuhr, is not a menace but that Jerry Falwell is a great one. Professor Hauerwas is, of course, speaking as a theologian and making a different point: that religion itself, including mainstream Christianity, is threatened by the corruption of Constantinianism. The Great Society, the Vietnam War and our contemporary politics, domestic and international make this warning not only pertinent but vitally important.[19] A period of disengagement might well be good for Christianity though, again following Tocqueville, it might not be good for Christians or for American democracy.

NOTES

1. John Howard Yoder, *The Priestly Kingdom: Social Ethics as Gospel* (Notre Dame: University of Notre Dame, 1984).

2. Robert Bellah et al., *Habits of the Heart: Individualism and Commitment in American Life* (Berkeley: University of California Press, 1985).

3. Richard Neuhaus, *The Naked Public Square: Religion and Democracy in America* (Grand Rapids: W. B. Eerdmans, 1984).

4. Stanley Hauerwas, "A Christian Critique of Christian America", in this volume; Yoder, *Priestly Kingdom*, pp. 165–66.

5. Walter Rauschenbusch, *The Righteousness of the Kingdom* (Nashville: Abington Press, 1968).

6. Hauerwas, "Christian Critique."

7. I have in mind the kind of "neo-liberalism" philosophically developed by Niebuhr in such works as Reinhold Niebuhr, *The Children of Light and the Children of Darkness* (New York: Scribners, 1945) and idem, *Moral Man and Immoral Society* (New York: Scribners, 1932).

8. Alexis de Tocqueville, *Democracy in America* (New York: Vintage, 1945), vol. 1, chap. 17; also, Phillip E. Hammond, "Another Great Awakening?" in *The New Christian Right,* Robert C. Liebman and Robert Wuthnow (New York: Aldine, 1983).

9. Tocqueville, *Democracy in America*, chap. 17.

10. See Note 4.

11. Cf. Robert Wuthnow, "The Rebirth of American Evangelicals", in *New Christian Right,* Liebman and Wuthnow; also Furio Colombo, *God in America—Religion and Politics in the United States,* trans. Kristin Jarratt (New York: Columbia University Press, 1984).

12. Here, note the enormous importance of the "moderate majority" in theory and practice of American democracy from James Madison and *The Federalist* to the present day.

13. Especially Niebuhr, *Children of Light and the Children of Darkness*.

14. Hauerwas, "Christian Critique" sec. 3.

15. *Zorach* v. *Clauson*, 343 U.S. 306 (1951), p. 313.

16. Neuhaus, *Naked Public Square*.

17. Cf., Theodore M. Kerrine and Richard John Neuhaus, "Mediating Structures: A Paradigm for Democratic Pluralism", *Annals of the American Academy of Political and Social Science* (1979), vol. 446, p. 10.

18. Gunnar Myrdal, *An American Dilemma: The Negro Problem and Modern Democracy* (New York: Harper and Bros., 1944), chap. 1 and app. 1.

19. For religious groups concerned about overstepping, A. James Reichley provides some useful guides. A. James Reichley, *Religion in American Public Life* (Washington, D.C.: Brookings Institution, 1985). Adapting freely, the gist of these is:

> 1. Avoid detailed policy stands: for instance, endorsing specific dollar amounts in the budget. We should be wary, as Jackie Gleason has said, of "born again" Christians who claim they receive daily stock-market tips from on High.
> 2. Do not dominate the mediating instruments such as party organs or legislative committees.
> 3. Do not operate tactically like ordinary pressure groups.
> 4. Do not demand a specific ideology as a condition for support: for example, Jerry Falwell's saying that one could not be a Christian and a liberal.

To this list of four, one might add a fifth: Do not identify the kingdom with any one earthly solution.

7

THE WALL OF SEPARATION AND LEGISLATIVE PURPOSE

LOUIS HENKIN

I

Professor Hauerwas has provided a perceptive analysis of contemporary Christian attitudes towards the perennial tension between the demands of God and of Caesar as that tension is reflected in the United States today. His own views are particularly noteworthy in that they are "ec-centric" within the Christian universe and stand in contrast to what is increasingly heard from Christian spokesmen. They contrast, as well, with the views of some representatives of some other religions, and with more idiosyncratic views such as those of the anonymous, secular Jewish philosopher cited by Professor Hauerwas.

Professor Hauerwas asks Christians to avoid Constantianism, to distance themselves from and shed responsibility—as Christians—for the corruption of pagan Caesar. His Jewish interlocutor, on the other hand, insists that since in our society Christians inevitably have Caesar's power, it is desirable that their power be governed by their Christianity. To that end he is willing to have Caesar—political authority—take measures to make Christians into good Christians.

Neither Professor Hauerwas, nor his anonymous interlocutor, places his views in a framework of political or ethical theory. Professor Hauerwas says he will not "reach for law" to further Christian morality, but that restraint apparently is not from any scruple rooted in democratic principle or in constitutional doctrine. He would not legislate Christian morality for political, practical reasons: because it could not be done in our political system; because such laws could not be enforced and would be divisive. His secular interlocutor, on the other hand, would apparently accept, say, prayer in the classroom, in the hope that it would help make the United States more authentically Christian and therefore more civilized. We do not know whether he would also favor spending public funds to support Christian institutions, or enacting laws forbidding the desecration of the Christian sabbath, or buttressing Christian morality by outlawing obscenity.

In effect, Professor Hauerwas offers Christian support for a constitutional jurisprudence of strict separation of church and state. Many Christians—and many non-Christians—who do not share his theology or ideology, support strict separation on other grounds. Some of us do so from commitment to individual human rights, including freedom of religion and conscience, because we believe that such freedom is furthered by avoiding even the marginally coercive effects of religious entanglement with political life. Others might accept that, at least in our pluralistic polity—a society that includes different kinds of Christians, religious non-Christians, many in various religions who (like Professor Hauerwas) wish to maintain their religion distinct from public life, as well as many who are nonreligious—strict separation is essential for the *good society*. The particular reason why one supports separation may determine the character of the separation one seeks, or how much less than strict separation one is prepared to accept.

II

As constitutional doctrine, separation is a rough, colloquial translation of the mandate of the First Amendment: "Congress shall make no law respecting an establishment of religion"—a prohibition later held to apply to all forms of official federal action, as well as to governmental acts of the states. The contemporary interpretation of that clause is doubtless not quite what the framers contemplated, as our society is not the society the framers knew or anticipated. To a large extent, separation, as defined and refined by constitutional jurisprudence since the Second World War, is the response of a liberal, "humanist" *Zeitgeist* in a pluralist society.

The difficulty some of us have with the recent intimacy between religion and politics is indeed that it brings the danger of Constantinianism against which Professor Hauerwas warned— danger to religion as well as to democratic values and individual freedom. We are not sure where that intimacy will stop; we are fearful as to where it might lead. We had come to rely on the courts to contain that danger but recent trends in judicial opinion have not been reassuring. The Supreme Court of the United States has held it not to be a breach in the *wall of separation* for a municipality to expend public funds for a creche, among other Christmas symbols, and to erect it on public property.[1] By an equally divided vote, the Supreme Court let stand a decision that required an *unwilling* polity to allow private persons to establish Christian symbols on public land, although the city council had voted not to allow them because to do so would be divisive.[2] In that case, the lower court had ruled that to prohibit such symbols would limit the freedom of religious expression of the proponents. But maintaining the symbols on public land was not intended merely as a private religious statement, nor was its location on public land necessary to give the private statement greater publicity; a private statement could have been made as effectively on private property open to public view. The purpose of erecting the creche on public grounds was apparently to render it an expression by the polity. Even had all of its members wished to make such a community statement, a Christian statement by the polity is an instance of the Contantinianism which the First Amendment sought to preclude.

III

Constantinianism raises issues for both Constitutional jurisprudence and moral philosophy, but in respect of religion, Constitutional doctrine and ethical principles are not congruent. The Constitution expressly forbids law prohibiting the free exercise of religion; such prohibitions would also raise moral concerns for individual autonomy and liberty. The other clause in the First Amendment, however, forbidding law "respecting an establishment of religion," reflects an additional and distinct value particular to United States Constitutional jurisprudence. We insist on nonestablishment, on separation of church and state, even if there were no evidence that establishment, or some particular manifestation of establishment, significantly limits the free exercise of religion. In other liberal states, which share our ideological conceptions in other respects, separation is not of constitutional dimension in principle or in fact.

In United States jurisprudence, separation requires lines to be drawn. Some points on the guidelines are reasonably clear. Separation bars official participation in religious activity as well as official promotion of private religious activity. On the other hand, separation does not bar some public benefits to religion, such as tax exemption for religious institutions as for other not-for-profit organizations, or tax deductions for private contributions to religious organizations as to other "charitable" organizations. In those respects, neither what separation permits nor what it prohibits raises significant moral issues.

One aspect of the jurisprudence of separation, however, implicates issues of permissible legislative purpose, an inquiry that in other contexts has been also the concern of political and moral philosophy. Separation bars laws and other governmental regulation that serve a religious rather than a secular purpose. In 1986, for example, a sharply divided Supreme Court invalidated a law requiring a "moment of silence" in the classroom that was clearly designed to promote religious prayer, but most of the Justices strongly intimated that a moment of silence not linked to religion in purpose or content might serve a secular purpose and would survive.[3] A distinction between religious and secular purpose was implied in the creche case: The Court recognized that the Constitution prohibited a municipal government from making a Christian statement since that would serve a religious purpose, but the majority concluded that for the municipality to recognize Christmas with what the Court deemed to be non-religious symbols was permissible as serving a secular community purpose. In 1987, the Court will presumably decide whether a law requiring the teaching of "creation science" (as well as evolution) is invalid as furthering a religious purpose, or whether it can be upheld as serving some secular educational purpose.

A distinction between religious and secular purpose is not always easy to apply, and is complicated by the conception of public purpose in Constitutional jurisprudence generally. The United States is a modified "liberal state." Its constitutional jurisprudence, reflecting a conception of "ordered liberty,"[4] of liberty subject to due process of law, inevitably has raised issues about the proper purposes of government. In the nineteenth century, United States jurisprudence accepted that government may legislate to serve "public" but not "private" purposes, and public purposes were defined as including "safety, health, morals and the general welfare."[5] But what is a public purpose, and the concept of "general welfare" in particular, have proved to be neither simple nor clear. For example, it is accepted that legislation serves a public purpose—the general welfare—if it serves the interests of the majority even if it disserves the minority. But legislation is also for the general welfare if immediately it serves the interests of only selected individuals or groups, as in legislation that protects or promotes the welfare of minorities, or that taxes all to promote the arts or to further developed aesthetic values, or to provide assistance to the handicapped. If so, may the state legislate to benefit individual religious persons, however many or few?

If the nonestablishment clause forbids legislating for a religious purpose, and if the distinction between religious and secular purpose is to have meaning, it cannot be that a state's concern for the welfare of religious persons, in respects related to their religion, may be treated as a permissible nonreligious purpose serving the general welfare. Presumably, a state cannot be heard to claim that giving pleasure—even "religious pleasure"—to groups of citizens, or protecting their sensibilities—even their religious sensibilities—is a secular purpose. Surely, a state may not give financial support to a religious denomination, though the state's purpose be not to further religious purposes of the denomination but only to give pleasure or confer financial benefit upon religious persons. Similarly, it is accepted that a state may not prohibit sacrilege or blasphemy in order to protect the sensibilities of religious persons. If a state may outlaw homosexuality it must be on grounds other than that the practice offends the religious sensibilities of others.[6]

Yet the Supreme Court had allowed—even required—a state

to exempt persons from a general societal requirement that
would offend their religious scruples or burden their exercise
of religion. Thus, in 1965, Mrs. Sherbert was discharged by her
employer because she would not work on her Sabbath; she could
not find work with other employers for the same reason. The
state of South Carolina refused her unemployment compensation under a law that denied such benefits to workers who failed,
without good cause, to accept "suitable work when offered."
The Supreme Court held that since the state law had the effect
of "penalizing" Mrs. Sherbert for observing her Sabbath, it bur-
dened Mrs. Sherbert's free exercise of religion.[7] Similarly, the
Court has held that a state may not apply its compulsory education law to compel an Amish father to send his child to public
high school against the tenets of the father's faith.[8] Exemptions
from military service for those who refuse to serve on religious
grounds are well established.[9] Some states have provided by
law that a doctor is not to be penalized for refusing to perform
an abortion on religious grounds.[10]

Constitutional jurisprudence has seen these cases as an attempt to accommodate the principle of nonestablishment to the
values of the free exercise of religion. Reasonable men may
differ as to how to balance those values, while accepting the
accommodation in principle. It is plausible to argue that in those
cases the state's purpose is not to further religion, but to serve
the secular purpose of easing the burdens for those who suffer
some extraordinary "limitation," even if it be a religious limitation. The Court has not told us, however, why a state may
protect religious persons against such discomfort or disadvan-
tage but not from offense to their religious-moral sensibilities.
The Court has not provided a relevant calculus of personal interests that might enable a state to distinguish among various
kinds of benefit to religious persons in respect of their religion,
and to relate such distinctions to the purposes of the Establishment Clause.

IV

Another point of contact between constitutional jurisprudence
and moral philosophy that remains insufficiently explored is

whether one can distinguish religious from secular morality. Some years ago I suggested that laws against obscenity are essentially "morals legislation," and do not respond to a secular morality; they make crime out of that which is only sin.[11] I asked whether a society committed to separation of church and state may properly legislate in support of values, including moral principles, that are exclusively religious. If separation bars such legislation, laws against obscenity, and laws regulating sexual acts between consenting adults—fornication, adultery, homosexual activity or incest—would be acceptable only if they could be found to serve a secular societal purpose.

The task of distinguishing religious from secular morality is particularly difficult in a society such as that of the United States, with a culture having deep religious roots and where the large majority of its members continue to be more or less committed to religious values. The difficulty of drawing a line between religious and secular morality need not trouble the mainstream of the criminal law. One may readily conclude that laws prohibiting injury to person or property have an independent secular purpose since such laws, though perhaps religious in ancient origin, are accepted as the purpose of every society and are common to all societies today, including secular and even atheistic ones. The "harm principle"—that law should prohibit only that which does injury to another—was recognized even by the French Declaration of the Rights of Man and of the citizen during the Age of Reason, as by John Stuart Mill without any religious basis a century later. "Paternalistic" laws, too—such as those that forbid euthanasia or suicide, or the use of drugs, or riding a vehicle without a seat belt or a helmet—may not satisfy the harm principle but may serve other secular purposes. Even laws strongly espoused by religious communities do not necessarily serve purposes that are exclusively, or primarily, religious. For a prominent contemporary example, a state that would outlaw abortion might insist that it is not moved by religious values: Secular morality, too, might accept that a fetus is a person from conception, and that the state is entitled, indeed obligated, to protect that person as it does one who is a "little older" and already born. In the Sabbath "Blue Laws" cases of a generation ago, the United States Supreme Court found a secular purpose

in maintaining a common day of leisure.[12] Does the regulation
of sexual activities between consenting adults serve primarily,
authentically, a secular societal purpose?

The suggestion that separation bars legislation motivated by
religious morality exclusively has not been explored by the
courts.[13] If the demarcation between secular and religious morality is constitutionally crucial, it deserves attention it has not
had. The harm principle could serve as a starting point: Legislation must protect individual interests against injury. But the
protection of interests of a kind not safeguarded by virtually all
societies is subject to scrutiny for undue religious influences.
One might attempt to trade the development of such laws in
the United States and to identify their roots and purposes. One
might explore whether a particular kind of law is to be found
among states that do not have strong religious traditions. One
might seek guidance in the doctrines and justifications of various ethical schools, attempting to determine—and exclude—
those that have a theistic basis. The basis of such scrutiny is not
hostility to religion. Its purpose is to ensure that legislation does
not impose sectarian values in a pluralistic society.

NOTES

1. *Lynch v. Donnelly*, 465 U.S. 668 (1984).
2. *Board of Trustees, Village of Scarsdale v. McCreary*, 739 F.2d 716 (2d
   Cir. 1984), affirmed by an equally divided court, 469 U.S. 915
   (1985).
3. *Wallace v. Jaffree*, 472 U.S. 38 (1985).
4. Justice Cardozo's phrase in *Palko v. Connecticut*, 302 U.S. 319, 325
   (1937).
5. See, e.g., *Lochner v. New York*, 198 U.S. 45, 53 (1905).
6. Compare *Bowers v. Hardwick*, 478 U.S., 106 S. Ct. 2841 (1986). In
   upholding the Georgia anti-sodomy law, the religious roots of these
   laws were not addressed either by the majority or by the dissent,
   but Chief Justice Burger, concurring, noted that "condemnation
   of those practices is firmly rooted in Judaeo-Christian moral and
   ethical standards."
7. *Sherbert v. Verner*, 374 U.S. 398 (1963).
8. *Wisconsin v. Yoder*, 406 U.S. 205 (1972).
9. See, e.g., *United States v. Seeger*, 380 U.S. 163 (1965); Gillette *v.
   United States*, 401 U.S. 437 (1971).

10. Compare the Massachusetts statute, Mass. Gen. Laws Ann. c 112, §121, protecting doctors against sanctions for refusing to perform or participate in an abortion "on moral or religious grounds."

    In 1985, the Supreme Court held that a statute that prevents an employer from dismissing an employee because he would not work on his Sabbath is unconstitutional because the statute advances religion. *Estate of Thornton v. Caldor,* 472 U.S. 703 (1985). The decision to invalidate the Connecticut statute could perhaps be supported not on the ground that the state legislation advanced religion or served a religious purpose but because there—unlike the case of Mrs. Sherbet—the state cast the burden of its regulation on the private employer.

11. Louis Henkin, "Morals and the Constitution: The Sin of Obscenity," *Colum. L. Rev.* 63 (1963): 391.

12. *McGowan v. Maryland,* 366 U.S. 420 (1961).

13. But compare *Stanley v. Georgia,* 394 U.S. 557 (1969), where the Court held that a state cannot punish private possession of pornographic materials.

8

RELIGION, PUBLIC MORALITY, AND CONSTITUTIONAL LAW

DAVID A. J. RICHARDS

The proper balance between moral pluralism and community is, I believe, a pervasive interpretive issue in American constitutional law in the constitutional jurisprudence of state neutrality required by the religion clauses, free speech, and constitutional privacy. State abridgements of religious liberty, for example, are justifiable, if at all, only on a strong showing of neutral state purposes.[1] In a recent book, *Toleration and the Constitution*,[2] I develop a general position on the role of history, interpretive conventions, and political theory in constitutional interpretation in general and try to show the interpretive fertility of this approach in terms of a unified theory of the value of constitutional neutrality pervasive in the interpretation of the religion clauses, free speech, and constitutional privacy. My analysis here elaborates an aspect of that argument, namely, how interpretations of religion-clause neutrality, shifting over time, can be plausibly understood in terms of an approach to constitutional interpretation that takes seriously the distinctive role of a certain kind of moral and political theory in making the best interpretive sense of our history and our changing interpretive conventions. On that basis, I make some correlative suggestions about how to understand comparable shifts in the interpretation of neutrality argument fundamental to the modern law of free speech and constitutional privacy. My larger theme is that the distinctively American constitutional commitment to liberties of religion, speech, and privacy self-consciously embodies an associated theory of constraints on state power that radically departs from traditional conceptions of enforceable public morality.

I. LOCKEAN TOLERATION AND THE RELIGION CLAUSES

The religion clauses of the First Amendment both use and elaborate the theory of religious toleration classically developed both in John Locke's *Letters Concerning Toleration*[3] and Pierre Bayle's contemporary *Philosophique Commentaire*.[4] Importantly, that theory incorporates interdependent critical and constructive aspects.[5]

The crux of Locke's and Bayle's critical attack on the theory and practice of Augustinian religious persecution[6] is its conception of a justly enforceable criterion for the erring conscience, namely, the Augustinian argument that conscience may be subject to criminal law when it expresses a willful failure to accept evident religious truths. Everyone, however, has a conviction of the truth of her or his beliefs, on the basis of which dissenting beliefs will be regarded as willful failures to acknowledge evident religious truths. Accordingly, the argument will justify universal persecution, which neither a just God nor the law of nature could have intended. At bottom, one theological system, among others equally reasonable, is made the measure of enforceable truths.

Such a biased conception of enforceable rational truth corrupts, in turn, the conception of just freedom of the person. The putatively irrational person is supposed, for that reason, to be unfree, marred by a disordered will. A judgment of unfreedom, alleged as the ground of coercive persecution, in fact viciously degrades the freedom that for Locke and Bayle, is the inalienable right of conscience: Conscience is made hostage to the judgments of others. The moral nerve of the argument for the right to conscience is that persons are independent originators of claims and that the demands of ethics and of an ethical God are only both known and practically effective in our lives when persons' right to conscience is appropriately respected. Otherwise, the demands of ethics are confused with public opinion or popular taste.

The association of religious conscience with ethical imperatives is, of course, pervasively characteristic of the Judeo-Christian tradition and its conception of an ethical God acting through
history.[7] Locke and Bayle are religious Christians in this tradition. They regard themselves as returning Christianity to its
ethical foundations, reminding Christians, for example, of the
toleration of the early patristic period.[8] Disagreements in speculative theology, which had grounded Augustinian persecu-
tions for heresy, were, for them, patent betrayals of essential
Christianity; they disabled people from regulating their lives by
the simple and elevated ethical imperatives of Christian charity.

Thus, Locke's and Bayle's deepest criticism of Augustinian
persecution was its corruption of religion, politics, and ethics,
and the motivation of their arguments for the inalienable right
to conscience is a new and constructive interpretation of what
ethics is, and how it connects to religion and politics. Locke
thus linked a free conscience to the autonomous exercise of the
moral competence of each and every person, as a democratic
equal, to reason about the nature and content of the ethical
obligations imposed on persons by an ethical God[9] and thought
of these obligations as centering on a core of minimal ethical
standards reflected in the Gospels.[10] And ethics, for Bayle, as
for Kant, is only a vital force in one's life when one independently acknowledges its principles oneself and imposes them on
one's life.[11] Bayle, who rejoiced in paradox, puts the point
bluntly: Beliefs in speculative religious truths did not insure
salvation. Such beliefs were often brigaded with the gravest irreligion, that is, barbarous failures of ethical obligation and
Christian charity, i.e., religious persecution; moreover, disbelief
in such truths, even atheism, was consistent with decent conduct.[12] The very point of respect for conscience, for Locke and
Bayle, is to ensure that each and every person is guaranteed
the moral independence to determine the nature and content
of ethical obligations. State enforcement of sectarian religious
beliefs taints this inalienable moral freedom by its enforcement
of speculative theological disagreements that distort the central
place of this democratic conception of ethics in what both regarded as true religion.

This new conception of ethics is, for Locke and Bayle, motivated by what they take to be the distinctive vision of God in

the Judeo-Christian tradition—God as personal and supremely ethical.[13] We come to know this personal God, in part, through the realization of our ethical nature, our creative moral powers of rationality and reasonableness, as persons, made in his image, in relation both to him and all persons. On this conception, religion does not embed us in ontological hierarchies characteristic of many of the world's cultural traditions,[14] but actually makes possible, indeed liberates a respect for persons expressive of our rational and reasonable freedom. The right to conscience has the focal role that it has in a just polity because it makes possible moral self-government.

This conception—that ethical independence and the right to conscience are mutually supportive—leads to a radical departure in political principle from other political traditions, namely, Locke's principle that sectarian religious ends are not a legitimate state concern.[15] Locke's principle was naturally opposed as undermining public morality and political stability, especially when it was later elaborated to include disestablishment in Virginia and under the First Amendment of the United States Constitution.[16] Political experience theretofore had associated religion with state coercive and other support, so that many wondered how a state could be stable when all religions were independent of it. Bayle and Locke responded that a peaceful civility can be restored only when religious persecution is abandoned; persecution itself creates the instabilities of intractable, sectarian conflict.[17] Indeed, their argument suggests that the older view of enforceable public morality, itself the product of religious persecution, was itself morally corrupt.

We should understand this claim of moral corruption in the content of a central puzzle for Christians and democrats like Locke: How is it that a religion like Christianity, a religion for Locke of democratic equality and civility, had long been associated in the West with the legitimation of antidemocratic institutions like hereditary monarchy? The question is particularly poignant for Locke and the Lockean revolutionary Americans a century later since they believed that, in fact, a properly understood Protestant Christianity supplied the ethics of personal self-government that made possible the theory and practice of democratic self-government. How, for millenia, could Christianity have thus betrayed its essential emancipatory purposes, degrading just human freedom into acceptance of morally arbitrary hierarchies of privilege and power? It is a distinguishing feature of the American democratic tradition that it chose to answer the question not in the terms of a Voltairean religious skepticism hostile to religion as such, a view that gravitates to the familiar British and European practice of a latitudinarian, established church that tames and civilizes religion to state purposes, along the lines of Rousseau's Erastian conception of civil religion.[18] Rather, American thought derives from an alternative analysis of how Christianity had itself been politically corrupted from its essential purposes by its role as an established church, thus suggesting an internally religious as well as ethical basis for attack on the very idea of an established church.

Thomas Jefferson, author of the Virginia Bill for Religious Freedom, thus argued, under the influence of both Kames[19] and Bolingbroke,[20] that the history of Augustinian intolerance in the West has corrupted Western ethics, including a proper understanding of the ethics of the Gospels, by speculative theology.[21] Indeed, Jefferson's commitment to the eighteenth-century theory of a moral sense gave a more potent sense to Locke's and Bayle's argument that Augustinian intolerance corrupted both religion and ethics.[22] The violation of the right to conscience was not construed, by Jefferson among others, as a corruption of the moral sense itself.[23] Jefferson's radical analysis of this moral corruption is associated with a radical cure envisaged neither by Locke nor Bayle, namely, an attack on established churches as such. Jefferson, in contrast to Locke, expressly elaborates the underlying moral ideal of respect for conscience to include not only free exercise, but any form of religious qualification for civil rights or any compulsion of tax money for support of religious beliefs, even one's own. For Jefferson, the very idea of an established church, associating state power with the support of sectarian religious belief, was the historical root of the corruption of Christianity from its essential emancipatory purposes: The dependence of religion on state power "tend only to beget habits of hypocrisy and meanness, are a departure from the plan of the holy author of our religion . . . and . . . hath established and maintained false religions over the greatest part of the world and through all time".[24]

On this view, Christianity fulfills its essential purposes of moral self-government and thus makes possible political self-government when persons, free of all state incentives, are guaranteed the ultimate right and responsibility as democratic equals to acknowledge, express, and revise the ultimate organizing aims of their personal and moral lives. A religion of democratic equality becomes the vehicle and support of such equality only when its independence of state power enables persons as democratic equals to understand and act on its ethics of democratic equality.

The upshot of both the critical and constructive aspects of the argument for religious liberty is, as Locke clearly saw, a politically operative distinction between the state's legitimate pursuit of state purposes broadly neutral among all forms of conscience and the illegitimate use of state power to either reinforce or endorse sectarian conscience. Bayle, though not a contractarian in his political theory, proposed a strikingly contractarian way of drawing distinction:

> "I would ask him first to hold himself aloof from his own personal interest and the manners of his country and then to ask himself this question: If a certain custom were to be introduced into a country where it has not been in usage, would it be worthy of acceptance after a free and critical examination."[25]

Locke's more explicitly contractarian argument defines neutrally acceptable state purposes as:

> "[c]ivil interest . . . life, liberty, health, and indolency of body; and the possession of outward things, such as money, lands, houses, furniture, and the like".[26]

The legitimate exercise of state power is thus limited to the pursuit of certain general goods that all persons would want as conditions of whatever else they might want. The idea is not that these goods define what makes a life ultimately valuable. Rather, state pursuit of such ends defines the limits of legitimate state power precisely because these goods do not themselves define ultimate questions, but are the all-purpose goods consistent with the kind of interpretive independence on such questions that respect for the inalienable right to conscience requires.[27] The Lockean theory of toleration would allow state power to forbid religious rituals involving child sacrifice (the taking of life, a general good) whereas a state prohibition on animal sacrifices (the taking of animal life not being a general good) might be forbidden.[28] Justifiability by neutral state purposes is thus to be interpreted by reference to a background theory of general goods, i.e., as the terms of secular justification for coercive state power acceptable to all persons committed as a normatively pluralistic community to the inalienable right to conscience as a background right.

The religion clauses of the First Amendment to the United States Constitution are clearly shaped by the Lockean argument to even more radical effect than Locke envisaged. James Madison, the architect of the First Amendment and the central Virginia advocate of successful passage of Jefferson's Bill for Religious Freedom, ensured that the First Amendment not only protect Locke's interest in religious free exercise, but also Jefferson's elaboration of Lockean argument to prohibit state establishments of religion.[29] Both the free-exercise and anti-establishment clauses clearly deploy the Lockean distinction between legitimate and illegitimate state purposes. Any infringement of the religious liberty of free-exercise can be justified, for example, only by a compelling secular state purpose,[30] and the anti-establishment clause demands that the state not support any form of sectarian religious teaching but pursue only neutrally acceptable secular purposes.[31]

Contractarian political theory has a powerful role to play in understanding these constitutional provisions in so far as a defensible form of contemporary contractarian theory best expresses their motivating conception. As I argue at length elsewhere, a contractarian theory that gives focal place to our moral powers of rationality and reasonableness meets that test.[32] This theory naturally enables us to understand and interpret the religion clauses as a coordinated protection of the inalienable right to conscience, the right to form, express, and revise our highest order interests in a rational and morally reasonable life.[33] The free-exercise clause thus protects expression of religious belief and ritual from state coercion; and the anti-establishment clause protects the formation and revision of ultimate personal and moral views from any state incentives. Both clauses limit state power in either area to the neutrally acceptable secular purposes defined by contractarian theory.[34]

II. The Scope of Religious Liberty

In order to understand how contractarian theory assists the task of interpreting the religion clauses, I examine here one abstract issue of moral and political theory that directly bears on a range of interpretive questions in religion clause jurisprudence, namely, the proper interpretation of constitutional neutrality. The issue at stake is the interpretive connection between religion clause jurisprudence and background conceptions of the nature of ethics. For example, background assumptions about the nature of ethics—Locke's theological ethics[35] versus the moral-sense theory of the American Enlightenment[36]—are an important source of interpretive disagreement over Lockean principles of toleration, and thus over the meaning of the religion clauses. Jefferson's refusal to follow Locke in excluding Catholics and atheists from the protection of the Virginia Bill for Religious Freedom reflects his own background assumptions,[37] and many later historical shifts in the interpretation of these clauses pivot on similar changes in thought. When Justice Story, for example, dubbed Protestant Christianity the de facto established church of the United States, he assumed that Protestantism was a just proxy for ethics itself. Accordingly, Story found no violation of constitutional neutrality in state imposition of prayers or Bible reading in public schools, or prosecutions for blasphemy, or exclusion of atheists from public office.[38] If we today take constitutional objection to such practices, this must turn on background shifts in our ideas of whether Protestant Christianity can any longer justly be regarded as a proxy for ethics as such.

These disagreements do correspond to the moral motivations of the argument for universal toleration stated contemporaneously by Locke and Bayle: The motivation of their argument for the inalienable right to conscience is, as we have seen, a new interpretation of what ethics is, namely, an ethics of the moral independence of democratic equals, and how it connects religion to democratic politics. However, because both Locke and

Bayle understand moral independence as a quest for an ethical God's uncompromisable demands, they exclude atheists from the scope of universal toleration.[39] Though atheists may act morally, as Bayle clearly acknowledges,[40] they lack the appropriate epistemic attitude of mind open to ethical demands, the uncompromisable demands of a personal and ethical God.[41] And the exclusion of Catholics from toleration is directed not against their worship (Bayle condemns such coercion and much else),[42] but against what Locke and Bayle took to be their commitment to intolerance and their seditious advocacy of the overthow of legitimate Protestant government.[43]

Accordingly, the sense of the political theory of toleration is linked to a cognate moral philosophy of democratic ethics by the very structure of the argument for toleration. Interpretation of the religion clauses, including the scope of toleration, will turn on how these background questions of political theory and moral philosophy are resolved.

We may, indeed, map a range of alternative positions on the scope of religious liberty onto their associated theories of democratic ethics—for example, the Massachusetts theocrats, Locke and Bayle, moral-sense theorists, and contemporary moral philosophers. The Massachusetts theocrats supposed natural knowledge of ethics to be corrupted by the Fall and associated ethical knowledge with reading the Bible in a certain highly specific way.[44] Locke and Bayle believed that we may come to know ethics by our natural reason inferring God's existence and his will for us; they believed that the Bible both assists and is assisted by such inquiry into ethical knowledge.[45] Moral-sense theorists argued that we know what is ethically right by our uncorrupted moral sense independent of God's will, a sense confirmed, however, by a proper reading of the Bible and reenforced by belief in an afterlife.[46] Contemporary moral theory—whether deontological, utilitarian, or intuitionist—standardly analyzes ethical reasoning independently of religious reasoning or belief in an afterlife.[47] Presumably, all these ethical theories, in the order roughly arranged, will dictate a correspondingly broader inclusive ambit for universal toleration: from belief in God and reading the Bible a certain way (the Massachusetts theocrats), to belief in God and reading the Bible (Locke and Bayle), to belief in God (some moral-sense views), to belief in God as well as agnosticism and atheism (other moral-sense views and contemporary moral theories).

Attitudes about Bible interpretation are a useful historical guide to the enlarging ambit of toleration, and an important background issue in controversies over religion clause jurisprudence in the United States. We should put these controversies in the context of the historical tradition they reflect and elaborate. Both Locke and Bayle, for example, are religious Christians in the Protestant tradition, a tradition in search of a pure Christianity of the Bible, to which one alone looked for guidance, *sola scriptura*.[48] But the metainterpretive diversity encouraged by humanism and the Reformation also unleashed diversity in styles of Bible interpretation (Erasmus, La Peyrere, Richard Simon, and Spinoza).[49] Both Locke and Bayle took seriously the wide range of disagreements over Bible interpretation that reasonable persons could, in view of this metainterpretive diversity, entertain; indeed, they conceived of respect for the right to conscience, the ground of universal toleration, as facilitating the exercise of reasonable judgment, including both epistemic and practical rationality.[50] So understood, the essence of their argument for toleration is that the state may not itself dictate standards of Bible interpretation (as Catholic intolerance did),[51] but must allow the exercise of the independent epistemic and practical rationality of persons as democratic equals in adopting, expressing, and revising standards on their own. All reasonable persons, once afforded opportunity to study the Bible, must believe in God and must believe that the Bible is the word of God; but they must be allowed rationally and reasonably to determine by their own standards what the truth is. This freedom alone ensures a pure religion and a practical ethics. Elisha Williams, a kinsman of Jonathan Edwards, makes precisely this point in his 1744 defense of conscience and toleration so typical of the evolving American normative consensus on these matters, gravitating to the unique American constitutional commitment to anti-establishment principles.[52]

Locke and Bayle, as well as Elisha Williams, implicitly concede that universal toleration must extend much further if rational and reasonable judgment, guaranteed the right to conscience, achieves their underlying ethical aims: an ethics of the

moral competence of democratic equals. While Catholic standards of Bible interpretation cannot be enforced by law, persons' reasonable adoption of such standards must be respected
if it is consistent, as it certainly is, with a tolerant respect for
the rights of others. Once conceptions of moral reasonableness
are, under the impact of moral-sense theory, not linked to God's
will, respect for independent rational and reasonable judgment
may not require either belief in God in general or in the Bible
in particular. Jefferson, for example, believed in a deist God,
in an afterlife, and, like Locke, in the essential ethical wisdom
of the gospels, suitably edited (see the Jefferson Bible).[53] But
apparently his lifelong study of and interest in pagan ethics led
him to doubt that the cultivation and exercise of moral reasonableness required such belief.[54] An acute sensitivity to issues of
reasonable metainterpretive diversity about ethics and its sources
led Jefferson to believe that the argument that Christian ethics
was superior to pagan ethics was *an argument* with which reasonable persons could disagree.[55] The implicit premise of this
argument is that rational and reasonable persons might realize
and express personal and ethical integrity through beliefs other
than Christian focussing on the Bible, religious beliefs, or beliefs in an afterlife.[56] If rational and reasonable persons could
realize their integrity through other kinds of beliefs and other
texts besides the Bible, respect for conscience must be accorded
them. The conception of the scope of universal toleration thus
expands for Jefferson to include not only Catholics but atheists.

If this was so in Jefferson's historical context, contemporary
notions of universal toleration can hardly be less generous. Undoubtedly, the nineteenth-century American consensus on religion-clause jurisprudence reflected an understanding of ethics closer to Locke's than to Jefferson's. This is the consensus
that Justice Story articulated when he appealed to the de facto
establishment of Protestant Christianity in the United States,
and justified state impositions of prayers and Bible reading in
the public schools, blasphemy prosecutions, and excluding
atheists from public office. But the nineteenth and twentieth
centuries saw a number of developments in Bible criticism and
in science, sharper demarcation between religious and ethical
claims, and even criticism of religion on ethical grounds. These

developments have, I believe, irretrievably undermined Justice Story's conception.

To summarize a long and complex story: Developments in historiography and Bible criticism have permanently eroded any monolithic conception of the essential beliefs and sources of Protestant Christianity.[57] Developments in science have further expanded such metainterpretive diversity, for example, over how to reconcile the epistemic claims of science, such as evolution, with traditional Bible interpretation.[58] Correlative with the radical metainterpretive diversity regarding essential religious beliefs and sources, a more critical appreciation is accorded the autonomy of ethics,[59] motivated by our need for a common ethical basis in the face of radical metainterpretive diversity, that is, for an ethics of equal respect centering on all-purpose general goods. Indeed, an autonomous ethics may be required from an internally religious perspective if it better expresses, as it may, the ethical motivations of a religion in which our moral powers fully express themselves in an ethics of equal respect for all persons whose dignity is the image of God in us.[60] From this perspective, the ethical independence even of the unbeliever may better express the spirit of ethically prophetic religion than the attitude of the conventional religious believer whose views mirror, and do not ethically examine, the often callous inhumanity of conventional morality.[61]

Furthermore, some influential contemporary perspectives criticize religion itself as ethically repressive, and claim that alternative nontheistic, or even atheistic, views are more expressive of realizing a community of equal respect.[62] Such a conception would, if true, turn the traditional exclusion of atheists from universal toleration on its head; advocacy of religion, not atheism, would be excluded from universal toleration.

None of these developments requires us to say that belief in God or in the truth of the Bible is false, or that any of the alternative propositions claimed is true. But they do establish the general line of Jefferson's thought: Persons may realize their personal and ethical dignity, expressing their moral powers of rationality and reasonableness, through belief in any of these propositions. Our conception of reasonable metainterpretive diversity, in the exercise of our freedom of conscience, has widened, if anything, beyond Jefferson's idea of reasonable arguments and sources. The scope of universal toleration must be correspondingly larger.

This kind of analysis clarifies the shifting scope of universal toleration over time and cognate constitutional arguments about the meaning and application of the constitutional neutrality commanded by the religion clauses of the first Amendment. For example, consistent with the analysis here proposed, the anti-establishment clause has been interpreted to forbid any form of state endorsement of religious teaching, for example, state-endorsed prayers in the public schools,[63] or adaptation of the curriculum to sectarian religious belief as in the creationism controversies.[64] And an important thread of religion clause jurisprudence suggests that the central right protected by the religion clauses cannot be confined to conventional forms of theistic belief.[65]

This analysis may clarify as well larger themes of moral pluralism and community, explaining how and why an interpretive dynamic of universal toleration has powerfully motivated an internal linkage of a more generous moral pluralism and a more encompassing and fair-minded conception of the legitimate scope of moral community. Constitutional interpretation here, and in the cognate areas of free speech and constitutional privacy, expresses a critical reflection on the enduring strands of arguments of principle and how they should be elaborated over time consistent with their motivating political and moral theory. So to interpret our constitutional law is also to interpret our history, but not slavishly or stupidly. Indeed, interpretive reflection may make possible an illuminating understanding of the contradictions of our constitutional tradition, a tradition with the most complete guarantees of religious liberty yet capable, as John Stuart Mill bitterly observed, of the most savage religious persecution (of the Mormons).[66] Such reflection may enable us to see otherwise unconnected developments in the jurisprudence of the religion clauses, free speech, and constitutional privacy as a self-critical coming to terms with contradiction and incoherence, indeed as motivated by an integrity of common arguments and principles. I briefly exemplify this program by an examination of the current jurisprudence both of free speech and constitutional privacy.

III. The Scope of Free Speech

The interpretive structure of the current law of free speech in the United States tends to enlarge the class of communications protected by the free speech and press clauses of the First Amendment and to forbid a state restriction on communications aimed at what is said, a content-based restriction on speech, unless there is a clear and present danger of some very grave harm. The modern law of free speech is remarkable both for its expansion in the scope of protected speech and its highly demanding requirements for satisfaction of the clear and present danger test. Each development is, I believe, clarified by the contractarian analysis here proposed.

We begin by noting that the judiciary has sharply eroded or contracted the traditional understanding that a range of communicative utterances (clearly "speech" in any reasonable sense of that term) is exempt from protection by the values of free speech. The traditional list included subversive advocacy,[67] fighting words,[68] libels both of groups and individuals,[69] obscenity,[70] commercial advertising,[71] and the like. The modern Supreme Court has now reexamined and recast such traditional exemption of these forms of speech from free speech protection: Subversive advocacy[72] and group libel[73] are now fully protected, and much that was traditionally fighting words,[74] obscene,[75] and advertising[76] is now more fully protected than previously.

I believe this expansion in the scope of free speech protection rests on the same kind of shift in the application of constitutional neutrality already examined in the area of religion-clause jurisprudence. For the same reason that no form of distinction among forms of conscience (religious or nonreligious) appears any longer consistent with equal respect for moral independence, traditional exclusions from free speech protection now compromise the kind of equal respect for communicative integrity that constitutional values of free speech command in service of freedom of conscience itself. American constitutional law has come to understand, for example, that neutrally applicable protections of free speech cannot exclude subversive advocacy, for this advocacy is often precisely the kind of independent expression of ultimate social, political, and moral criticism essential to respect for the diverse forms of moral independence in a pluralistic society.[77] Even the traditional scope of the idea of the obscene has, I believe, been eroded in the face of a range of forms of legitimate moral pluralism in styles of sexuality and life unthinkable in the morally homogeneous and sexually repressive society that dictated the way in which puritanical reformers in Britain and the United States enforced Victorian sexual morality through the obscenity laws.[78] If that sexual morality is now conscientiously debated in society at large, as itself arguably immorally repressive and unjust, the traditional scope of the obscene must now appear no longer neutral because of a shift in underlying assumptions similar to the reasons that the traditional scope of religion-clause jurisprudence is no longer neutral.[79]

Correlative with the expanding scope of constitutionally protected speech, the Supreme Court has been increasingly demanding in the showing of a clear and present danger required for a content-based restriction on protected speech. The Court has thus moved from its highly deferential tendency test,[80] to a less deferential but still weak test of aggregate expectable harm,[81] to its current quite demanding requirements of very grave harms both highly probable and not rebuttable by the normal pattern of dialogue and discourse in society at large.[82] This modern interpretation of a clear and present danger is, I believe, the elaboration in free speech jurisprudence of the test for legitimate state action first stated by Jefferson in his Virginia Bill for Religious Freedom as a criterion for interfering in religious liberty: "that it is time enough for the rightful purposes of civil government for its officers to interfere when principles break out into overt acts against peace and good order", and that the normal course for rebuttal of noxious belief, consistent with respect for the right to conscience, is "free argument and debate."[83] Jefferson formulates this test as a way of insuring that mere objection to a certain system of religious belief cannot of itself justify abridgement of exercise of that belief, for democratic majorities will often confuse their unhappiness with and disapproval of the claims of an unfamiliar religion with a threat of secular harms. Accordingly, the state must limit any restrictions on religious belief to cases where there are such secular harms, for example, Locke's example of a religious ritual of child sacrifice. But the same pattern of intolerance familiar in unjust religious persecution occurs as well in censorship of speech, and the modern Court has correctly understood that the same protections of moral independence fundamental to our Jeffersonian conceptions of religious liberty apply, as a matter of principle, to free speech as well. The lesson of the McCarthy witchhunts is, as the name suggests, precisely the common wrong of and remedy for religious and political persecution.[84]

IV. CONSTITUTIONAL PRIVACY

Finally, the same erosion of the traditional understanding of legitimate moral debate—that we have seen in the areas of religious liberty and free speech—explains as well the development in modern American constitutional law of the constitutional right to privacy. My understanding of the constitutional right to privacy is that it centrally protects from state coercive interference the right to form intimate relations of which the traditional exemplar was, of course, the marriage relation.[85] That right was, I believe, quite clearly one of the reserved unenumerated rights protected by the Ninth Amendment, the Privileges and Immunities Clause of Article IV, and, eventually, the Privileges and Immunities Clause of the Fourteenth Amendment.[86] However, the need to protect this constitutional right, as a live constitutional issue, arose in the relatively recent modern era when the traditional understanding of constitutionally neutral moral argument eroded in ways we have already seen in the areas of religious liberty and free speech. When the Supreme Court validated the criminal prosecution of Mormon polygamy in *Reynolds v. United States*,[87] as consistent with the constitutional guarantee of religious free-exercise in the First Amendment, it did so on grounds that assimilated the moral neutrality of the prohibition of bigamy to the prohibition on the murder of children or one's wife in a religious sacrifice or ritual. That decision could not, I believe, be decided with the same ease today precisely because our moral views of family law are so profoundly in dispute among feminists and society at large. My larger point is not the rightness or wrongness of

Reynolds then or now, but the kind of reigning American consensus on the morality of marriage relations at the time of *Reynolds* which made almost any prohibition applicable to marriage
relations appear based on constitutionally neutral, not sectarian, grounds and thus justly enforced at large. On this view,
the constitutionally required burden for abridging a fundamental right like marriage was satisfied for the same reasons
that abridgement of the right of religious free-exercise was satisfied, and thus arguments of constitutional privacy were not
elaborated.

The development of the right to constitutional privacy under
American law reflects the erosion of the belief in the neutrality
of such moral prohibitions. When the Supreme Court recognizes the constitutional right to privacy in *Griswold v. Connecticut*,[88] it protects the right of married couples to use contracep-
tives because any justification for the criminal prohibitions of
contraceptive use appeared then clearly sectarian, and so not
neutral. Such laws could not be justified by any plausible argument of secular harms either to others or to self. To the contrary, contraceptive use enabled married couples to limit population growth in ways politically desirable to society at large,
and advanced the rational good of married couples in general
and married women in particular through enabling them better to control reproduction and to explore the sexual dimension of personal relations in a humanely fulfilling way. In this
context, the traditional moral condemnation of contraception
as a kind of homicide against the unborn (St. Thomas)[89] must
appear as a metaphysically non-neutral view that cannot justly
be enforced on society at large. The perceptions underlying the
view are simply not the broadly shared premises that leave the
state neutral among competing sectarian interpretations of various general goods. Rather, the enforcement of such perceptions through prohibitions of contraception use enlists the state
in the support of sectarian conscience in a core area of the just
moral independence of both women and men in the exercise
of constructive moral powers defining permanent value in living. Since the moral justification for the prohibition of contraception appeared non-neutral, it became invalid, and the Supreme Court understandably extended the constitutional right

to privacy to protect a traditionally recognized fundamental right.[90]

Both the empirical and normative components of many traditional moral views, about contraception and the like, may once have commanded broad consensus, embracing the most tolerant and enlightened people. From the perspective of such uncontroversial beliefs, state prohibitions even of central human rights like conscience, speech, and privacy are justifiable to all reasonable persons,[91] and are thus constitutionally adequate justifications for abridgements even of fundamental rights. Often, however, empirical and normative assumptions become subject to much reasonable criticism on grounds of empirical mistake or changing social circumstances or new elaborations of central principles of fairness or humanity. The previous universal consensus about these beliefs is shattered, and so too is the justifiability of their constitutional neutrality as the basis for abridgement of fundamental rights. What once were the normative assumptions common to all forms of reasonable conscience are now the subjects of sectarian debate and division. Their enforcement through law is hence the functional equivalent of the injustice that Locke and Bayle identified as the imposition of speculative theology through law: the invention of orders and hierarchies that corrupt and degrade the essentially human moral powers for self-government. In short, coercive laws no longer satisfy the constitutionally required burden of neutral justification for abridgement of fundamental rights, and a right like constitutional privacy is properly elaborated in our law, and properly applied to contraceptive use.

The Supreme Court's later elaboration of the constitutional right to privacy (its application to abortion[92] and pornography use in the home,[93] its failure of application to consensual homosexuality)[94] is, of course, enormously controversial, and I cannot discuss such disputes here.[95] My more abstract interpretive point is that the constitutional right to privacy is a principled elaboration of and argument over the impact of background shifts in the understanding of constitutional neutrality in the area of traditionally recognized fundamental rights, here the right to marriage, elsewhere the right to conscience and free speech.

V. Conclusions

The general theme that unites these developments in the constitutional jurisprudence of religious liberty, free speech, and constitutional privacy is the impact of the enlarging scope and understanding of legitimate moral pluralism on a constitutional tradition centrally committed to toleration for forms of conscience, speech, and ways of life that do not impose secular harms on others. That impact is, I have suggested, the consequence of a central contractarian commitment of American constitutional law to the inalienable right to conscience, viz., to our self-determining moral powers of rationality and reasonableness.[96]

This way of connecting politics, religion, and ethics was historically original, linking, as it does, constitutional guarantees of basic liberties of conscience, speech, and privacy to respect for exercise of moral powers essential to self-government. Persons, on this view, are no more naturally or necessarily embedded in hierarchies of privilege and power than they are fatalistically chained to some metaphysical order of being. Rather, a just society is so structured as to allow persons to live in a cooperative community fully expressive of their rational and reasonable freedom, a community in which self-respect and respect for others are complementary resources of personal, moral and political life.

A just community, thus understood, must continually review and revise its conceptions of the scope of neutrally enforceable state power in light of these values. Otherwise, traditional assumptions of the natural order of things (for example, of women's role) may, on critical reflection, express yet another hierarchy of domination corrupting to a decent respect for our constructive moral powers. The constitutional command of neutrality expresses, I have suggested, this imperative and this constraint on the coercive power of the state to enforce traditional morality. Our examination of the constitutional jurisprudence of religious liberty, free speech, and constitutional privacy shows how this command is naturally sensitive to the ways in which the scope of legitimate ethical debate has opened to include critical debate about traditional morality that bears upon certain fundamental rights. Much of traditional morality will not bear upon these rights, and much that does will survive the analysis, for example, the prohibition of intrafamilial murder or rape or violence, all of which are secular harms that satisfy the constitutional burden required for state interference even in sensitive areas of intimate relations. But we retain legitimate state prohibitions not because they are traditional, but in service of the ethics of self-governing moral freedom which, I have suggested, is the distinctive morality of constitutional liberty.

NOTES

1. See, e.g., *Sherbert v. Verner*, 374 U.S. 398 (1963); *Wisconsin v. Yoder*, 406 U.S. 205 (1972).
2. David A. J. Richards, *Toleration and the Constitution* (New York: Oxford University Press, 1986).
3. See *The Works of John Locke* (London: Thomas Davison, 1823), vol. 6.
4. Pierre Bayle, *Philosophique Commentaire sur ces paroles de Jesus Christ "Contrain-les d'entree", Oeuvres Diverses de Mr. Pierre Bayle* (A la Haye: Chez P. Husson et al., 1727). vol. 2, pp. 357–560 (hereinafter *Philosophique Commentaire*).
5. For a fuller analysis, see Richards, *Toleration and the Constitution*, pp. 89–98.
6. Ibid., pp. 86–88.
7. For the distinctive force of this conception in the Old Testament's narrative style and sharp repudiation of different conceptions of divinity in surrounding cultures, see Herbert Schneidau, *Sacred Discontent: The Bible and Western Tradition* (Baton Rouge: Louisiana State University Press, 1976); Dan Jacobson, *The Story of Stories* (New York: Harper and Row, 1982); Robert Alter, *The Art of Biblical Narrative* (New York: Basic Books, 1981).
8. See, e.g., Bayle, *Philosophique Commentaire*, pp. 387–88.
9. See, in general, John Colman, *John Locke's Moral Philosophy* (Edinburgh: Edinburgh University Press, 1983).
10. See John Locke, *The Reasonableness of Christianity*, ed. I. T. Ramsey (Stanford: Stanford University Press, 1958).
11. Bayle, *Philosophique Commentaire*, pp. 367–72, 422–33.
12. See Walter Rex, *Essays on Pierre Bayle and Religious Controversy* (The Hague: Martinus Nijhoff, 1965), pp. 51–60, 62–65.
13. On the importance of this conception in shaping Old Testament narratives and revulsion against surrounding religions, see

Schneidau, *Sacred Discontent*; Jacobson, *Story of Stories*. On the impersonality of India's concept of the divine, see Arthur Danto, *Mysticism and Morality* (New York: Harper, 1973), pp. 40–41. On the personality of the Western conception of the divine and its broader cultural significance for Western ethics, politics, and science, see Denis de Rougemont, *Man's Western Quest*, trans. Montgomery Belgion (Westport, Conn.: Greenwood, 1973).

14. Van Leeuwen thus notes peculiarly Western anti-ontocratic concerns. See, in general, Arend Th. van Leeuwen, *Christianity in World History*, trans. H. H. Hoskins (New York: Scribners, 1964). Cf., William Albright, *From the Stone Age to Christianity* (Garden City, N.Y.: Doubleday Anchor, 1957).

15. The statement of this principle is the subject of the first *Letter Concerning Toleration, Works of John Locke*, pp. 5–58.

16. For example, opposition to total disestablishment of the Anglican Church of Virginia, led by Patrick Henry and Richard Henry Lee, centered on the idea that some form of multiple establishment was necessary to preserve public morality in the state. See H. J. Eckenrode, *Separation of Church and State in Virginia* (New York: Da Capo Press, 1971), p. 74.

17. For Locke, see *Works of John Locke*, pp. 7–9; for Bayle, see Bayle, *Philosophique Commentaire*, pp. 415–19.

18. See Jean Jacques Rousseau, *The Social Contract* in *The Social Contract and Discourses*, trans. G. D. H. Cole (New York: Dutton, 1950), pp. 129–41.

19. See Henry Home Kames, *Essays on the Principles of Morality and Natural Religion*, ed. R. Wellek (New York: Garland Publishing, 1976), pp. 136–49.

20. See Lord Bolingbroke, *The Works of Lord Bolingbroke* (London: Frank Cass, 1967), vol 3, pp. 373–535.

21. See Adrienne Koch, *The Philosophy of Thomas Jefferson* (Gloucester, Mass.: Peter Smith, 1957), pp. 9–39. For Jefferson's own linkage of religious persecution with moral and religious corruption, see Thomas Jefferson, *Notes on the State of Virginia*, ed. William Peden (Chapel Hill: University of North Carolina Press, 1955), pp. 159–61; and the Preface to Bill for Religious Freedom, in *The Papers of Thomas Jefferson, 1777–1779*, ed. Julian Boyd (Princeton: Princeton University Press, 1950), vol. 2, pp. 545–46. In his later life, Jefferson subscribed to Joseph Priestley's views on the corruption of true Christianity. See, in general, Dickinson Adams, ed., *Jefferson's Extracts from the Gospels* (Princeton: Princeton University Press, 1983), pp. 14–30; Jefferson's own attempts at Bible criticism were actuated by the desire to distinguish the gold from the dross.

22. Both Shaftesbury and Hutcheson, who shape the moral-sense theory of the age, specifically deny that the concept of ethics depends either on God's will or on divine punishment. See, e.g., Third Earl of Shaftesbury (Anthong Ashley Cooper), *An Inquiry Concerning Virtue, British Moralists*, ed. L. A. Selby-Bigge (New York: Dover, 1965), pp. 15–16, 23–24, 45–47; Francis Hutcheson, *An Inquiry Concerning the Original of our Ideas of Virtue or Moral Good, British Moralists*, ed. L. A. Selby-Bigge (New York: Dover, 1965), vol. 1, pp. 71–72, 79, 85–86, 90–92, 122–23, 125. Since the experience of ethics is defined by an independent moral sense, the very content of such ethics depends on the exercise of this natural sense, in terms of which we define our concept of a good and just God, not conversely. Accordingly, the corruption of this moral sense will corrupt, in turn, our capacity to know God's will. Since for Locke, in contrast, knowledge of ethics requires knowledge of God's will, not conversely, only corruption of specifically religious truth would corrupt ethics. For eighteenth-century believers in the theory of the moral sense, corruption of ethics itself is the root of all other corruptions.

23. See note preceding.

24. Jefferson, Preface to Bill for Religious Freedom, p. 545.

25. *The Great Contest of Faith and Reason: Selections from the Writings of Pierre Bayle*, ed. Karl Sandberg (New York: Frederick Ungar, 1963), pp. 45–46.

26. *Letter Concerning Toleration, Works of John Locke*, p. 10.

27. See John Rawls, "Social Unity and Primary Goods," in *Utilitarianism and Beyond*, eds. Amartya Sen and Bernard Williams (Cambridge: Cambridge University Press, 1982), pp. 159–85.

28. See *Letter Concerning Toleration, Works of John Locke*, pp. 33–34.

29. See, in general, Thomas Curry, *The First Freedoms: Church and State in America to the Passage of the First Amendment* (New York: Oxford University Press, 1986), pp. 134–58, 193–222.

30. See, e.g., *Sherbert v. Verner*, 374 U.S. 398 (1963).

31. See, e.g., *Lemon v. Kurtzman*, 403 U.S. 602 (1971).

32. I defend the proposition that contractarian theory is the best such theory in David A. J. Richards, *Toleration and the Constitution* (New York: Oxford University Press, 1986). See also John Rawls, *A Theory of Justice* (Cambridge: Harvard University Press, 1971); "Kantian Constructivism in Moral Theory," *Journal of Philosophy* 77 (1980): 515. Cf., David A. J. Richards, *A Theory of Reasons for Action* (Oxford: Clarendon Press, 1971).

33. See, in general, Richards, *Toleration and the Constitution*, pp. 121–62.

34. Ibid.

35. See, in general, Colman, *Locke's Moral Philosophy*.
36. See note 22.
37. For Locke's exclusions, see Locke, *Works of John Locke*, vol. 6, pp. 45–47 (Catholics); p. 47 (atheists). For Bayle's comparable exclusion, see Bayle, *Philosophique Commentaire*, pp. 410–15 (Catholics); p. 431 (atheists). In contrast, Jefferson's Bill for Religious Freedom makes no exception for Catholics or atheists, and Jefferson's notes on Locke make clear that the omission is intended. Pointing to the Lockean exceptions, Jefferson states: "But where he stopped short, we may go on," Jefferson, Preface to Bill for Religious Freedom, p. 548.
38. See Joseph Story, *Commentaries on the Constitution of the United States*, excerpted in *Church and State in the United States* in *Papers of the American Historical Association*, by Philip Schaff (New York: Putnam, 1888), vol. 2, no. 4, pp. 128–30.
39. See note 37.
40. See Rex, *Essays on Pierre Bayle*, pp. 51–60, 62–65, and text accompanying.
41. For Bayle, like Kant, acting in accord with ethics, as atheists could, must be distinguished from acting on ethical motives properly understood, as Bayle believed atheists could not.
42. For example, Bayle insists that Catholics should not be subject to stigma, nor should their possessions be threatened, nor should their right to bring up their children according to their beliefs be disturbed. See Bayle, *Philosophique Commentaire*, p. 412.
43. See note 37.
44. See, for example, Perry Miller, *Orthodoxy in Massachusetts 1630–1650* (Cambridge: Harvard University Press, 1933).
45. See notes 9–12, and accompanying text.
46. See note 22.
47. Among deontological theories, see Alan Gewirth, *Reason and Morality* (Chicago: University of Chicago Press, 1978); Rawls, *A Theory of Justice;* Richards, *A Theory of Reasons for Action;* David Gauthier, *Morals by Agreement* (Oxford: Clarendon Press, 1986). Among utilitarian theories, see R. M. Hare, *Moral Thinking* (Oxford: Clarendon Press, 1981); Richard Brandt, *A Theory of the Good and the Right* (Oxford: Clarendon Press, 1979). Among intuitionist theories, see W. D. Ross, *The Right and the Good* (Oxford: Clarendon Press, 1930); H. A. Prichard, *Moral Obligation* (Oxford: Clarendon Press, 1949).
48. See Norman Sykes, "The Religion of Protestants," in *The Cambridge History of the Bible*, ed. S. L. Greenslade (Cambridge: Cambridge University Press, 1963), vol. 3, pp. 175–98.
49. See Louis Bouyer, "Erasmus in Relation to the Medieval Biblical

Tradition," in *The Cambridge History of the Bible*, ed. G. W. H. Lampe (Cambridge: Cambridge University Press, 1969, vol. 2, pp. 492–505, and Richard Popkin, *The History of Scepticism from Erasmus to Spinoza* (Berkeley: University of California Press, 1979), pp. 214–48.

50. Bayle, for example, quite clearly brings to Bible interpretation standards of moral reasonableness which he will not allow that an ethical God could have violated. See Bayle, *Philosophique Commentaire*, pp. 367–72. And Locke brings to the Bible as much as he finds in the Gospels, the minimum of ethical reasonableness. See Locke, *The Reasonableness of Christianity*.

51. See, e.g., *Works of John Locke*, vol. 6, pp. 26, 145, 194, 366 (express comparison of intolerance to the Pope's infallibility), 401, 407, 411, 412, 517, 531, 532; Bayle, *Philosophique Commentaire*, p. 438. Bayle also condemns assumptions of infallibility, p. 438.

52. See Elisha Williams, *The Essential Rights and Liberties of Protestants* (Boston: Kneeland and Green, 1744), p. 33.

53. See *Jefferson's Extracts*, Adams.

54. On Jefferson's religious and ethical views, see ibid., Introduction, pp. 3–42. Cf., Adrienne Koch, *Philosophy of Thomas Jefferson*, pp. 1–43.

55. See *Jefferson's Extracts*, Adams, pp. 3–42. Jefferson's attempt to integrate the study of classical moralists with the enlightened ethics of the Gospels reflects the tensions between classical and Christian sources characteristic of the metainterpretive diversity of the Reformation and the Enlightenment. See, in general, Peter Gay, *The Enlightenment: An Interpretation* (New York: W. W. Norton, 1966), vol. 1: *The Rise of Paganism*, pp. 207–419.

56. For historical background on the seventeenth-century debates over an afterlife, see, in general, D. P. Walker, *The Decline of Hell* (Chicago: University of Chicago Press, 1964).

57. See, e.g., Jerry Brown, *The Rise of Bible Criticism in America, 1800–1870* (Middletown, Conn.: Wesleyan University Press, 1969); Stephen Neill, *The Interpretation of the New Testament 1861–1961* (New York: Oxford University Press, 1966); Nathan Hatch and Mark Noll, *The Bible in America* (New York: Oxford University Press, 1982); James Barr, *The Bible in the Modern World* (London: SCM Press, 1973). On the resulting divisions within Protestantism, see William Hutchison, *The Modernist Impulse in American Protestantism* (Cambridge: Harvard University Press, 1976); Martin Marty, *Righteous Empire* (New York: Dial Press, 1970); Ernest Sandeen, *The Roots of Fundamentalism* (Chicago: University of Chicago Press, 1970); George Marsden, *Fundamentalism and American Culture* (New York: Oxford University Press, 1980). On the erosion of distinc-

tions between believers and unbelievers, see Martin Marty, *Varieties of Unbelief* (Garden City, N.Y.: Anchor, 1966); idem, *The Infidel: Freethought and American Religion* (Cleveland: World Publishing, 1961).

58. See, in general, Charles Gillispie, *Genesis and Geology* (Cambridge: Harvard University Press, 1951); John Greene, *The Death of Adam* (Ames: Iowa State University Press, 1959). On the response to Darwin by American religion, see Sidney Ahlstrom, *A Religious History of the American People* (New Haven: Yale University Press, 1972), pp. 766–72.

59. See, in general, Gene Outka and John Reeder, *Religion and Morality* (Garden City, N.Y.: Anchor, 1973); Paul Helm, ed., *Divine Commands and Morality* (Oxford: Oxford University Press, 1981). Cf. Philip Quinn, *Divine Commands and Moral Requirements* (Oxford: Clarendon Press, 1978); Basil Mitchell, *Morality: Religious and Secular* (Oxford: Clarendon Press, 1980).

60. Cf., Gordon Allport, *The Individual and His Religion* (New York: Macmillan, 1950).

61. See, in general, Marty, *Varieties of Unbelief.*

62. See, e.g., Kai Nielsen, *Ethics Without God* (Buffalo, N.Y.: Prometheus Books, 1973). Cf., David Muzzey, *Ethics as a Religion* (New York: Frederick Ungar, 1951).

63. See, e.g., *Engel v. Vitale,* 370 U.S. 421 (1962); *Abington School Dist. v. Schempp,* 374 U.S. 203 (1963); *Wallace v. Jaffree,* 105 S.Ct. 2479, 466 U.S. 924 (1985).

64. See *Epperson v. Arkansas,* 393 U.S. 97 (1968); *McLean v. Arkansas Board of Education,* 529 F. Supp. 1255 (E.D. Ark. 1982).

65. See *United States v. Ballard,* 322 U.S. 78 (1944); *Torcaso v. Watkins,* 367 U.S. 488 (1960); *United States v. Seeger,* 380 U.S. 163 (1965). But cf. *Wisconsin v. Yoder,* 406 U.S. 205, 216 (1972). For commentary, see Richards, *Toleration and the Constitution,* pp. 129–33, 141–46.

66. See John Stuart Mill, *On Liberty,* ed. Alburey Castell (New York: Appleton-Century-Crofts, 1947), pp. 92–93.

67. See, e.g., *Gitlow v. New York,* 268 U.S. 652 (1925).

68. See, e.g., *Chaplinsky v. New Hampshire,* 315 U.S. 568 (1942).

69. See, e.g., *Beauharnais v. Illinois,* 343 U.S. 250 (1952).

70. See *Roth v. United States,* 354 U.S. 476 (1957).

71. See *Breard v. Alexandria,* 341 U.S. 622 (1951).

72. See *Brandenburg v. Ohio,* 395 U.S. 444 (1969).

73. See *Collin v. Smith,* 578 F.2d 1197 (1978), *cert. den.,* 439 U.S. 916 (1978).

74. See, e.g., *Gooding v. Wilson,* 405 U.S. 518 (1972).

75. See, e.g., *Miller v. California,* 413 U.S. 15 (1973).

76. See, e.g., *Virginia Pharmacy Board v. Virginia Consumer Council,* 425 U.S. 748 (1976). But see *Posadas de Puerto Rico Associates v. Tourism Company of Puerto Rico,* 478 U.S.—(1986).

77. For fuller discussion, see Richards, *Toleration and the Constitution,* pp. 178–87.

78. For fuller discussion, see David A. J. Richards, "Free Speech and Obscenity Law: Toward a Moral Theory of the First Amendment," *U. Pa. L. Rev.* 123 (1974): 45.

79. For fuller discussion, see Richards, *Toleration and the Constitution,* pp. 203–9.

80. Under this test, it sufficed that dangerous speech, for example, subversive advocacy, might have some tendency to frustrate legitimate state purposes. See, e.g., *Schenck v. United States,* 249 U.S. 47 (1919).

81. This test focussed on the result of discounting the prospective harm by its judged improbability, so that even subversive advocacy with very little probability of being effective could be abridged if the prospective harm, for example, the overthrow of constitutional government in the United States, were so grave that the low probability multiplied by the very grave harm would be a large amount. This was, of course, the theory that allowed the Supreme Court to legitimate abridgement of the advocacy of the American Communist Party: while the likelihood of success was admittedly infinitesimal, the harm was so grave as to justify abridgement under the applicable test of aggregate expectable harm. See *Dennis v. United States,* 341 U.S. 494 (1951).

82. See *Brandenburg v. Ohio,* 395 U.S. 444 (1969).

83. *Papers of Thomas Jefferson,* p. 546.

84. If, as I have suggested, the background right to conscience must today be interpreted to include all forms of conscience (theistic, agnostic, and atheistic), then suppression of Marxism is itself a kind of religious persecution in the constitutionally condemned sense: One of the great secular religions of the modern age is unjustly suppressed by law. On Marxism as a religion or heretical anti-religion, see Joseph Needham, *Science in Traditional China* (Cambridge: Harvard University Press, 1981), pp. 122–31.

85. See Kenneth Karst, "The Freedom of Intimate Association," *Yale L.J.* 80 (1980): 624.

86. See Richards, *Toleration and the Constitution,* pp. 232, 256.

87. *Reynolds v. United States,* 98 U.S. 145 (1878).

88. *Griswold v. Connecticut,* 381 U.S. 479 (1965).

89. Thomas Aquinas elaborates Augustine's conception of the exclusive legitimacy of procreative sex in a striking way. Of the emission of semen apart from procreation in marriage, he wrote:

"[A]fter the sin of homicide whereby a human nature already in existence is destroyed, this type of sin appears to take next place, for by it the generation of human nature is precluded." Thomas Aquinas, *On the Truth of the Catholic Faith: Summa Contra Gentiles,* trans. Vernon Bourke (New York: Image, 1956), pt. 2, chap. 122(9), p. 146.

90. For fuller discussion, see Richards, *Toleration and the Constitution,* pp. 256–61.

91. Cf., T. M. Scanlon. "Contractualism and Utilitarianism," in *Utilitarianism and Beyond,* pp. 103–28.

92. *Roe v. Wade,* 410 U.S. 113 (1973).

93. *Stanley v. Georgia,* 394 U.S. 557 (1969).

94. *Doe v. Commonwealth's Attorney,* 403 F. Supp. 1199 (E.D. Va. 1975), *aff'd without opinion,* 425 U.S. 901 (1976); *Bowers v. Hardwick,* 54 U.S.L.W. 4919 (decided June 30, 1986).

95. I discuss these issues in Richards, *Toleration and the Constitution,* pp. 261–80.

96. Does the way of thinking I here defend depend on contractarian theory in contrast to other political theories (for example, utilitarianism)? I argue that contractarian theory, suitably understood, is the best way to understand these issues in Richards, *Toleration and the Constitution.*

9

DIVINE SANCTION AND LEGAL AUTHORITY: RELIGION AND THE INFRASTRUCTURE OF THE LAW

LISA NEWTON

Is religion necessary for law? By implication, must a secular state that rules by the authority of law preserve the practice of religion within its boundaries in order to maintain its own authority? In a nation whose Constitutional foundations include the separation of church and state, must the state, ultimately, protect and support the church?

Affirmative answers to these questions must be less than welcome to liberals in the time of an administration that seems to be trying to take us back to a Puritan theocracy as part of its evangelical conservative mission. And part, at least, of the philosophical problem has been solved: We know that God and the action of God are not needed as logical underpinning of any coherent morality or fundamental law. Whether we follow J. S. Mill in deriving a perfectly adequate and humane morality from the simple fact that people attempt to obtain happiness, Immanuel Kant in pegging the working out of morality from the simple imperative to be moral, or H. L. A. Hart in deriving a perfectly usable fundamental "natural law" from the mere attempt to survive in human bodies with human needs, we can deduce most of the morality that religion has taught from very simple observations.[1] If we want to be quite ambitious about reproducing the work of moralists of religious motivation, we can even duplicate the Ten Commandments, not at all implausibly.[2] We need no *"Dominus dixit"* to back up our fundamental moral convictions. But law, as we are interested in law, is not a logical exercise, but a practice enmeshed in the pressures of human need, greed and weakness. If we do not need God in our equations to make them come out right, we might still need the church to provide a bridge from human nature to the demands of the law. So, at least, it has been argued.

In what follows, we shall take up that argument. In the first section, we shall, very briefly, set up the problem by demonstrating (1) that our ancient and medieval forebears left us with answers profoundly at variance on the appropriate role of religion in the legal life of the state; and (2) that the moderns have achieved no consensus on the subject.

The second section will set forth three major roles that the church seems to play in the modern state, focusing on the third as deserving further examination. Throughout the paper, by "church" we shall mean no more than any organized religion, or association formed to give expression to religious feeling or conviction.

The third section will explore that third role, of reinforcer of the unenforceable infrastructure of the law, and, on reconsideration of all three roles, will conclude that indeed, the law needs religion, although not the way it thought it did. It needs religion as the escape hatch for those driven to their limits by the unrelenting material pressures of the state and as the free space within which new ideas can incubate and as the protector of those ideas, when presently unwelcome, until the state can be taught to accept them. Above all, religion is needed as a counterweight to the vast and bumbling power of the state, as a glue for all that area of associative life that predates and is presupposed by the state, in which law operates most effectively and humanely. The state does not need the church, by the way, to maintain and extend its power, as monarchists and anarchists alike have thought for centuries; on the contrary, to the extent that the church is effective, it limits the range and power of the state.

Assumed in all that follows is a necessarily very limited concept of "the state"—unless specified otherwise, we will be referring to the modern Western democratic state, and no other.

Assumed also is an even more limited understanding of church or "religion", referring only to the Judeo-Christian tradition at best, or more accurately to the Christian tradition, since no self-respecting Jew will acknowledge any hyphenated Christianity as part of his tradition. The limitations imposed on the analysis will become obvious as we go along; however limited, the analysis seems to be worth pursuing.

I. PUTTING FIRST THINGS FIRST

Does law need religion? In ancient political thought, from which we all begin, the answer seems to be yes, but not very much. In *The Republic,* Plato's masterpiece of political philosophy, 133 lines (27 pages in the Grube edition)[3] are devoted to the literary and musical education of the Guardians, seen as essential to form their characters, which characters will determine whether the entire spirited sector of the Republic will succeed or fail. But to establish the appropriate religious practice of his state—the entirety of the citizens' relation with the gods—he sends a casual mission to Delphi to find out what they ought to do.[4]

In Aristotle's *Politics,* the treatment is similar. Chapters 1 and 2 of Book I of the *Politics* are dedicated to articulation of the secular forms of law and association: the family (citing Hesiod, "First house and wife and an ox for the plough"), where law is simply the rule of paterfamilias (citing Homer, "Each one gives law to his children and to his wives"); the tribal village law (again citing Homer in his denunciation of the "tribeless, lawless, hearthless one"); and the polis itself, the political association, self-sufficient, adequate to provide for all the needs of human beings. Aristotle's account of the forms of law and association essential to humankind culminates in his assertion that "It is evident that the state is a creation of nature and that man is by nature a political animal."[5] Succeeding chapters in that book, and succeeding books, elaborate upon the nature and needs of those three associations, especially the polis. Not until Book VII, Chapter 9, does Aristotle find time to place religion in his ideal state. Who shall be the priests? The old men, it turns out, of the two classes of citizens, because it is proper that "Citizens who have thus spent themselves in long service should both enjoy their retirement and serve the gods."[6] In short, if you're too old to do anything else, we'll put you in charge of religion.

It could be argued, of course, that the Greek understanding of religion was far narrower than ours and that the true wisdom and transcendant spirituality that we associate with God and conventional religion both Plato and Aristotle would have put elsewhere in their philosophy. The comparison, then, hardly stands. We would reply that that is just the point. Whatever else the deities may have meant to the ancients—and no one had to tell a Greek, or a Roman for that matter, that the gods were powerful and could be very dangerous—they were not a source of law, wisdom, and authority, such that they were necessary to ground the authority of the state. Our notion of God as lawgiver was derived from the Hebrews, and was imposed on the notions of nature and of natural law derived from the Greeks. (It is not clear to us whether the Jewish concept of God as lawgiver entailed that only religious, God-given and priest-interpreted law was valid law for the state, or whether the concept permitted a secular state that made its own laws by secular means and merely protected the observance of religious law for those who wanted it. From the disputes that presently wrack the state of Israel, we conclude that we are not alone in our unclarity.)

Once the two notions have been combined, they permit a powerful and persuasive notion of law that came down to us as the natural law, primarily as articulated by Thomas Aquinas. After defining law by its four causes in Question 90 of the *Summa Theologica*, ticking off the various kinds of law there may be in Q 91, and affirming, with Aristotle, that the effect of law should be to make people good (Q 92), Aquinas sets out to show the grounds of obligation for the law. On his understanding of God the lawgiver, this task is simple: In Article 1 of Q 93, he establishes the reality of the eternal law as (quoting Augustine) "the sovereign type, to which we must always conform," for "As the type of the Divine Wisdom, inasmuch as by It all things are created, has the character of art, exemplar, or idea; so the type of Divine Wisdom, as moving all things to their due end, bears the character of law. Accordingly the eternal law is nothing else than the type of Divine Wisdom, as directing all actions and movements." In A 3, he completes the derivation: "Since then the eternal law is the plan of government in the Chief Governor, all the plans of government in the inferior governors must be derived from the eternal law. But these plans of inferior governors are all other laws besides the eternal law. Therefore all laws, in so far as they partake of right reason, are derived from the eternal law. Hence Augustine says *(De Lib. Arb.* i 6) that *'in temporal law there is nothing just and lawful, but what man has drawn from the eternal law.'"* And any law that is just, he concludes in Q 96 A 4, obligates those to whom it applies, not just as obliging them to obey for fear of punishment, but as binding them in conscience and imposing obligation moral as well as legal: citing Proverbs, Chapter 8, verse 15, *"By Me kings reign, and lawgivers decree just things."*[7]

For Aquinas, then, putting first things first meant putting God's wisdom first, that part of wisdom discernible by human reason as the font of human law and identical with justice, and specifying several times that (citing Augustine, *De Lib. Arb.* i. 5) *"that which is not just seems to be no law at all."* To be sure, the source of governance is the reason of the prince, not the inspiration of the priest; but the stage is set for all subsequent appeals to the authority of God over the authority of man—all revolution, all secular protest against immoral policy, and, as we are well aware, all affirmation of the rights of man against the power of the state. Thus does the Old Testament tradition of prophecy enter the modern world.

We now have two roots of the Western political tradition before us incorporating two starkly contrasting views of the relative positions of religion and law. A third root, which deserves some mention at this point before emerging in the third section in a new and unexpected guise, might be that of St. Augustine, who portrayed two cities, ancestral church and ancestral state, with totally different sources, missions, and possibilities, yet constrained to live together and, somehow, to protect each other, even as each fundamentally rejects the legitimacy of the other. The city of man "consists of those who wish to live after the flesh, the other of those who wish to live after the spirit; and when they severally achieve what they wish, they live in peace, each after their kind."[8] The cities cannot understand each other, having been "formed by two loves: the earthly by the love of self, even to the contempt of God; the heavenly by the love of God, even to the contempt of self."[9] Clearly the city of God is superior (given only those two descriptions, which one would *you* claim as your own?), but it condescends not only to tolerate, but even moderately to support the city of man in its quest for earthly peace, remembering always, however, that ultimately the city of man is to be utterly destroyed and consigned to eternal torture by a just and angry God at the Last Judgment.[10] For mortals, after all, even saved mortals, need the civic peace that the king can provide.

> The heavenly city, or rather that part of it which sojourns on earth and lives by faith, makes use of this peace only because it must, until this mortal condition which necessitates it shall pass away. Consequently, as long as it lives like a captive and a stranger in the earthly city, though it has already received the promise of redemption and the gift of the Spirit as a seal of this promise, this city makes no scruple to obey the laws of the earthly city whereby the things necessary for the maintenance of this mortal life are administered; and thus, as this life is common to both cities, there is harmony between them in regard to what belongs to it.

Truce is off, of course, should any "hindrance to the worship of the one supreme and true God" be introduced.[11] The compromise does not sound like a happy one, and the advance of years has not made any easier the coexistence of those who think they live in the city of God and those whom they think live in the city of man.

The moderns of course, Machiavelli to Dewey, have occupied every conceivable position entailed in the ancient and medieval writings mentioned above—from the Ultramontanes' insistence that the king should be subject to the Pope in all matters of consequence[12] to Machiavelli's assumption that the appeal to God was no more than a device cynically used to obtain the compliance and belief of citizens who would otherwise resist good laws. Or as Rousseau put it: "This sublime reason, so far above the comprehension of vulgar men, is that whose decisions legislators put in the mouth of the immortals, that those might be led along under the sanction of divine authority, whom it might be impossible for human prudence to conduct without it. . . . After this, I should not conclude, with Warburton, that politics and religion have with us one common object, but that, in the origin of nations, the one serves as the instrument of the other."[13] Review of the 57 varieties of possible relation would not serve our purposes well. All we need to proceed to the next phase of the thesis is that there is no consensus; that the origins of the church in the West and the streams of Western thought are such that an array of positions on the subject is supportable; and that, especially given that third root above, it may be dangerous to assume that the relation will be a peaceful one.

II. Functions of the Church

The tradition then, as so far presented, permits at least three roles for the church, for organized and established religious practice, vis-à-vis the law, the organized and established political and legal system. It can be an auxiliary of the law, fundamentally its ally, helping it teach the virtues of civic order and cooperation that the state needs to survive; it can rule the law, establishing and expounding the great moral truths to which the law must conform its practices and directives; or it can exist very uneasily side-by-side with the law, scorning its objectives and denying its ultimate legitimacy, while cooperating with it in day to day operations in order to avoid causing pain for those unable to live as Christians. The latter roles have received well-merited attention in the last few decades; the first, while undisputed, seems so obvious as to require no comment. To redress the balance, we shall concentrate on that first role in the third and final section of this paper. For the present, we shall take a brief look at the other two, starting with the third.

One of the things the church should do best is simply be the church. As the church, it symbolizes, teaches and embodies a permanent possibility of life that is not of this world, not subject to the ills and compromises of this world, a life rooted in eternity. This world, or "city", as Augustine would call it, with its own practices, objectives, and rules for entry, provides a readily available route of withdrawal for those whose disillusionment with the state-governed world forces them to reject its secular ways. This escape hatch has generally been regarded by secular rulers as potentially dangerous—remember Pentheus's determination to crush the Bacchae in Euripides' play of that name. Mysticism worries even established churchmen (where do the mystics *go* when they go into those trances?), and when personal religious enthusiasm collectivizes into sects, as in the recurrent emergences of the Anabaptists, secular rulers tend to take alarm. The alarm is certainly justified, at least in part, by claims to exclusive truth made by most of those small religious groups we call "sects," and by the potential for warfare therein inherent. State persecution of the church in this separatist form follows as mushrooms after rain, and the fate of these groups has not been happy, save during that window of opportunity provided in the seventeenth through nineteenth centuries by the availability of land in the New World. It is commonplace that the history of that New World came out as no one intended: Each immigrant (or American-born, for that matter) sect wanted only to impose its holy way upon everyone else as secular law, for it was the city on the hill, the church incarnate; but then it discovered that the next town over was also a city on the hill, only with a different (unholy) set of beliefs; the two could not conquer each other so they settled for the right to be left alone, and that's how we got religious toleration in America. Now the number of sects, each one more mystical and irrational than the one before, can expand without limit.

But that result is not necessarily dangerous for the law. Laurance Moore has argued in *Religious Outsiders and the Making of Americans*,[14] that the proliferation of sects, or "outsider religious groups", by providing a legally protected safety valve for the very discontent, serves as a protection of the law and the state. As long as the religious enthusiast will keep his behavior within the bounds of the secular law, he is at liberty to define for himself the reality that encloses that law. Augustine asked for no more. Church, then, unintentionally strengthens secular law by making it bearable; in the emotional security of religion, I lose interest in revolutionary activity. Just as error can be tolerated with safety as long as truth is left free to combat it, just so intolerance can be tolerated and even encouraged, as long as tolerance for *all* intolerances is maintained. We may yet discover the unsafety of this arrangement, should one of the intolerances capture a majority in the statehouse.

That last possibility leads us to the next role of the church in the state—that of giver, or at least of judge, of the laws. The prophets of the Old Testament did not hesitate to denounce the laws of the state when they found them contrary to God's word or God's will. Prophecy has continued as part of the church's understanding of its own role in the state, with greater or lesser emphasis, to the present day. The word "prophecy" is being used broadly here: all instances have in common only the intention of the body doing the prophesying to instruct the society in which it prophesies on some moral truth or truths that the society seems to have forgot. The instances are distinguished by the size and power of the body, the size and power of the relevant society, and the purported effect of the prophecy.

At one end of the spectrum, the single unheard individual, "the voice crying in the wilderness" to no one at all, does witness before God to his beliefs, perhaps by quietly resigning from or refusing to cooperate with, secular power being used for immoral purposes. At the other end of the spectrum, an organized church with irresistible majority power dictates laws to obedient princes. Between the two we have an immense variety of religiously motivated prophets:

> individual monks who set themselves on fire to dramatize their opposition to war—like the voice again, only this time in from the wilderness; through small groups known to us as "activists" who seek public fora to preach against some perceived moral evil; through the larger groups of Left and Right, organizing in living rooms to carry on campaigns against comic books, the manufacture of nuclear arms, pornography, corporate irresponsibility or investment in South Africa or both, the purchase of goods from communist countries or South Africa or both, reproductive technology and the destruction of the environment; through the larger bodies of organized religion, seeking an end to the practice of elective abortion or racial discrimination, and working to see their views transformed into laws; and, finally, to the great social movements like the enthusiasms for Savanarola, fundamentalist Islam, or the current growth of conservative Christianity, which without the official status of the established Church, nevertheless present such formidable political power that no government, democratic or otherwise, can possibly ignore them.

We have deliberately included in that list movements of several political stripes. Theory seems to show no way to distinguish, although we are all very good at it in practice, between the liberal black pastor protesting the humiliating treatment meted out to black citizens, and the conservative small-town white pastor protesting the cartoons of women's legs and buttocks in stocking advertisements: The object of both protests is a perceived insult to human dignity, and if we tend to see merit in one of those protests and not in the other, that may be because our perception is skewed. Nor is it easy to sort the prophets into categories by size, for the continuum is perfectly logical: If I think I am right (all alone), it is reasonable to attempt to persuade others to my view and form a group; if I wish to persuade others, it is reasonable to seek publicity and involve the news media; and if I truly believe that what I advocate is right for all, it is reasonable, indeed imperative, that I attempt to persuade public bodies to endorse my view and transform it into policy. Thus the Interfaith Center on Corporate Responsibility (sponsored and run by the National Council of Churches) appropriately engages in attempts "to change corporate behavior in a manner that the church considers socially responsible," citing John D. Rockefeller, Jr., to the effect that "Its mission [the mission of the church] should be the righting of wrongs and the active pursuit of the great Judeo-Christian values."[15] Its choice of means, primarily shareholder resolutions doomed to overwhelming failure at the annual meetings, may strike us as silly, but they may not be as futile in the long run as the confrontations, demonstrations and boycotts favored by IN-FACT in its attacks on Nestlé for its infant formula marketing practices and its current campaign to get General Electric to stop making nuclear warheads.[16] And it is certainly as logical for the Roman Catholic church to attempt to persuade legislators to declare abortion illegal as it was for Martin Luther King, Jr., to work to ban lynching; Both attempts are seen by their proponents as simple applications of the current prohibition of murder. And then it is ultimately logical for a Christian majority to impose its moral beliefs on any minority through the legislature, as Lord Devlin thinks it must;[17] after all, if a majority can impose a law for any reason at all, why not for good reasons of morality and religion? There is no discontinuity between the voice in the wilderness and the church triumphant; I am inconsistent if I simultaneously assert both that what I believe is right and that I have no interest in having others agree with me or in seeing the whole society conform its practice to my views—unless, of course, I accept pluralism as a ruling value in itself and for its own sake, in which case I am not a church nor inspired by religion.

On the surface, the two responses of the church to the secular state presented in this section—the reaction of psychological withdrawal to the heavenly city, on the one hand, and on the other, the reaction of activism, the attempt to impose religious morality on the secular state as a whole, to make the city of man obey God willy nilly—might seem to be incompatible with each other. We have suggested that they are no such thing, but that the rejection of the secular world implied in the first response mutates naturally into the desire to dominate that world as soon as the requisite power is available. The competing cities on the hill that form our pluralistic religious heritage never said they *liked* peace and pluralism; they just decided to keep quiet about their imperialistic dreams until such time as the means to subdue the others might be available. We have been saved from this outcome so far by the rapid secularization of the society, rendering most sectors of the nation impervious to the persuasions of all preaching alike. The New Fundamentalism may have changed all that. The church standing in opposition to the secular law, insisting on the Right and abjuring all responsibility to care for the Wrong, or Left, part of the citizens, may prove to be a loose cannon on the deck of the ship of state.

The third tradition of interaction of religion and the secular realm presents a striking contrast to the others. Here the church is the firm ally of the state, carrying its bidding to the private homes where the state cannot easily reach, teaching on subjects that the state cannot easily monitor, like sexual mores, and teaching purity of mind and emotion, which lie completely beyond the observation of the state and its agents. Thus Thomas Aquinas deduces the need for a "Divine Law" in addition to the natural law and the human law, to govern the "interior acts" of the citizens.[18] From Aristotle onward the political philosophers have assumed that the church would teach the citizens not only to do good and avoid vice, but also to be kind and compassionate to each other and honest to the tax collector, all of which would make it possible for the state to govern. "Community depends on friendship," Aristotle asserts, and holds it to be the highest duty of the ruler to promote it.[19] All of this indentifies the church in a totally different role: not of working for change but of preserving the status quo of respect for authority, not as carrier of prophecy but as protector of order. We think that a radical reinterpretation of this view is in order: that the church as keeper of order stands against the state as firmly as, and much more effectively than, the church as prophet. It is this project of reinterpretation that will occupy our inquiry in the next section.

III. The Private Sector's Self-Defense Pact

From Aristotle to Machiavelli to the present, religion has been portrayed as teaching citizens that basic morality without which the state could not function. Should this teaching be neglected, the thesis seems to be, the people would be at each others' throats; no taxes would ever be collected, and the state would collapse in impotence. Church shores up state, over a wide range of activities; hence, state should be grateful to, and support, its strongest natural ally. On this thesis, if we are anarchists, and some of us tend to be, we should oppose the church not just in its historical, institutional role of ally-in-fact with whatever monarchy happened to be in power in the country where the anarchists were operating, but as necessarily a bulwark of the kind of brutal and coercive authority that the anarchists were attempting to abolish.

In this section we shall defend a different assumption, at odds, but not incompatible, with the standard one. We shall argue that at least in this day of technologically advanced governments, the idea of the state's simply collapsing of its own weight because the people it governs are insufficiently moral is an idle dream. We do not need people to be honest in order to collect our taxes; with sufficient electronic controls, we can monitor every penny of their income, sales or profits, and collect taxes on it before they even see it. We do not need people to consider the poor and needy and give to charity; we can tax them and distribute welfare payments to the poor. (In different administrations, different classes of people will qualify as "truly needy" and therefore deserving of welfare payments, but that is to be expected.) We do not need private, individual or corporate support for education or environmental preservation; to the extent that these causes can be shown to contribute to governmental viability, we can simply levy more taxes to create public institutions to fill the gaps left by the disappearance of private ones. In short, the private virtues, and the private institutions that embodied those virtues, so far from being essential to the running of the public space, are replaceable without exception by public effort. Law does not need virtue or the church, to keep itself going as the law; where private institutions falter, omnipotent government is there to bail them out, drain off their market, and finally to take over their function completely. We do not find this fact reassuring.

In *The Quest for Community*, Robert Nisbet argues that the collapse of all private institutions—clubs, schools, voluntary organizations for service, for charity, and for recreation; families, villages, ethnic solidarity groups—and their replacement by agencies of the state would be a disaster for human freedom, power and dignity. We are free, he suggested, citing the anarchist Proudhon as his authority, insofar as the diversity of our group memberships makes it possible for us to choose our own allotment of time among them: A plurality of groups gives us a plurality of role identifications that we can parlay into flexibility in dealing with our obligations. And even as our freedom profits from a rich assortment of voluntary associations, so does the opportunity for us to maximize our personal effectiveness and power. I cannot (I may have discovered from experience) have very much personal influence on the state as a whole, but I can influence the small groups in which I participate. So I experience achievement in my limited strength; but more importantly, so I learn the responsible exercise of personal influence or power, just in case I do find myself in a position to affect the lives of others to a significant extent. In recognition of this relation, the Founding Fathers insisted on the federal system; but the range of small groups goes well beyond the town government that was expected to be its smallest unit. And in the combination of personal freedom and personal power, we discover the person, the moral agent who alone has dignity rather than price, the fundamental unit of moral reasoning. So

ιe groups, the primary associations of our lives,
ɔ our humanity, at least in the political setting so
ı argue, and there seems much merit in what he
ʌ interesting update of Nisbet's thesis, Sara Evans
Boyte argue that religiously oriented intermediate
ʌs, in particular, have provided the ideas and impetus
for ⸱   ⸳ democratic change in this country by furnishing the
"free spaces," free from government sponsorship and supervision, in which people can discover their own dignity, independence, and vision. This layer of association seems to be the locus of creativity, analogous to the pre-conscious layer of the
mind, where accepted ideas or traditions can interact with new
problems and initiatives, to produce innovative solutions to social dilemmas.[21]

For purposes of this section, we will define a "private sector"
in the lives of the citizens as that portion of their lives carried
on in the primary and intermediate associations that Nisbet,
Evans and Boyte are talking about; institutions developed by
nongovernmental persons or groups, for purposes of satisfying
directly human needs or desires, operated by persons not on
the payroll of any government or responsible to an electorate
directly or indirectly. The private sector does not operate without government regulation or sanction—a sector that did we
might call the "outlaw sector"—but in its day-to-day operations
it does not orient itself toward, or deal necessarily with, any
government or government official. Thus we can put private
schools in the private sector even though they must satisfy state-
accreditation requirements, not to mention municipal fire regulations, because their income is derived primarily from voluntary contributions and the sale of educational services, not
from government subsidy. The significance of the difference,
just in case our agenda is not already clear, is that in day-to-
day operations the private school must orient itself to the needs
of its immediate beneficiaries, the paying students, and the desires of its friends, or rapidly go out of business; the public
school of necessity must orient itself to political agendas of the
governmental entity that sponsors it. Hence in the periodic Legion of Decency attacks on school libraries, the public schools
cannot afford to reject the calls for censorship out of hand; the
private schools can. It is a credit to the courage of public em-

ployees that often public sector institutions do mount very effective resistance to these campaigns. The disappearance of the private school would leave none but politically sensitive public schools in the field; the disappearance of the whole private sector would leave only the state in the field.

Accordingly, it would seem that the preservation of the private sector of the citizens' lives is of utmost importance. Vis-à-vis a monolithic state, the individual is alienated and powerless. Democracy, taken as meaning no more than voting, is no defense. Robert Paul Wolff once suggested a fine way that citizens could vote, not just for the candidates, but for or against every proposition before Congress, by pushing buttons on their television sets, resulting in a world where universal democracy needs no more than universal franchise and universal television.[22] We would hesitate to call this life a life of freedom, for it is characterized by a total absence of accountability; the notion of "standing up to be counted", crucial to democracy, entails that one can be seen by others, in public view, through most of the moments of the political process, the secret ballot being an exception to the rule. Moral agency may be impossible to develop in the kind of alienation so posited; agency requires responsibility, and that in turn grows incrementally in a variety of small associations, the associations of the private sector. Yet the prevailing trend seems to be against the private sector and toward the progressive politicization of all social functioning. Before this process is complete, we might examine the philosophical infrastructure of this sector to see how it works and therefore how it might be protected; if no other purpose is served, we shall at least have brought to consciousness a set of unconscious presuppositions in daily use at present, so that we might have a look at them before they disappear forever.

The infrastructure of the private sector is an intricate interdependency of individual virtue, social practice, corporate structure, corporate virtue, individual and social benefit. Let us take an example, say the individual virtue of personal honesty. As a recognized virtue, it is as well accepted as any could be; Cephalos, the first of Socrates' interlocutors in the *Republic*, identifies honesty in word and deed, telling the truth and paying your debts as the essence of the life according to justice. If ethicists would quarrel with this proposition, they might be re-

minded that academic disputes as well as ancient Greek social
life depend upon the ability to trust the word of another. (Why
else do we use footnotes?) More to the point, the entirety of
our economic enterprise depends on it. The willingness of businessmen to trust each other's honesty was the foundation of
our international law and remains the precondition of all com-
merce; competitors as well as suppliers tend to deal honestly.
To varying degrees, they also trust their employees—with the
supplies, the telephone, the inventory, sometimes even with the
crucial tools of the business.[23] Their further willingness to trust,
by and large, our honesty, makes economic enterprise much
more profitable for all concerned, considering that all security-
oriented activities are completely nonproductive, i.e., noneco-
nomic. Thus the value of a social practice to its participants, in
this case the entirety of what we know as business, presupposes
the societal presence of an individual virtue, which it can reinforce, but can by no means teach. But since business can presuppose it (by and large; businessmen who presuppose too much
do not stay in business very long), the structure of businesses
aim at convenience rather than security, and everyone profits.
The virtue then appropriately generalizes: If all persons who
participate in business enterprise have been taught honesty from
the cradle, and if each business enterprise depends on honesty,
it would hardly be acceptable for a corporation to be dishonest;
if for no other reasons, corporate dishonesty would make suppliers uneconomically distrustful, employees cynical and oppor-
tunistic, and customers hostile.

Taking "honesty in business dealings" as a typical private sector virtue, then, we may characterize these virtues generally as
follows:

1. They are primarily individual dispositions, to do and/or
   forebear.
2. Universal manifestation of these virtues is never presupposed, but deviance from the expected behavior is taken as
   seriously wrong.
3. They are not simply expressions of altruism, love for others,
   or of pure devotion to duty, but are strongly inculcated and
   reinforced by social institutions by appeals to self-interest and
   promise of long-run reward.

4. The social product of aggregate individual behavior in accordance with these dispositions is of enormous benefit to the society as a whole.
5. They generalize well to larger entities, corporations and other groups.
6. Government at any level is not needed to enforce them, since it supplies nothing essential to the interrelated individuals and the relevant social practices.

These virtues, in sum, are too important to be left to the vagaries of individual altruism, too close to home to leave to government to enforce, and manifestation is expected at the corporate level as well as at the individual level.

Honesty is not the only virtue that satisfies these conditions. Others that qualify would include the disposition to take good care of one's own property (prudence, we might call it, or a branch of prudence: possibly "ownership", as parallel with that "stewardship" we are expected to exercise with the property of others); the disposition to use one's wealth, goods or time to relieve human pain or enhance human life (philanthropy); and the disposition to care for one's own children, and to worry about and if possible to make provision for one's own children and grandchildren. Ordinarily we tend to take the second one as a function of altruism, of sacrificing oneself to benefit others, just as we tend to take honesty as at least a limitation on the pursuit of self-interest, and to take the first and third of the list—care for one's own property and one's own children—as manifestations of selfishness. But that distinction rests on a mistaken notion of the self, or rather, two notions of the self. Narrowly conceived, the self is just that, an individual totally defined by his or her own skin at this very moment, for the future person, occupying different time, is as "other" to me as someone occupying different space. For such a self, concern for material goods beyond those needed for immediate satisfactions is just as much an exercise in altruism as concern for the condition of the national parks and small individuals who happen to be genetically related are just as "other" as the abstract "neighbor" we are enjoined by the Gospels to love. A person who held to such a conception of the self might turn out to be an altruist, and gladly care for property and children, but he would do it as an altruist, not out of self-interest. But the self can also be broadly conceived, rooted in history, place, and society, extended over time and the community. For this self, property and family are only extensions of the self, but so is the entirety of the home community, and honesty vis-à-vis that community, and support of its institutions through philanthropy are simply ways to protect and improve the self.

On this more comprehensive understanding of the self, the dispositions listed above—the "ordinary virtues," they might be called to complement Judith Shklar's "ordinary vices"[24]—are the very essence of self-interest, as well as, and in part because they are, enormously beneficial to the society. Individually and collectively we are better off if people will privately undertake to bear, raise and educate the next generation of citizens, maintain and enhance the productive facilities of the nation, and take care of those persons and enterprises which are not self-supporting. Done by us, these things can be expensive; done by the state—which they will be, if we fail to do them well enough—they are still expensive, *and*, in addition to the expenses of the jobs themselves, we have to pay the salaries of the government functionaries who do the jobs for us *and* the salaries of the tax collectors who take the money from us to pay the salaries of the functionaries doing the job as well as the expenses of the jobs themselves, and of course that's much more expensive. The social good is best served by having these enterprises privately funded; the condition for that, as Aristotle pointed out in his criticism of Plato's "ideal state", is that they be left in private hands, subject to individual choices.[25]

Given the overwhelmingly good economic reasons not to statify (give over to the state, nationalize, socialize) the primary associations and economic activities of a society, political theorists from Aristotle to Adam Smith to Proudhon to Ronald Reagan have denounced state interference with the private sector and insisted that the public sector should be, as far as possible, reprivatized. Yet the sphere of government activity does not contract; it expands without limit. The reason for this is not far to seek; Any normal failure in the private sector must be accompanied by personal disaster (tragic deaths and the like), which in general we will not accept and which we insist must be remedied by government. As soon as some failure is remedied by the government, someone's salary depends in part on continued government involvement there. Immediately there is pressure to keep government intervention going, and therein is one very simple explanation for the continued expansion of the range of the government. It is too simple, of course. A more potent factor lies in our occasional willingness to adopt, as a people, projects the execution of which is much too complex for any combination of private initiatives, like New Deals, atom bombs and space explorations, not to mention crusades against Communism. But another, and less justifiable, explanation lies in our willingness, as individuals or more likely as small special interest groups, to appeal to government to intervene with regulations and laws and agencies without number against our private sector enemies, to make our cause triumph and theirs fail. This *group* recourse to government is, as analogy, a collective manifestation of our notorious individual litigiousness, our disposition to take our disputes with our neighbors to the law, to vindicate us, to confound them, and to extract for us large amounts of their money. Christians, however, are enjoined not to take each other to the law, but to settle our disputes privately;[26] not that Christians pay much attention to that these days, but Paul's injunction will serve as a re-entry point for our original topic: what can the role of the church, of organized religion, be in a secular law-governed state?

The church can serve as theorist, leader, and enabler of a self-defense pact for the private sector. The church above all has no interest in the progressive advance of the State, for by our Constitution, where the state is, there the church cannot be. As the church, it has access to the rest of the private sector. The family is traditionally its domain; charity is its most appropriate duty, and businessmen, nervously contemplating needles' eyes between them and heaven, have usually been respectful. In addition to access to the private sector, the church has experience as a societal coordinator. We are not that far away from the time when the parish was the unit of local government, and there are areas, even in this country, where the local church is still the focus of community activity. The theory required is already present, for the church in any of its manifestations articulates a vision of society that operates completely on trust, compassion and mutual respect, where recourse to courts, regulatory agencies, compulsory taxation to feed the poor, and government power generally, is unnecessary. The educational apparatus to teach individual morality, along the lines indicated above, is already in place. The leadership required is already existent in the very traditional, and therefore very well accepted, hierarchies of the various branches of the church. Every pastor of every denomination is already vested and charged with the responsibility of leading a congregation; the role need not be changed in its extension to cover more of the citizenry. The enablement can, again, be accomplished by simple extensions of the sorts of activities churches carry on now— community gatherings, teaching, consultations, meetings without end or number, counseling, and the provision of channels for the energies of the participants where they are needed for the community good. The private sector will disappear completely if it cannot stick together; the church can be its glue.

But what of the unchurched, those who want nothing to do with anything organized or religious, especially religious? The analysis provides no answer, which is only one of its deficiencies. Its worst deficiency is that the church, at the height of its power and unity, continued, Paul to the contrary notwithstanding, to rely on the secular arm to protect its rights and enforce its laws. It is theoretically possible to live indefinitely on love, trust, and mutual respect, but humans have never found it possible to put this particular theory into practice. Universality is simply not claimed for this suggestion. All that is claimed is that where the church is—and that must be the domain of the private sector since it is forbidden in the public—it should stay and serve that sector as its leader, comforter, reinforcement, teacher, theorist and guide. It is the private sector that still, at least in this country and at least to a significant extent, raises the children, cares for the environment, produces the goods and services, sponsors the arts, and takes care of the poor and does it far more efficiently and agreeably than government ever could. To continue to operate, it needs citizens with dispositions to take responsibility: for people who need care, for land and other property, for the cultural heritage from the past and for the fate of the future. The church, teacher of values and custodian of virtues, finds its oldest and best role in preparing citizens for that kind of responsibility.

IV. Summary

Of the traditional functions of the church—refuge, prophet, lawgiver and keeper of order—we have been chiefly concerned with the last. From its inception, and of necessity, the church has stood over against, if not actively opposed to, the state. We have suggested that the church finds its best employment providing alternative order for the citizens' nonstate activities, rather than in attempts to guide or coerce the state into change that the church finds desirable. The state is strong enough as it is; should it undertake to enact the dictates of any religious group and secure for itself a total alliance of the two cities, we citizens would be left with no place to hide in this world or the next.

Notes

1. See J. S. Mill, *Utilitarianism* (New York: Library of Liberal Arts [Bobbs Merrill], 1957); Immanuel Kant, *Foundations of the Metaphysics of Morals* (New York: Library of Liberal Arts [Bobbs Merrill], 1959); H. L. A. Hart, *The Concept of Law* (New York: Oxford University Press, 1961), chap. 9.

2. See Bernard Gert, *The Moral Rules* (New York: Harper and Row, 1966).

3. Plato, *The Republic*, ed. G. M. A. Grube (Indianapolis: Hackett Publishing, 1974), 376E–403C, pp. 46–73.

4. Ibid., 427B, p. 92.

5. Aristotle, *Politics* 1.–2. 1252b9–1253a38.

6. Ibid., 7.9.1329a37.

7. Thomas Aquinas, *Summa Theologica* Part II, I qq. 90–97, (The "Treatise on Law") (Chicago: Great Books of the Western World, vol. 20, Encyclopedia Britannica, 1952.).

8. Augustine, *On the Two Cities*, selections from *The City of God*, ed. F. W. Strothmann (New York: Frederick Ungar, 1957), p. 54.

9. Ibid., p. 63.

10. Ibid., chaps. 15, 20.

11. Ibid., chap. 19, pp. 103–4.

12. See Gerald R. Cragg, *The Church and the Age of Reason, 1648–1789* (Baltimore: Penguin Books, 1960), p. 23.

13. Jean-Jacques Rousseau, *The Social Contract*, Book II, Chap. VII: Of the Legislator, (New York: Washington Square Press, 1967).

14. Laurance Moore, *Religious Outsides and the Making of Americans* (New York: Oxford University Press, 1986).

15. Prakash S. Sethi, *Up Against the Corporate Wall: Modern Corporations and Social Issues of the Eighties*, 4th ed. (Englewood Cliffs, N.J.: Prentice Hall, 1982), chap. 6, Corporations and the Church, pp. 450–80.

16. The most thorough account of the infant formula controversy is probably to be found in Senate Committee on Human Resources, *Marketing and Promotion of Infant Formula in the Developing Nations: Hearings before the Subcommittee on Health and Scientific Research*, 95th Cong. 2d sess., 1978. For more typical accounts, see Leah Margulies, "Baby Formula Abroad: Exporting Infant Malnutrition," *Christianity and Crisis* 10 (November 1975): 264–67; Leah Margulies, "Bottle Babies: Death and Business Get Their Market," *Business and Society Review* (Spring 1978): 43–49; Douglas Clement, "Nestle's Latest Killing in the Bottle Baby Market," *Business and Society Review* (Summer 1978): 60–64; and Barbara Garson, "Bottle Baby Scandal: Milking the Third World for All It's Worth," *Mother Jones* (December 1977): 33–40.

17. Lord Patrick Devlin, *The Enforcement of Morals* (New York: Oxford University Press, 1965).

18. Aquinas, *Treatise on Law*, Q 91 A 4.

19. Aristotle, *Politics* 1.1295b25.

20. Robert A. Nisbet, *The Quest for Community* (New York: Oxford University Press, 1953).

21. Sara M. Evans and Harry C. Boyte, *Free Spaces: The Sources of Democratic Change in America* (New York: Harper and Row, 1986).

22. Robert Paul Wolff, *In Defense of Anarchism* (New York: Harper and Row, 1970), chap. 2.

23. Numerous stories of success through trust are cited in the best-selling book by Thomas Peters and Robert Waterman, *In Search of Excellence* (New York: Harper and Row, 1982).

24. Judith N. Shklar, *Ordinary Vices* (Cambridge: Harvard/Belknap, 1984).

25. Aristotle, *Politics* 2.1261b15–1264b25.

26. 1 Cor. 6:1-8.

10

BRINGING THE MESSIAH THROUGH THE LAW: A CASE STUDY

ROBERT M. COVER

I. Introduction

I intend to present to you some history and a text related to an attempt to bring the Messiah through the law that took place in Safed, the Galilee, in 1538. First, I want to explain briefly my interest in the event in terms of a concept of law I have been trying to develop.

Law is a bridge in normative space. It connects the world we have to a world we can imagine. But there are many possible worlds and many ways to connect them. Not all these futures—not all the bridges to them—can plausibly be called "law." Elsewhere, in trying to evoke the peculiarities of law as a bridge to the future, I wrote, with an excess of metaphoric rhetoric, that "Law is that which holds our reality apart from our visions and rescues us from the eschatology that is the collision in this material social world of the constructions of our minds."[1]

I, thus, had in mind an idea that law bridged *two* "moving worlds." The normative world we have is a changing or moving one. Our concept of our normative selves and environment is in flux. But, as our concept of where we are (normatively) changes, so does our concept of the possible world to which our

Editors' note: We wish to thank Susan P. Koniak for her generous assistance in the preparation of this manuscript.

law impels us to go. A world with "law" is a world in which there are:

(a) particular processes (bridges) for getting to the future;
(b) particular kind of futures that one can get to;
(c) always (new) future worlds that are held over against our current normative world with an implicit demand that they be striven toward.

I think I am making a strong claim here for the *teleology* implicit in law and for what is entailed in that teleology: namely a generative capacity through which law not only generates new law but also is at least linked to—if it is not determinative of—the generation of new concepts of the worlds we strive to realize.

The idea that a particular "bridge" with its implicit teleologies be a product of "law" seemed to me inconsistent—in a loose way—with apocalyptic eschatologies. I would have supposed—I did suppose—that Messianism in its customary apocalyptic form was the antithesis of lawful transformation. I suppose, in writing the above quoted passage, I accepted the notion that Messianism typically had an antinomian cast to it. Since I then chose, and continue to choose, to treat the juxtaposition of implicit alternative futures to current concepts of reality as central to the idea of law, the immediacy of the end of days (like revolutionary transformations), seemed inevitably to tend to undermine the "normal" tension between present and future, that which is real and that which is to be realized. Thus, I concluded, elliptically, that law "rescues us from . . . eschatology."

In defense of the obvious fallacies in this line of reasoning I can only plead in retrospect that I was not making an argument about the logical or necessary relation between law-life and eschatologies, but one about tendencies. It may be that—as a general matter—the tendencies have been as I had supposed, though I am no longer confident about that. In any event, I have been exploring in an intense way over the past year or so, at least one very significant case of Messianic immediatism that is powerfully and positively related to religious law. It seems to me an important case study for several reasons closely connected to the idea of law I set forth in "Nomos and Narrative." Before setting forth those reasons I hasten to add that I would be surprised if there were not similar instances of legal apocalypticism in other religious traditions in which law and Messianism draw from a common culture of narrative literature. Thus, for example, I would expect parallels in Islam and Christianity. However, because of my own relatively greater familiarity with the sources and the language of Judaism, I have undertaken an analysis of a prominent instance of the phenomenon in Jewish history. I come to the study of any history of religion as a rank amateur seeking elaboration of a jurisprudence—not as an historian or philosopher of religions, certainly not as a comparatavist.

The interest of "legal" Messianism for my general thesis is threefold. First, any thesis is illuminated by examining limiting cases—cases at the margin of applicable conditions. I have set forth a view of law that sees the essential law-creating act as requiring creation of strong worlds by strong communities with attendant commitments to realize those worlds over time. The concept of a world realized at the *end* of time is an obvious limiting case. Second, my thesis in "Nomos and Narrative" was that the creation of the world-of-now; the creation of a world-to-be-realized; and the bridge between them—law—are made meaningful in large part through narratives. Moreover, I pointed out that narratives resist the kinds of social control typically exercised over what are sometimes denominated strictly 'legal' materials—statutes, official court decisions, codes and constitutions. Historians of religion have time and again demonstrated that Messianic and apocalyptic narratives have not only proven resistant to social controls, but also that their manifest content creates a potential challenge to any presently constituted authority. Thus, for one who would elevate the significance of narrative for law, the special category of Messianic/apocalyptic narratives are particularly significant. Such narratives most clearly exemplify resistance to control precisely at the point that they are taken most seriously as meaningful guides for conduct. Finally, I had stressed in "Nomos and Narrative" the role of commitment in any community creating a law for itself. In *Nomos* I was concerned primarily with the role of commitment relative to violence. For the modern state's definition of itself in terms of *territorial monopoly on violence* requires that any group that seeks to hold an independent concept of reality and realization either see its worlds as contingent upon the tolerance of the dominant state elites, or see itself as prepared—when necessary—to suffer and/or inflict violence for its "law."

However, as important as the relation of violence to commitment may be, it is not the only way in which commitment operates to constitute law for a community. The serious encounter with new, strange worlds also requires commitment. It may appear to risk not death but a form of madness. Messianism requires a commitment that entails loss of present social life, authority, and reality in exchange for that which can only be imagined.* A lawful messianism entails a special form of commitment that holds to the immediacy of a privileged and strange transformation while insisting on a highly unusual capacity for familiar transformational institutions.

In the next section of this paper I shall present a brief outline of the events in Safed in 1538 taken largely from an earlier paper. In section III, I present my translation and annotation of one of the surviving texts from the Safed affair, the initial proclamation of the sages of Safed. Finally, in section IV, I will offer some comments on the way in which the Act of the Rabbis of Safed was a driving of their legal culture to its extreme intellectual limits while acting within its behavioral paradigms. I shall then offer some brief generalizations.**

II. The Renewal of Semikhah at Safed, 1538

Jewish law has traditionally distinguished between the authority exercised by ordinary judges and that exercised by truly ordained judges. Ordination, or Semikhah, the laying on of hands, was a transference of authority that supposedly traced back through an uninterrupted chain to Moses, himself. Only a truly

---

*Editors' note: Here Professor Cover intended to insert a discussion of "whether the loss of the present world is something which is 'given up' through commitments or 'taken away' by conditions destructive of ordinary social life that are 'objective' preconditions of messianic movements." He died before writing this discussion.

**Editors' note: Professor Cover died before writing section IV.

ordained judge could decide certain classes of cases, especially those involving fines or criminal penalties. Sometime, probably in the fourth century, the chain of ordination was broken.[2] Indeed, Roman authorities had tried to prohibit semikhah much earlier, though according to the Jewish sources they never totally wiped it out.[3] The end of the chain of semikhah, shrouded in mystery, did not bring a sudden or catastrohpic change in the actual practices of Jewish courts. For one thing, most elements of criminal jurisdiction had been taken from these courts by Roman authorities centuries before the end of semikhah. Moreover, to the extent that non-Jewish authorities permitted a measure of criminal jurisdiction to the Jewish courts, Jewish law evolved doctrinal ways of permitting that power to be exercised by judges who did not have true semikhah. Categories of penalties imposed by virtue of the exigency of the hour were exempted from the semikhah requirement. In short, as one might suppose would happen, legal fictions and categories were created to accommodate the formal requirements of the system to reality.[4]

The formal characteristics of the system continued, however, to have some impact. Certain penalties—those biblically mandated—were not carried out by unordained judges. Moreover, the cosmological significance of human jurisdiction was impaired. For example, according to the Talmud many transgressions are punishable by "excision."[5] This penalty is signaled by the biblical phrase, "And he shall be cut off." Rabbinic law had taught that this penalty meant that the person who transgressed would die an untimely death and, perhaps, that he would not have a place with Israel in the world to come after the Messiah.[6] But the penalty of excision could be avoided by the experience of the very this-worldly punishment of flogging for the violation in question.[7] However, precisely in this respect the fictions surrounding the exercise of rabbinic authority cut deeply, for the floggings imposed by the Bible were among the true biblical penalities that unordained judges could not impose. On the other hand, they could impose flogging for rebellion against rabbinic authority. But were floggings imposed for rebellion efficacious in preventing the penalty of excision? Of such stuff are academic legal discussions made. And you can be sure that such academic discussions there were in the thousands. But even academic discussions may become pressing matters, if conditions are ripe.

In 1492 the Jews were exiled from Spain, the home of the most important and brilliant of Jewish communities in the world. The disaster of that exile existed at several levels. Homelessness and economic losses were catastrophic. Cultural loss was equally great as the dominant scholars and artists of the Jewish world lost their communities and tried to start afresh as refugees and wanderers. If communities in Turkey and the East profited greatly from the dislocation, it was at a great cost to those who were themselves dislocated. Among the refugees were many who had undergone at least nominal conversion to Christianity during the disastrous years attending the exile. Those crypto-Christians or Marranoes frequently viewed themselves as having committed a grievous sin—one punishable by excision—in the acts attending their conversion. Their attempt to find solace, or more precisely penitence, was an important phenomenon, particularly among the most religiously active and pious of the refugees. A second phenomenon of importance was the wave of Messianic anticipation that attended the disasters in the wake of the exile.[8]

Both of the phenomena mentioned above raised the problem of the true status of Jewish courts and judges. The penitents needed, or so some of them thought, a tribunal that could impose upon them the true biblical-lashings that would absolve them from the penalty of excision, especially now that there were signs of the coming of the Messiah. The coming of the Messiah, itself, was related to the renewal of semikhah. For, in Isaiah, Chapter 1, we have a Messianic proof text: "I will return your Judges as of Old, your counselors as at the beginning; And [then] you shall be called the faithful city."[9] All rabbinic authorities agreed that the return of the judges referred to true judges: namely those ordained in the tradition that went back to Moses. The text from Isaiah thus provided an occasion for the use of law to express powerfully needs and aspirations that are not themselves necessarily legal.[10]

The precise legal question that was raised was whether it was possible to reconstitute semikhah—true ordination—once it had been lost, as all agreed it had been, long before the sixteenth century. For the position that such a bold act of jurisdiction-creation was possible, there was the word of the greatest of medieval Jewish authorities, Maimonides, himself. There were two texts in the Maimonidean corpus in which the issue was addressed as a legal question. In Maimonides' *Commentary on the Mishnah,* written while Maimonides was a young man and completed in 1168, the Great Eagle wrote that if all the sages of the Land of Israel should agree to reinstitute semikhah and should all agree on one of their number to be the head of the academy, then that person would be truly ordained and would have the power to pass on the ordination to others.[11]

In his great code, the Mishneh Torah, written in 1180, Maimonides takes a somewhat more equivocal position:

> It seems to me that if all the sages in the land of Israel agree to appoint judges and to ordain them then they would thereby be ordained and could judge matters of fines and could ordain others. . . . And the matter requires reflection.[12]

These texts suggested a blueprint for the reinstitution of ordination, even if it was not clear what the reflection on the matter would yield. Maimonides, himself, reasoned that there had to be a formal, legal process for reinstitution of semikhah, in part because he was not prepared to take an apocalyptic perspective on Messianism. Indeed, Maimonides held that the Messiah himself could do nothing against the law. He would have no power to change or transform the law, but only to oversee its more perfect implementation. Thus, it was necessary that the verse "I will renew your judges," be amenable to realization without postulating any extra-legal act by the Messiah or by God.[13]

Maimonides' texts and the texts surrounding the renewal of semikhah in Safed leave little doubt that for this legal civilization "true jurisdiction" was a sacred aspiration, a part of Messianic fulfillment. The justice that was rendered as part of their daily lives—and these rabbis were all judges in their communities—was an inadequate and pallid reflection of the justice that could be rendered by true courts. The active approach to Messianism taken by many in the generation after 1492 included the view that those acts that were necessary *preconditions* to the Messiah that could be done by human beings should be done by them to hurry the Messiah on his way. Among those acts was the renewal of Semikhah—the return of the judges.[14]

By the 1530s there was a geographic center to the Messianic yearnings, to the kabbalistic approaches to manipulation of the cosmos, and to the legal scholarship that in Judaism had never been divorced from the esoteric approaches to religion. That center was Safed, a small city in the Galilee. There probably had been speculation and preparation for a renewal of semikhah in Safed for a year or two prior to 1538.[15] Jacob Berab, the dominant scholar in the town, seems to have attempted to create an academy of colleagues that enacted his vision of what the Great Sanhedrin had been and would be. Berab was able to mold a community out of such great, and often conflicting figures as Joseph Karo and Moses b. Isaac Trani (The MaBIT).[16] While we do not know a lot about the communal processes that led up to the fateful renewal of semikhah, we can guess that there must have been an intense interpersonal atmosphere of moral energy and collegial pride to produce such an act, for the act was an act of supreme juridicial *chutzpah* (nerve).

Rabbi Jacob Berab, the head of the Academy of Safed,[17] the acknowledged leader if not the acknowledged master among them, was made the head of the academy as outlined by Maimonides and was given semikhah. The sages of Safed were unanimous in their appointment of Berab and in their intent to renew semikhah. They proclaimed their act through a message sent to the sages of Jerusalem by one of their number.[18] In the message sent to Jerusalem, they also purported to confer upon the leader of the sages of Jerusalem, Rabbi Levi Ibn Habib, ordination by virtue of the new authority of Berab.[19]

In fact, Ibn Habib considered the missive from Safed and quickly concluded that it had no basis in law according to the normal canons of standard legal reasoning. A war of pamphlets ensued between Berab and Ibn Habib with some assistance from others on both sides. Eventually, a request for a formal opinion was also sent to Rabbi David Ibn Abi Zimra (RaDBaZ), one of the great authorities of the time, then residing in Egypt. He sided with the sages of Jerusalem and, by his own account, sent them a responsum denying the power to renew semikhah.[20]

We can hardly ignore the fact that for the rabbis of Safed

this was not a case of standard legal reasoning. Indeed, the most eloquent testimony to this fact is a "dog that didn't bark." Rabbi Joseph Karo was, as I have said, among the academy that conferred semikhah on Berab. Moreover, he, himself, was one of four disciples of Berab who received semikhah from him when Berab had to leave the country a year later. Finally, we know that Karo used the authority of semikhah he had received to ordain still a third "generation" of sages, his disciple Moses Alshekh.[21] None of this would be surprising in itself. However, in all of Karo's large legal corpus there is very little that indicates his opinion on the validity of this audacious act. Indeed, Karo wrote a commentary to the Mishneh Torah of Maimonides in which there is a gloss to practically every legal provision in the sections covered by the commentary. The provision in which Maimonides makes his creative and by no means uncontroversial suggestion draws no substantive comment or expression of approval from Karo. It is almost as if Karo managed to keep his legalistic oeuvre mentally separated from this act, the reasons for which were not standard legal reasoning but the necessity to hasten the Messiah.[22]

There is in the Act of Safed, a daring commitment and a risk of madness. The daring commitment is in this: *One of law's usual functions is to hold off the Messiah.* Messianism implies upheaval and fairly total transformation. Law ordinarily requires a cautious discernment among commitments: Some of these we are prepared to undertake *now* with total subordination of other values; some we are prepared to undertake only after specified preconditions shall be met; and some we are not prepared to commit ourselves to concretely though we may yet acclaim their value. The readiness to move into a pre-Messianic mode of judicature is a readiness dramatically to increase the range of current legal commitment. It is to evince not only dramatic dissatisfaction with the world as it is, but a looming responsibility for drastic change. Now the natural understanding for a court confronting a gap between what is affirmed as right and the world as perceived, is that the *world* will be changed. Courts exercise power to that end. But we know, from the study of failed Messiahs, that the failure of inflated expectations may entail complex compensations in the *perception* and understanding of a reality that cannot be brought to coincide with the demand made upon it. The risk, in short, is that the gulf between the redeemed world and the unredeemed will be bridged not by our committed practical behavior, but by our "inner life"— our spiritual and psychological realities. The Safed, which was to have been the home of the Great Court or Sanhedrin, became the home of Lurianic Kabbalah, increasingly spiritual and esoteric; psychologically demanding; and powerfully expressive of the chasm between the unredeemed, fractured world of mortal human kind and the hope and vision that could no longer be grasped through law. Such powerful, expressive movements of the inner life may have revolutionary potential, realized in this case in the Sabbatian Movement in the 1660s. But such movements, though they bring a Messiah, do not do so through law. Sabbatai Sevi was hardly the Messiah Maimonides, Berab, or Karo had projected for the world.[23]

III. The Text

The principal texts of the Safed-Jerusalem controversy—at least some of them—were collected by one of the principal actors in the affair, Rabbi Levi Ibn Habib of Jerusalem. (The RaLBaH) The RaLBaH collected his own and Berab's pamphlets on the matter. They have been published as an addendum to the editions of RaLBaH's responsa since the seventeenth century. Dimitrovsky has discovered and published other relevant documents. The legal discourse in these works is interesting in several ways—principally in the treatment of decision-making processes and in the problem of interpretation and authority of Maimonides' texts. In this section, however, I wish to present— in stark form—the document that proclaimed the daring act of Safed together with a preliminary trial at a notes apparatus for that text:

A COPY of the document of the Rabbis of Safed with their agreement, sent to us, signed with their names. From the goodness of their integrity and modesty they left it to us to preserve [perhaps 'uphold'] its validity with our names with the signatures of our hands:

"Behold, this one People:"[a] "these are the People of God,"[b] "kingdom of priests, Holy Nation"[c]—"Established from the be-

[a]Gen. 11:6. The text of the semikhah announcement is a truly remarkable collage of biblical quotations. This first quotation is, itself, extraordinary as the commencement of the announcement. The quotation is from the story of the Tower of Babel, as God descends to see the city and the work and says: "Behold this one people with a single language. This is what they begin to do. And now, nothing will be withheld from them which they schemed to do." (Gen. 11:6). Thus, the quotation itself suggest the daring and presumptuous quality of the act which it announces. Moreover, it also suggests a kind of forcing of the divine hand. The Tower, had it succeeded, would have left nothing withheld from man. So, the act of renewing semikhah, because of its revolutionary Messianic implications would leave nothing withheld from man. Whether all these implications are intended, as with all richly connotative systems of expression, is difficult to ascertain. On its face, the three words from Gen. 11:6 are simple and could almost be unintentional as a quotation except for the initial word "he" which together with Am Ehad uniquely locates the quote in the Tower of Babel story.

The connection between the God-forcing character of the one people in the Tower story and the God-forcing aspiration of the sages to bring the Messiah is a connection that is already made explicitly by the principal text of the kabbalists, the Zohar. The Commentary of the Zohar on this very verse of Genesis concludes: "And if since they had a single will and Heart and spoke in the Holy Tongue, it is written, Nothing will be withheld from them which they initiated to do and the Judgment of On High could not rule over them, then We, the Comrades who are engaged in Torah, and We are One Heart and One Will, how more so—."

[b]Ezek. 36:20. Just as the first quoted appellation of the people suggests the daring, God-forcing act of the Rabbis of Safed by invoking the Tower of Babel, so this second quoted appellation for the people suggest the sorry sin-stained state from which the daring act is designed to rescue them. The full passage from which the three words are quoted reads:

"And when they came to the Nations into which they came they profaned my Holy name, in that men said of them *'These are the people of God* gone out from His Land.' "

The passage goes on to prophecy that God will, for the sake of His Name and not merely for the sake of Israel, establish Israel in its land, flourishing, cleansed of sin and shameful at its former iniquity. The land, itself, which had been calumnied as a land that eats its inhabitants will be like Eden.

Once again the particular three word phrase "Am Yhwh Eleh" (These are the people of God) is uniquely and unmistakably located in Ezek. 36:20. and brings with it, to the reader who knows the texts by heart, the sin, shame and reproach of exile together with the impending, immediate promise of redemption through the Holy Land.

[c]Ex. 19:6. "And you shall be to me a kingdom of priests and a Holy Nation." This quotation with its Sinaitic context suggests a "Jurisgenetic" event of first magnitude. The text is more or less "framed" by two Sinaitic quotations: this

ginning, before ever there was earth."[d] "To which the Nations shall go aseeking."[e] Oh where are the rigors, where the disciplining of Judges and officers who rule the people for praise and honor and glory, but now, that "they have transgressed the Teachings (toroth); they have changed the law."[f] The anger of God is kindled against His people. He "breaks them with breach upon breach."[g] There is no king, no officer, no mighty man nor man of war in the wars of Torah. The "cunning craftsman" and the "eloquent orator" have ceased, come to an end.[h] They have rotted away because of our sin which is great. And this nation of God has been "scattered and dispersed."[i] "We have all, like sheep, gone astray; each has turned to his own way."[j] "Our sins have increased over our heads."[k] "The crown of our

one and the quotation from Ex. 18:23 at note ee infra. The fourfold appellation of Israel which is the sound of this great call thus invokes three distinct texts and three great themes:

1. One nation (or, singular nation)—Babel, God-forcing, presumption and daring.

2. These are the people (or nation) of God—shame and sin of exile to be transformed by redemption in the land.

3. Kingdom of priests and holy nation—the covenant of law: the commandments of Sinai.

All three themes are central to the deed of the rabbis of Safed.

[d] A quotation with small syntactical changes from Prov. 8:23: "I was established from everlasting, before ever Earth was."

[e] Isa. 11:10: "On that day it shall be, that the root of Yishai which stands for a banner to the nations, to it shall the nations seek and its resting place shall be glory."

[f] Isa. 24:5.

[g] Job 16:14: "He breaks me with breach upon breach." From Job's answer to his comforters.

[h] The previous two sentences refer unmistakably to the prophecy of Isa. 3:1–3: "For behold, the master, Lord of Hosts, takes away from Jerusalem and Judah the stay and the staff, the whole stay of bread and the whole stay of water, *the mighty man, and the man of war,* the judge and the prophet, the diviner and the elder: the *officer* of fifty, the honorable man and the counselor, *the cunning craftsman and the eloquent orator.*" While the quote is not direct, the terms used to describe the sad state of affairs of the present time include all the underlined terms from this little section of Isaiah, describing what will be missing in the time when Judah will be oppressed both by itself and by others.

[i] Phrase from Esther 3:8.

[j] Isa. 53:6 which is part of the description of the suffering servant of the Lord and which continues in the same verse, "and the Lord has caused the iniquity of us all to fall upon him. He was oppressed but he humbled himself."

[k] Ezra 9:6.

head has fallen;"[1] our crown is profaned at the ground. There is no more a prophet teaching us righteousness; and there is none among us to judge fines,[m] nor to "rebuke the wicked for his blemish."[n] And should there come shortly a man who would repent to God, he would say in his heart, "Why do I labor in vain?"[o] What good will it do if I fast or if I walk mournfully? For if I were flogged forty lashes it would neither increase, bestow nor accumulate the power to exempt me from my penalty of excision.[p] "My sin is before me forever;"[q] "my shame will not be wiped away."[r] This was for our people "a stumbling block and a rock of offense"[s] that it not return penitent to God; that it hold fast to foolishness and the path of waywardness; that it lock the doors of repentance "And who is he and where is he"[t] that calls himself by the name of Israel[u] and would rely upon the God of Israel who can say to the Lord, it is I who will be girded for this thing. No tear falls from his eyes. "For the people of God go down to the gates."[v] "And now, for a little moment, grace has been shown by the Lord, our God, to leave us a remnant"[w] to preserve us to this day and to "raise us from

[1] Lam. 5:16: "The crown has fallen from our head, woe to us that we have sinned."

[m] To judge the law of fines is an expression which means to exercise a full jurisdiction which includes the power to set fines, that is, enact edicts and thus innovate (within limits) as necessary.

[n] Prov. 9:7 In context of the verse in Proverbs the meaning of the Hebrew is different from its meaning here in the text. "He who corrects a scorner brings shame on himself; he who rebukes the wicked [brings upon himself] his [the wicked's] blemish."

[o] Job 9:29: "I know I shall be condemned, why do I labor in vain?"

[p] Death at the hand of God or possibly denial of the afterworld.

[q] Ps. 51:5.

[r] Cf. Prov. 6:33: "his shame will not be wiped away."

[s] Isa. 8:14.

[t] Esther 7:5. Esther has just requested from King Ahasueros her life and the life of her people which are under threat. The King says: "Who is he and where is he that dares presume in his heart to do so?"

[u] Cf. Isa. 44:5.

[v] Judges 5:11. The line with small changes is part of the Song of Deborah who, of course, celebrates *her* willingness, readiness, eagerness to take on the leadership role of the people. It is barely possible, as well, that there is an allusion in the use of "gate of tears" which is open even when the "gate of prayer" is closed. See Babylonian Talmud, Berahoth, 32b.

[w] Ezra 9:8.

the gruesome pit"[x] of exiles and destructions which "were knit together and came up upon our necks" (like a yoke),[y] in the lands of the nations. And He has brought us to this place which He chose, and to this city upon which His Name is called. "He has given us a secure anchorage in His holy place."[z] Therefore, upon all the matters of this epistle we have arisen; we shall encourage ourselves—we the lesser of the flocks of the Holy Land—to be zealous for the honor of The Name. For how (else) will the "None [who] calls in righteousness"[aa] begin to return to God with all his heart and the "none [who] are judged in faith/truth."[bb] And so we said to each other "Be courageous and let us be strong for our people and for the cities of our God."[cc] We shall raise up the banner of the Torah which has been flung to the ground as if it were for trampling in the streets.

Therefore we have chosen the greatest from among us in wisdom and worth [lit. number], the complete sage, the great Rav, our teacher the Rav Berab—may the Rock watch over him and save him—that he be ordained and the head of the Academy, and that he be called Rav.[dd] He may then place some from the most wise among us next to him; and they will be called Rabbis. They will be ordained forever, always carrying out the judgments of Torah in truth and equity to judge the mighty [violent]. And if the wicked be deserving of blows then he will be brought before them and they will beat him according to the Torah to the extent that he can bear it. He will, thus, become exempt from the punishment of excision [either divinely administered premature death, or, alternatively, being cut off from the world to come] and will draw nigh to God, Eternal. "And all this nation, as well, will go to their place in

[x] Ps. 40:3.

[y] Lam. 1:14.

[z] Ezra 9:8. This phrase completes the full, nearly exact quotation from Ezra 9:8 which begins above, note w, with "And now for a little moment . . ." The other material, including quotations, are in a sense a parenthetical inserted within the thought of a foothold in the Holy place which the verse from Ezra describes.

[aa] Isa. 59:4.

[bb] Isa. 59:4.

[cc] II Sam. 10:12.

[dd] See RaLBaH's textual note (p. 129 infra) and note 19.

peace."[ee] This deed of righteousness and peace is, first and foremost, for the redemption of our souls; that we may be "a crown of glory in the hand of our Lord and a royal diadem in the hand of our God . . ."[ff] May He, in His mercy, cause the Shehinah to rest upon the work of our hands and fulfill the words of His servant: "I will restore your Judges as of yore, your counselors as of Old, and afterwards you will be called the city of righteousness, a faithful city."[gg] Amen, amen.

Thus far, the language of the text. It is signed by twenty-five. First come the greatest among them. Then follow the rest of the colleagues and students.

NOTES

1. Cover, "Nomos and Narrative," 97 *Har. L. Rev.* 4, 10 (1983).
2. *Encyclopedia Judaica,* sub nom. Semikhah.
3. Babylonian Talmud, Sanhedrin, 13b–14a.
4. For an interesting compilation of these fictions and subterfuges see E. Quint and N. Hecht, *Jewish Jurisprudence: It's Sources and Modern Applications,* vol. 1 (Hardwood Academic, 1980), 139–213. The terms "fictions and subterfuges" is mine and would not, I think be an acceptable characterization of "exigency jurisdiction" to Quint and Hecht themselves. For a much more aggressive posture on the application of exigency jurisdiction, see J. Ginzberg, *Mishpatim Le' Israel: A Study in Jewish Criminal Law* (Hebrew) (Harry Fischel Institute for Talmudic Research, 1956).
5. See Mishneh K'ritoth, I, 1.
6. Maimonides, *Mishneh Torah: Laws of Repentance,* ch. 8, par. 1.
7. Babylonian Talmud, Makkoth, 23a–b.
8. In particular, there was a major Messianic anticipation surrounding the life and martyrdom of Solomon Molcho (1500–1532). Molcho, himself, was a reconverted Marrano. He had predicted

[ee] Ex. 18:23. A very apt quotation from Jethro's advice to Moses to set up a system of jurisdiction of inferior courts or judges to judge the people.

[ff] The phrase with the possessive suffixes changed from second person to first person plural is taken from Isa. 62:3. It is perhaps worth noting the context here. Isa. 62:1–3: "For Zion's sake I will not hold my peace; for the sake of Jerusalem I will not be still; until her righteousness goes out radiantly and her salvation like a burning torch. And the nations shall see thy righteousness . . . Thou shalt be a crown of glory."

[gg] Isa. 1:26.

that a Messianic event would occur in 1540, and many of his followers believed he had been miraculously saved from the stake in 1532. For the Messianic background to the Safed events, see e.g., R. Werblowsky, *Joseph Karo: Lawyer and Mystic* (Jewish Publication Society of America, 1977), 97–99; Y. Maimon, *Hidush Ha Sanhedrin Be Medinnatenu Ha Mehudesheth* (Mossad Harav Kuk, 1967). See also *Encyclopedia Judaica*, supra note 2, sub nom. Molcho, Solomon.

9. Isa. 1:26.

10. For examples of law as a medium of expression, see Cover, "Nomos and Narrative," supra note 1, at 8.

11. Maimonides, *Mishneh Commentary*, Sanhedrin I, 3: "And I reason that if there be agreement from all the students and sages to appoint a man of the Academy—that is that they make him Head—on condition that this be in Israel—then behold that would make that person ordained and he could ordain whomever he wished."

12. Maimonides, *Mishneh Torah: Laws of Sanhedrin*, ch 4, par. 11.

13. Maimonides, see note 11. Maimonides' reasoning in this respect led later commentators to engage in elaborate textual exegesis to determine whether there were proof texts for a scenario in which Maimonides' requirement for a return of judges without abrogating the law could be satisfied without also postulating some concrete legal act for reinstituting semikhah. See e.g., the commentary of Yom Tov Heller on Mishneh Sanhedrin 1, 3 (Tosephoth Yom Tov) suggesting that Elijah the Prophet, who undoubtedly has semikhah, will precede the Messiah and will ordain the judges.

14. On the connection between Messianism and the renewal of Semikhah see R. Werblowsky, supra note 8, at 122–25.

15. On Berab's role in creating the academy and its spirit, see Dimitrovsky, "Rabbi Ya'akou Berab's Academy," 7 *Sefunot, Annual for Research on the Jewish Communities in the East* 41–102 (1983). See also R. Werblowsky, supra note 8, at 125.

16. On the later conflicts between Karo and Trani see Dimitrovsky, "A Dispute Between Rabbi J. Karo and Rabbi Moses Trani," 6 *Sefunot* 71–134 (1962).

17. See Dimitrovsky, supra note 15.

18. The messenger was R. Solomon Hazzan or possibly Hasson.

19. The proclamation of semikhah and the polemical literature between R. Levi Ibn Habib and R. Jacob Berab were collected by Ibn Habib and published by him as a sort of appendix to his responsa. It has become known as Kunteres Ha Semikhah and may be most conveniently found as a separately numbered addendum to the She'eloth U'Teshuvoth HaRaLBaH reprinted, Jerusalem 1975. Two additional items in the controversy have been found

and published by H. Dimitrovsky, 10 *Sefunot,* 113–192 (1966). These documents are also included in the modern reprint edition. Some of the documents are also reprinted in Y. Maimon, supra note 8.

20. See gloss of the RaDBaZ, in Maimonides, supra note 12, ch 4., par. 11.

21. On Karo, see R. Werblowsky, supra note 8, at 122–29. On Alshekh, see Porges, *Introduction to She 'Eloth U'Teshuboth Maharam Alshekh* (1982).

22. R. Werblowsky, supra note 8, at 124. There are several references, sometimes oblique, to the Semikhah incident in the strange work, Maggid Mesharim, a sort of mystical diary attributed to Karo in which the Mishneh personified speaks to and through Karo. The authenticity of the attribution was long in doubt though Werblowsky has established the work as Karo's to the satisfaction of those competent to judge (of whom I am not one). Id. ch. 2–3. One must note that the Kesef Mishneh was the last of Karo's major works to be completed and he must have looked back at the Semikhah incident from a perspective of its having failed. On the other hand, the MaBIT in his commentary on the Mishneh Torah does explicitly relate the incident. See the MaBIT's Kiryath Sefer ad loc.

23. See, e.g., N. Cohn, *The Pursuit of the Millennium* (Oxford University Press, 1961); L. Festinger et al., *When Prophecy Fails,* (University of Minnesota Press, 1956). See more pointedly, the complex social responses to the collapse of the Sabbatian Messianic expectations, G. Scholem, *Sabbatai Sevi: The Mystical Messiah* (Werblowsky trans.) (Princeton University Press, 1973) especially at 689–93. See also G. Scholem, *"The Crypto-Jewish Sect of Donmeh* [Sabbatians] in Turkey," in *The Messianic Idea in Judaism and Other Essays on Jewish Spirituality* (Schocken, 1972).

11

NATURAL LAW AND CREATION STORIES

RONALD R. GARET

I. NATURAL RIGHT AND NATURAL COMMAND

Natural law is one of the chief ideas that religious ethics, political philosophy, and jurisprudence share. In this chapter, I will suggest an interpretation of natural law that situates it within these three fields. In particular, I will make use of some perspectives from religious studies, with a view toward deepening our understanding of natural law as a specifically *naturalist* theory. For natural law, as I understand it, is a human-nature-naturalist theory of basic juridical concepts such as justice, rights, and law itself.

By a human-nature-naturalist theory, I mean a theory that associates its claims about the ordering of basic social relations with claims about human nature. Natural law theories elaborate a vision of human nature and attempt to make that vision available to political philosophy. Yet just what it means to associate an anthropology (conception of human nature) with a political theory, or to make the former available to the latter, is not at all clear.

It is for the purpose of casting some light on this relation that I will call upon certain ideas and observations stemming from religious studies and religious ethics. In particular, I will draw upon a theme that is of importance in Judaism and Christianity, and indeed throughout the sphere of human religious experience and speculation: the theme of the creation of the

218

world (cosmogony) and the creation of humankind (anthropogony). In drawing upon creation stories as a source of insight into the relation between nature, politics, and law, I do not mean to be making any claim about the primacy of cosmogony in religion generally, or in Judaism or Christianity. I do not claim that cosmogony and anthropogony are the essence of religion, or of any particular religion. But creation stories are surely vehicles for the crystalization and expression of certain religious outlooks; and it is with that view of them in mind that I will approach them here.

That creation stories are somehow involved in efforts by religious groups to put forward a normative conception of nature and of human nature will come as no surprise to those of us who are aware of attempts by certain fundamentalist movements to place so-called "creation science" in the public school curriculum.[1] Creation science may suggest to many that the political and ethical function of creation stories is to provide a mythological foundation for dogmatically asserted divine commands, especially those divine commands that hold us to fixed roles such as gender roles and sexual identities. By locating creation stories in the larger context of natural law, I mean to contest both of these conclusions. Creation stories have no inner connection to a "divine command" ethics or to a view of human nature that attaches groups to an immutable hierarchy of ends or divine purposes.

Creation stories illuminate the relation between nature and juridical concepts in natural law by clarifying two aspects or "moments" of natural law, both independently and in their interrelation. I will call these aspects "natural right" and "natural command." I will say that natural right responds to the "justificatory moment" of natural law theories, and natural command to the "presentational moment." I will give a brief account of these distinctions and indicate why they are important to an understanding of natural law, and indeed to an understanding of religious ethics more generally.

By natural right, I mean the teaching of nature concerning both the good life for humankind and the just regime most hospitable to that good life. The underlying notion is that careful observation of nature permits us to understand which regime or basic social structure is best suited to beings such as ourselves. It should be obvious that natural right in this sense is not at all the same as "natural rights," conceived as the thesis that we have certain rights just because we are human beings. Natural right simply claims that there is a way of life and a correlative political regime that is "naturally right," correct, or righteous. On the other hand, it is the *job* of natural right theories to take a stand on such questions as whether we have natural rights; if so, what they are, how they are to be balanced (if at all) against other rights and interests, and so on.

This usage is not very common, and is perhaps a bit confusing. Nonetheless, it does convey one of the meanings carried by the continental natural law vocabulary. In phrases such as *ius naturale, droit naturel,* and *Naturrecht,* the words *ius, droit,* and *recht* in part mean "just" or "right." As we will see, this meaning is inherited from classical Greek ideas concerning the "life according to nature" and the *physei dikaion,* or naturally right/just. Hence natural right identifies one of the major sources of the specifically "naturalist" ethical content of natural law.

I take the phrase natural right from Leo Strauss, who made extensive use of it in his book *Natural Right and History.*[2] This book, which in many respects anticipated Alasdair MacIntyre's more celebrated *After Virtue,*[3] makes a strong if idiosyncratic case for classical political theory. For Strauss, it is not Aquinas but Plato and Aristotle who exemplify the natural law tradition, or, as Strauss calls it, "natural right." While Strauss is painfully shy in defining the term, it is clear from *Natural Right and History* and from Strauss's other writings that it is meant to signify the thought of Athens as against that of Jerusalem. A central aim of this essay, and especially of section five, is to take issue with this simplistic distinction, and to fold natural right within natural law as an aspiration that emerges from both classical culture and Biblical faith.

Natural right, as I conceive it, functions within a natural law theory to identify the content of an ethics and politics, and to justify that content by tracing it back to nature. That is, it satisfies the needs of the justificatory moment of a natural law theory. For example, in the *Republic,* the content of the good regime, namely the structure of its hierarchical organization and the placement of the wise in the position of rule, is provided by inspection of human nature, which likewise is hierarchically organized. Yet the naturalist derivation of a proper political organization does not suffice to locate that organization and the deeds and practices that will be required to create and maintain it, unequivocally within the sphere of the ethical. Where political philosophy strives, as in the *Republic,* to show us nature writ large, it may construct accounts of ideal organization that have little connection if any to what might be called ordinary ethical experience: feelings of devotion and respect, of claiming and of being claimed, of entitlement, guilt and fault, and so on. These are the experiences that we sometimes identify with the conscience. To the extent that this identification is valid, we can say that natural right systems that construct a model political regime and justify that regime by deriving it from nature typically fail to convince us that their subject-matter is indeed ethical in the sense of responsive to conscience.[4]

Ethics, like any other subject-matter, must be presented to thought, as a domain that deserves thought and that does not disappear under the influence of thought. This means that any ethical theory must have what I call a presentational moment, a presentation of ethics as a subject-matter. Natural law theories identify the subject-matter of ethics as the conscience. The aspect of natural law theories that performs this identificational and presentational function I will call "natural command." Natural command theories, in short, are specific naturalist conceptions of conscience.

Biblical references to the divine law "written upon the heart" are instances of such conceptions. Thus Jeremiah contrasts the old covenant that God made with the people when Israel was redeemed from exile, to a "new covenant . . . which I will make with the house of Israel. . . . I will put my law within them, and I will write it upon their hearts; and I will be their God, and they shall be my people."[5] Even Paul, no admirer one might think of natural law, puts forward in his letter to the Romans a natural command conception of conscience.

> When Gentiles who have not the law do by nature what the law requires, they are a law to themselves, even though they do not have the law. They show that what the law requires is written on their hearts, while their conscience also bears witness.[6]

It is worth pausing for a moment to consider how one ought to interpret these two passages in light of the fact that it is common to deny that Hebrew Scripture embraces a notion of natural law and common to read Paul in the light of Luther's vigorous rejection of natural law.[7] If the passages do not by themselves amount to a natural law theory—and I do not think that they do—this is for either or both of two reasons.

First, it may be that while these passages speak of God as writing the covenant or law upon our hearts, they do not convey any distinctively naturalist dimension of these imperatives. In short, perhaps the divine commands are not represented as being promulgated by or in *nature* in any distinctive sense. It may be helpful to compare these biblical passages to a cosmogonic declaration in the Qu'ran.

> Lo! Your Lord is Allah who created the heavens and the earth in six Days, then mounted He the Throne. He covereth the night with the day, which is in haste to follow it, and hath made the sun and the moon and stars subservient by His command. His verily is all creation and commandment.[8]

Here we see a somewhat different view of promulgation, in which "commandment" is clearly linked to "creation." Allah has created the world in such a way that everything is subservient to him; his commands are built into nature itself. The biblical passages, by contrast, do not associate the law written upon the heart with creation.[9] The Qu'ranic passage comes closer than the biblical passages to expressing an idea of natural command, insofar as it associates command with its ruling conception of nature, namely Allah's creation. Even in the Qu'ranic passage, however, nothing is said that might help us to make sense of the idea that nature or human nature speaks in a voice of command.

Indeed, the very genius of Islam is that it emphasizes the idea of Allah's command, and the correlative idea of human subservience—Islam itself means "submission to Allah"—to such a point that the command cannot truly be located even in the creation. This position is taken to an extreme by Shi'ite and especially by Ismailite theologies that disvalue the creation in Gnostic fashion and seek to obtain salvation through the coming of a final redemptive Imam.[10] Even in Sunni Islam, however, the orthodox insistence upon the absoluteness of Allah

and upon the human believer as Allah's slave rules out any notion of natural command that does not primarily restate divine
positive law. In the presentational moment, Islam presents the
subject-matter of ethics not as natural command but as the
command of Allah.

Even if I am wrong in my assessment of the moves that Islam
makes in the presentational moment, it would still be false to
say that Islam offers an example of a natural law theory. For
even if Islam presents the subject matter of ethics as natural
command, it does not derive the content of its ethics or law, or
seek to justify that content, by reference to inferences drawn
from the observation of nature and of human nature. In other
words, Islam clearly lacks a theory of natural right. Since it does
not make use of a natural-right theory of justification, Islam
cannot count as an instance of natural law in my sense; for
natural law, as I see it, is a conjunction of natural command
and natural right.

II. Divine Command Theories of Religious Ethics

Islam develops the idea of divine command, and the correlative
idea of human submission, to a point unequalled in most other
faiths. More than any other aspect of religious ethics, however,
the idea of divine command has captured the public imagina-
tion as embodying the essence of religion's distinctive contribution to ethics, law, and politics. From the internal viewpoint
of a Barthian Protestant, for example, recognition of the utter
primacy of the commands of God is the *sine qua non* for a
Christian life, since only in this way can the Christian acknowledge God's sovereignty. From the external viewpoint of the
modern secularist, however, it may be difficult to distinguish
the religious orientation of the Barthian Protestant from that
of the Moslem who aspires to be the "slave of Allah." Inclined
to think that we have had enough of slavery in all its forms and
that a readiness to offer rational and empirical justifications for
our normative positions is required by intellectual honesty and
mutual respect, the secularist sees little value and much danger
in the divine command ethics that he or she takes to be characteristic of religion.

A number of questions must be distinguished here. Is divine

command ethics somehow essential to all religion as such? Is it essential to some or all of the biblical faiths? Is it empirically widespread among religions, even if not essential to religion as such, or to biblical religions? To the extent that some religious ethics are divine command ethics, how are such ethics experienced and discussed within the internal point of view? Viewed externally, are there any characteristic social consequences that flow from the existence of religious groups entertaining a divine command ethics?

Unfortunately, as might be expected, reliable answers to any of these questions are not easy to find. I venture to suggest, however, that in many cases divine command ethics names just an external stereotype for a much more complex view that resembles the orientation that I am calling natural law. In section five, I will offer some brief accounts of creation stories to support the idea that religious ethics resembles natural law more than it resembles divine command. Nevertheless, I certainly do not want to make anything like the strong claim that natural law represents the definitive ethics of religion in general or of biblical religions in particular. In fact, the very idea of natural law, as it has come down to us from ancient traditions of thought, bears the marks of recurring arguments within which the meaning and possibility of natural law are hotly contested.

To illustrate this fact, in the following section I will give a very brief account of the emergence of natural law as a contested idea from sources in the religion of Israel, Christianity, and Gnosticism. Because of the fateful interaction of the biblical religions with classical philosophy in the Hellenistic world, and because its contribution to the contested status and meaning of natural law are independently significant, the classical distinction between *nomos* and *physis* must be included in this account.

III. The Emergence of Natural Law as a Contested Idea

For the religion of Israel, recognition of the primacy of the commands of God functioned as the strongest insurance of monotheistic faith. At the same time, however, the ethics of the religion of Israel could never simply be equated with an ethics of divine command. Among the complex moral messages transmitted by the biblical narratives, I want to draw attention to two.

The first of these supplements or challenges to the primacy or exclusivity of the divine command is the history of God's saving acts *(Heilsgeschichte)*, and the recordation and embodiment of these saving acts in the establishment of a covenantal relation between God and people. As the quote from Jeremiah, above, makes clear, the law that God gives to the people is transmitted from within the matrix of this ongoing relation of mutuality. The stories of deliverance, covenant, and law-creation—what Robert Cover aptly calls "jurisgenesis"[11]—give rise to relationships and expectations that assert their own authority. The authority of these stories and expectations presupposes equally the existence of divine commands, the autonomy of the narratives that report them, and the immunity of the traditional interpreters of those narratives.

The Babylonian Talmud, in recounting a halakhic (legal) dispute between rabbis Eliezer and Joshua, makes this point with great subtlety. To prove the correctness of his interpretation of the law, R. Eliezer invoked three miracles. But R. Joshua denied that these miracles have standing to prove the validity of an interpretation of the law. Hence R. Eliezer said, "If the halakhah agrees with me, let it be proved from Heaven!"

> Whereupon a Heavenly Voice cried out: "Why do ye dispute with R. Eliezer, seeing that in all matters the halakha agrees with him!" But R. Joshua arose and exclaimed: *"It is not in heaven."* What did he mean by this? Said R. Jeremiah: "That the Torah had already been given at Mount Sinai; we pay no attention to a Heavenly Voice, because Thou has long since written in the Torah at Mount Sinai, *'After the majority must one incline.'* "
>
> R. Nathan met Elijah and asked him: "What did the Holy One, blessed be He, do in that hour?" "He laughed [with joy]," he replied, "saying: 'My sons have defeated Me, My sons have defeated Me.' "[12]

The adjudicative function of such stories presupposes their authority to expound the law. The story of R. Eliezer mobilizes support for that supposition. Certain texts, the story suggests, have standing to shape or govern the understanding of the law. The Heavenly Voice, by contrast, lacks such standing. The authority of the canonical texts is traceable to the divine commands that the texts mediate; yet the texts enjoy an autonomy that the Holy One celebrates.

The second aspect of the Biblical narratives that does not neatly fit into a simplistic picture of divine commands is the cosmogonic aspect: the creation stories of Genesis, and their echo throughout the Hebrew Bible. The natural order that God has created is in many ways a source of moral insight and instruction. The book of Job, for example, draws ethical instruction from our created nature.

> If I have rejected the cause of my manservant or my maidservant, when they brought a complaint against me; what then shall I do when God rises up? When he makes inquiry, what shall I answer him? Did not he who made me in the womb make him? And did not one fashion us in the womb? [13]

This ethical instruction is further linked to the created order of nature, and to the curse that has befallen it.

> If my land has cried out against me, and its furrows have wept together; if I have eaten its yield without payment, and caused the death of its owner; let thorns grow instead of wheat, and foul weeds instead of barley. [14]

Yet the sense of law emerges from the deliverance narratives, and the sense of natural order that emerges from the cosmogonic narratives, never combine in a natural law ethics that can be openly confessed and officially sanctioned. Indeed, it may be said that the notion of natural law might have struck the people of Israel as an oxymoron. The conventional view, at any rate, is that Israel was locked in a strict theological combat with its Canaanite neighbors, who were nature-worshippers. While other ancient religions sought to appease nature-gods, the religion of Israel was exclusively concerned with Yahweh's historical acts of redemption and with the commands and covenants that bound the people to their god. Since the religion of Israel looked to God rather than to nature as the promulgator of the law, there was no natural command. Since the justification of traditions and laws was sought in the history of the divine-human encounter rather than in the observation of nature, there was no natural right. These are the conclusions generated by the conceptual matrix in which notions of command, law, and nature were embedded. At the same time, it is by no means clear that the normative hermeneutic significance of the biblical narratives and symbols always could be contained within these offical structures of thought.

The inability of natural law to arise straightforwardly from the religion of Israel will come as no surprise to many modern dualists, who stand ready to divide Western civilization between Hebraism and Hellenism and to associate natural law with the latter rather than the former.[15] This association, however, is thoroughly misleading. Like the religion of Israel, classical Greek philosophy contributed to the development of a conceptual matrix that rendered natural law a divided and contested notion.

The Greek contribution to which I refer is the familiar distinction between *nomos* and *physis*. *Physis* meant nature, in the sense of the unchanging and the ideal, while *nomos* meant law, custom, or convention, which changes from time to time and from place to place. Hence *physis* was the opposite of *nomos;* there could be no "natural law."

What could be natural was not *nomos* but *dike* and its variations *(dikaion, dikaiosyne)*, meaning right or rightness, justice, or righteousness. In the well-known discussion with which he begins the seventh chapter of book five of the *Nicomachean Ethics,* Aristotle draws a distinction between changeable *nomos* and the "just by nature," or *physei dikaion.*

> What is just in the political sense can be subdivided into what is just by nature and what is just by convention. What is by nature just has the same force everywhere and does not depend on what we regard or do not regard as just. In what is just by convention, on the other hand, it makes originally no difference whether it is fixed one way or another. . . . Now, some people think that everything just exists only by convention, since whatever is by nature is unchangeable and has the same force everywhere—as, for example, fire burns both here and in Persia—whereas they see that notions of what is just change. But this is not the correct view, although it has an element of truth. Among the gods, to be sure, it is probably not true at all, but among us there are things which, though naturally just, are nevertheless changeable, as are all things human. Yet in spite of that, there are some things that are just by

nature and others not be nature. . . . [W]hat is just not by nature but by human enactment is no more the same everywhere than constitutions are. Yet there is only one constitution that is by nature the best everywhere.[16]

What is just by nature (*physei dikaion,* the right or just by nature, or natural right) is unchangeable. Among the gods it is utterly unchangeable, whereas "all things human" are changeable. Justice or rightness and the regime or constitution *(politeia)* by which society is ruled, change according to convention. Nonetheless, there is a natural justice/rightness and a naturally best *politeia.* Political philosophy, accordingly, is the juxtaposition of this natural justice/rightness and this naturally best *politeia,* to the sublunary world in which we "change our ways." Political philosophy is the confrontation between *physis* (nature conceived as the unchangeable) and *nomos* (changing human convention, or customary law).

In addition to meaning the unchangeable, *physis* for Aristotle also meant teleological perfection. Thus, Aristotle's declaration of our natural communality was an assertion that the state and society are *physei,* by nature (or in nature).

> When several villages are united in a single complete community, large enough to be nearly or quite self-sufficing, the state comes into existence, originating in the bare needs of life, and continuing in existence for the sake of the good life. And therefore, if the earlier forms of society are natural, so is the state, for it is the end of them, and the nature of a thing is its end. For what each thing is when fully developed, we call its nature, whether we are speaking of a man, a horse, or a family. . . .
> Hence it is evident that the state is a creation of nature, and that man is by nature a political animal.[17]

Now, it is evident that a thing's teleological development is a kind of becoming, hence a kind of change. Or so it appears to us, in any event. We regard teleology in human life as a kind of "perfectibilism," whereby in both individual and collective human life we progress toward our goal.[18] In perfecting ourselves, we are apt to think that we are not only changing ourselves, but creating or "realizing" ourselves. But to Aristotle, teleology was in fact the only possible form of unchangeability.

In thinking of *physis* as the "state of being fully what one can be,"[19] Aristotle meant changeless perfected being, as opposed to the changeable or variable shapes of the unperfected.

Unlike these simple pictures of ancient Judaism and classical thought in which nature and law are opposed, an equally simple picture of Christianity might regard the two ideas as correlatives. On this view of Christianity—a view which is in some respects Luther's—nature and law name only two of the four poles of a double-axis or quadratic conceptual opposition. The two poles needed to complete the quadratic structure are grace and Gospel. Christian thought, as understood in this simple model, has tended to associate nature and grace as the extremes or poles of an axis that defines the means of salvation. Similarly, law and Gospel are regarded as poles of an axis that defines God's revelation, and distinguishes its "old" [testament] and "new" [testament] forms. (See figure below.)

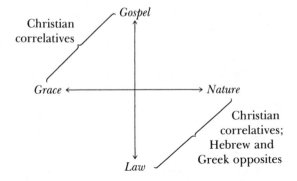

On this view, grace is to nature as Gospel to law. Grace saves us from our fallen nature; the Gospel saves us from the regime of Law. It is not hard to see that this conceptual structure identifies grace and Gospel as the positive poles, and nature and law as the negative poles. It identifies the northwest quadrant, the Gospel of grace, as what is to be affirmed; it brands the southeast quadrant, natural law, as the abyss.

When this form of Christianity superimposed itself upon the classical background, law remained the disvalued pole of a binary opposition. The new pairing of law vs. Gospel retained the valence of the classical pairing of law vs. nature, since the law pole was still disvalued in comparison to the non-law pole. But behind that continuity brooded a transvaluation of values. Aristotle disvalued *nomos* in relation to *physis* because *nomos* was the changeable; the good was *physis,* the invariant. By contrast, when Christianity disvalued law, it meant Jewish law; and the source of the disvalue was if anything that law's unchangeableness. The law condemned and killed; the Gospel brought life.

Christianity also worked a concomitant transvaluation of values in relation to nature, although this revolution was not completed until the Reformation. Just as Pauline thought added a second oppositional pole to *nomos,* so it added a second oppositional pole to *physis.* The opposite of nature in Pauline Christianity is grace. Nature is fallen, prey to sin; thus, it brings death. In this it is just like law, with which it cooperates in indicting us. Grace, by contrast, frees us from bondage to nature, just as it frees us from bondage of law.

While Christianity was decomposing the conceptual opposition of *nomos* and *physis,* flourishing Neoplatonic movements in Christianity broke down the fragile harmony between the Platonic and the Aristotelian sides of classical natural right, the *eidos* and the *physis.* Neoplatonic Christianity aligned God with the *eidos,* the timeless form. This as identified with the Johannine *logos* ("In the beginning was the Word, and the Word was with God, and the Word was God," John 1:1). But John goes on to say "And the Word became flesh and dwelt among us," John 1:14. In this view, *eidos* is anterior to *physis,* and superior to it as well, but not hostile to it. The fact that the Word became flesh is not to be understood to suggest a wastage or diminution of the divine nature; the Word does not "fall" when it becomes flesh.

Gnosticism, however, adopted precisely this interpretation of the relation between *eidos* and *physis.* In Gnostic systems of thought, and in the systems of alchemy that took their aims from Gnosticism, the Word of wisdom, the *nous* of rational mind, is threatened and captured by *physis. Physis* is symbolized by *meretrix* the whore, "who with passionate arms draws the Nous down from heaven and wraps him in her dark embrace."[20] Only the Gnostic, the possessor and transmitter of secret wisdom, can rescue the *nous* from its physical captivity. The Gnostic recognized a series of cosmic transformations that would liberate the captured spirit. The alchemist sought actually to effect those transformations. In either case, what counted was transformation, not the unchanging and unchangeable. All of this is exquisitely expressed by Zosimos of Panoplis, a third-century C.E. Gnostic and alchemist.

> Beautiful it is to speak and beautiful to hear, beautiful to give and beautiful to take, beautiful to be poor and beautiful to be rich. How does nature teach giving and taking? The brazen man gives, and the moist stone receives; the metal gives, and the plant receives; the stars give, and the flowers receive; the sky gives, and the earth receives; the thunderclaps give darting fire. And all things are woven together and all things are undone again, and all things are mingled with one another, and all things are composed, and all things are permeated with one another, and all things are decomposed again. And everything will be moistened and become desiccated again, and everything puts forth blossoms and everything withers again in the bowl of the altar. For each thing comes to pass with method and in fixed measure and according to the weighing of the four elements. The weaving together of all things and the undoing of all things and the whole fabric of things cannot come to pass without method. The method is natural, preserving due order in its inhaling and exhaling; it brings increase and it brings stagnation. And to sum up; through the harmonies of separating and combining, and if nothing of the method be neglected, all things bring forth nature. For nature applied to nature transforms nature. Such is the order of natural law throughout the whole cosmos, and thus all things hang together.[21]

The claim that "the order of natural law" is that "nature applied to nature transforms nature" takes us very far from Aristotle, especially when that maxim is understood within its Gnostic cosmological context. For in Gnostic cosmology, the fundamental truth about the world is not that it has a timeless form, but that behind this form lies a world of transformations. In the words of a Valentinian Gnostic,

> What liberates is the knowledge of who we were, what we became; where we were, whereinto we have been thrown; whereto we speed, wherefrom we are redeemed; what birth is, and what rebirth.[22]

While the Aristotelian philosopher could see beyond the changeable to the unchanging nature of things and could find in that nature the key to goodness and right, the Gnostic philosopher could see beyond the apparently unchanging world to the hidden drama of transformation. Gnosticism sought in transformation a redemption from nature *(physis);* classical natural right sought in nature a redemption from the changeable and changing.

IV. THE DENATURING OF NATURAL LAW IN RECENT JURISPRUDENCE

This brief and necessarily schematic history of the emergence of natural law as a contested idea provides a larger conceptual context within which my initial definition of natural law—as a human-nature-naturalist theory of basic juridical ideas—must be located. For natural law as I initially defined it has always represented a contested aspiration rather than an achievement. The very vocabulary that rendered the idea of natural law possible also operated to render it impossible.

Modern thought, I suggest, has tended to forget these complexities and the aspirations that animated them. This amnesia has been enabled by a reduction and simplification of the normative meaning of "nature" in fundamental ethical thought. The results of this process are visible in the meanings that Michael Moore, Ronald Dworkin, and John Finnis have assigned to natural law within the overall design of their major theories of jurisprudence.

While Moore, Dworkin, and Finnis characterize their theories as natural law theories, among them only Dworkin regards his theory as "naturalistic." Moore insists that a natural law theory need not choose between naturalism and nonnaturalism, while Finnis's natural law theory expressly repudiates naturalism. Neither Moore's position avoiding specifically naturalist commitments, nor Finnis's rejection of such commitments, preserves the aspiration to natural law as I have described it. On the other hand, what Dworkin calls naturalism is no closer to that aspiration.

Moore's natural law theory holds that the fundamental adjudicative questions—what is the law, what are the facts, how does the law apply to the facts, etc.—must be answered by reference to moral reality. Moore regards this requirement as the defining characteristic of a natural law theory.[23] Moore means by moral reality "real morals, not just conventional morality."[24] This oppositional connection between moral reality and convention is indebted to the classical distinction between *nomos* and *physis*. But Moore's notion of moral reality abandons the specifically naturalist meaning that originally attached to *physis*. To that extent, it would be more accurate to regard Moore's theory as a "moral realist theory of law" than as a theory of natural law.

While Moore says that "it is the nature of things, and not social conventions, that determines the extension of a moral word," he also holds that "[w]e should not classify moral qualities as being natural kinds."[25] Ultimately he declares that a realist should avoid a commitment to naturalism or nonnaturalism, and that "[n]othing forces the realist to characterize his position as either naturalist or nonnaturalist."[26] Accordingly, Moore's moral-realist theory of law can fairly be called a natural law theory only on two counts: (1) it distinguishes itself from conventionalism, as *physis* was distinguished from *nomos,* and (2) it distinguishes itself from positivism, by holding that the fundamental adjudicative questions must be answered by reference to moral reality. Moore's theory is not a natural law theory in the stronger sense, or at least what I claim to be the traditional sense, since it does not offer to show or effect a union of moral inferences from natural observation (natural right) and the voice of conscience (natural command).

While Moore calls his theory a natural law theory, Ronald Dworkin's initial presentations of his "rights thesis" avoided the term natural law. Dworkin's concern was to show that adjudication presupposes pre-existing rights discovered and applied by reference to moral principles embedded in the practices of the community and of legal institutions.[27] In a more recent essay, Dworkin admits that if "any theory which makes the content of law sometimes depend on the correct answer to some moral question is a natural law theory, then I am guilty of natural law."[28]

Dworkin goes on to call his theory "naturalistic." "According to naturalism, judges should decide hard cases by interpreting

the political structure of their community in the following, perhaps special way: by trying to find the best *justification* they can
find, in principles of political morality, for the structure as a
whole. . . ."[29] Two aspects of naturalism, so defined, may be
distinguished. One aspect is a source thesis: the "idea that the
standing political order is a source of judicial rights."[30] The
other aspect is a thesis about the right answers to cases, a thesis
that identifies such right answers with the "best justified" answers.

Both aspects, independently and in combination, seem very
far from naturalism. The source thesis, by asserting that "the
standing political order is a source of judicial rights," appears
closer to *nomos*-as-conventionalism than to *physis*, whether the
latter is conceived as moral realism or as a specifically naturalist
moral realism.[31] The identification of correct answers with best-
justified answers is likewise neither morally realist in general
nor naturalist in particular.[32]

Unlike Moore and Dworkin, John Finnis has developed a
natural law theory whose repudiation of naturalism is grounded
in a careful interpretation of the classical and Thomistic sources
of the natural law tradition.[33] Finnis distinguishes between a
naturalistic theory, which purports to draw prescriptive inferences from speculative reason (observations of human behavior
or human nature), and reason's practical activity in comparing
and evaluating the possible purposes for which action might be
undertaken. The latter, practical reasoning, asks "why" questions about prospective purposes until reason is satisfied, as it
is by certain inclinations or ends, such as knowledge or friendship, that are self-evidently worth pursuing for their own sakes.

I understand Finnis to make three claims for this account of
practical reasoning. First, he claims that this account, and not a
naturalistic theory in which prescriptions are inferred from human nature, is the core of Aquinas's theory of natural law.[34]
Second, Finnis claims that this natural law theory is a good description of what we do when we act, even if it is not always a
good description of our reflections on our action (since those
reflections may be influenced by theories, such as naturalism or
consequentialism, that Finnis regards as mistaken.) Third, Finnis claims that we ought to engage in practical reasoning as he
defines it.

In evaluating Finnis's first claim, it is helpful to remember that Aquinas must be interpreted not only in an Aristotelian but also in an Augustinian context. While Finnis sometimes interprets Aristotle as affirming the nonnaturalist theory of practical reasoning that Finnis calls natural law,[35] at other points he tries to distinguish or even to save Aquinas from Aristotle.[36] Given the strain inherent in giving Aristotle's conception of *physis* a nonnaturalist reading,[37] it might be better for Finnis to acknowledge that his interpretation of Aquinas is more faithful to Thomas's Augustinianism than to his Aristotelianism. When Finnis declares that "the right choice is one which is in accord with open-hearted love of all the basic human goods," or suggests that practical reason might embrace the "requirements of a reason-loving love of those things that can be humanly (humanely) loved," he is surely closer to Augustine's account of loving inclination than to Aristotle's *physis*.[38]

Finnis's second and third claims are of great importance, and should be addressed by any specifically naturalist account of natural law. They stand or fall upon the adequacy of a sharp binary distinction between speculative reason and practical reason. Naturalism denies the crispness of this distinction. More precisely, it acknowledges that one *can* define knowledge of human nature (speculative reason) and knowledge of what ought to be done (practical reason) in such a way as to render the latter autonomous in relation to the former, but questions the ultimate helpfulness or wisdom in dividing thought or experience along those lines. I am more inclined than Finnis to locate a stable or equilibrium terminus to the quest for practical reasons at a point where the central philosophical questions—Kant's "What can I know? What ought I to do? What may I hope? What is man?"—cohere, converge, or (perhaps) become indistinguishable from one another.[39]

If these three major recent natural law theories have rejected (in quite differing, even opposed ways) the sense and function of nature to which the natural law tradition has aspired, their denaturing of natural law finds support in the thorough modern repudiation of a familiar sort of naturalism: the teleological view of human nature that assigns different groups to different ranks in a hierarchy. A justifiably famous example of this type of natural law—remarks made by Justice Bradley in his concur-

ring opinion in *Bradwell v. Illinois* (an 1873 case in which the
Supreme Court upheld a law that forbade women to practice
law)—helps explain why there is currently little interest in natural law understood as a form of human-nature-naturalism.

> [T]he civil law, as well as nature herself, has always recognized a
> wide difference in the respective spheres and destinies of man
> and woman. . . . The constitution of the family organization, which
> is founded in the divine ordinance, as well as in the nature of
> things, indicates the domestic sphere as that which properly be-
> longs to the domain and functions of womanhood. . . . The par-
> amount destiny and mission of woman are to fulfill the noble and
> benign offices of wife and mother. This is the law of the Crea-
> tor.[40]

The reference to "the divine ordinance" suggests a divinely
promulgated positive law; the appeal to "nature herself," however, makes it clear that the divine positive law is embodied in
nature. Since the god to whom Bradley appeals is a Creator
god, nature and the divine command merge; nature is constituted by and renders visible "the law of the Creator." Yet the
passage exhibits no overall conception of human nature. On
the contrary, the operative premise of Bradley's argument is
that women differ from men in nature, in that the two sexes
occupy distinct "spheres," "destinies," "functions," "domain[s],"
"mission[s]," or "offices."

This series of distinguishing terms assumes that creation's
naturalistic function is teleological; God sends men and women
on distinct missions, toward distinct destinies, etc. In other words,
nature is a normative concept because nature provides us with
ends. The theological story appropriate to this teleological naturalism is one in which the god who creates us sets us on our
way equipped with a set of commands that constitute the ends
that we must reach (or at least pursue) if we are to flourish.
But because the destinies, missions, and so on, are not derived
from or through any natural right derivation or construction,
their only force is bestowed by dogmatic attribution to divine
command. At the same time, the ancient oppositional structure
that pitted nature and law against either one another or the
gospel of grace is utterly abandoned. This utter simplification

forgets the very strangeness of nature, its sublunary character, that once made it both attractive and repellent. Where nature is but the holy relic of an ancient teleological worldview, it is called upon only to sanctify commands and never to instruct, surprise, or raise a sense of wonder.

V. Cosmogonic Sources of Natural Law

A. The Sense of Fracture in Human Nature

Creation stories (cosmogonies), encountered almost universally among the peoples of the earth, convey a normative appreciation of nature. That appreciation, however, has taken a variety of forms, most of which long antedate the idea of natural law, or arise in non-Western cultures from which the familiar tributaries of natural law—Stoic philosophy, Roman law, Thomism—have not flowed. Only by attending carefully to the various moral forms of cosmogonies will we be able to retrieve their significance for a theory of natural law.[41]

The simplest of these moral forms consists of the experience of natural objects, such as stones or trees, as hierophanies—manifestations of the sacred—that are replete with meaning, and with an especially convincing reality, due to their symbolic participation in the cosmogonic events that occurred "once upon a time," or "in the old days." On this view, which Mircea Eliade has supported in the massive comparative studies that have been his life-work, value is simply equivalent to being and meaning.[42] A person who experiences objects and events in the world as sharing the sacred order of world-creation finds such objects and events to be overflowing with being and meaning, and in so finding them regards them with reverence. Life organized around such experiences forever repeats the cosmogonic acts, and shares the world-creating magical power.

Now this form of cosmogonic morality or spirituality is exceedingly simple; but, simple as it is, it is nonetheless subject to a crucial question. The question may be asked either methodologically, as a problem in the interpretation of the so-called "primitive" religious experience, or normatively. Putting the question first in the latter way, we are bound to ask: Should we regard human life so depicted as a zenith of creativity, or as an

abysmal and inauthentic subjection to traditionalism and repetition? In other words, should we admire the cosmogonic life,
or be repelled by it?

To ask this question is to treat the cosmogonic life as if it
advanced a conception of human nature and of the human good.
Of course, it does not advance any such conception in the familiar ways; it does not advance a view and defend it against
alternatives. It may be unaware of alternatives. But we might
say that the cosmogonic life *lives out* a conception of human
nature, one which identifies nature with creation and human
nature with the eternal recreation of the world. So conceived,
should this life be admired or abhorred?

Restated in a more methodological and interpretive way, the
question becomes: Is the cosmogonic life one of creation or one
of imitation? More precisely: Does the distinction between creation and imitation permit us to remain faithful to the experiences that constitute the cosmogonic life? This is a question about
phenomenology, a question which requires us, in part, to define the "phenomenology of religion," and to ask whether Eliade's
work can be regarded as an instance of the phenomenology of
religion.[43] Eliade's own terminology often seems not phenom-
enological but Platonist or Neoplatonic. He speaks of "archetypes" which the hierophanies repeat, and in relation to which
they acquire meaning. It may be fair to say of Eliade that he
assumes a distinction between signifier and signified, then *finds*
that while for the cosmogonic life the domain of what can be
signified is eternally frozen (everything means the sacred creation), the domain of the signifiers is infinite (everything is a
potential hierophany). The cosmogonic life thus understood is
creative only in a permanently imitative way. We might then
evaluate this life by comparing it with others: for example, with
a life in which the domain of the signified is infinite (anything
can be meant), but in which the domain of signifiers is restricted (stones and trees are not signifiers, except perhaps in a
code or a rebus.)

The problem shifts, however, if we abandon the assumed distinction between signifier and signified, in favor of the phe-
nomenological assumptions employed, for example, by Paul Ricoeur in *The Symbolism of Evil.*[44] In pursuing the ideas of fault,
sin, and evil, through the study of the symbolism of stain and

defilement, and through interpretation of creation myths, Ricoeur finds that "the most primitive and least mythical language is already a symbolic language;" that "We are not, therefore, reduced to the ineffable when we try to dig beneath the myths of evil; we still come up with a language;" that "The consciousness of self seems to constitute itself at its lowest level by means of symbolism and to work out an abstract language only subsequently, by means of a spontaneous hermeneutics of its primary symbols."[45] The experience of fault, for Ricoeur, is not a signified which is expressed by symbolic signifiers such as images of stain or pollution. Experience is not prior to symbolism, but always found in a matrix of symbols; conversely the symbols do not correspond to an independent moral reality, but are involved in the constitution of that reality.

It is crucial to observe two differences between Eliade's and Ricoeur's accounts of cosmogonic stories, human nature, and morality. The differences lie in *what* the creation stories say, and in *how* they speak. As to *what* the creation stories say: To Eliade they speak of perpetual human sharing in the creative action of the cosmogony, while to Ricoeur they speak of alienation and loss, of a fault that expels us from Eden. The tables are turned, however, in the matter of *how* the creation stories speak to Eliade and to Ricoeur. For Eliade, the creation stories are simply representational; in them, we see how people other than ourselves, "primitive" and "archaic" people, used certain signs that are still available to us (stones, trees, and so on) to signify forms or types that are largely lost to us, or in which we no longer believe. For Ricoeur, by contrast, we have no access to our own fundamental moral experience other than that provided by study of our symbolic and mythical expression.

> All the symbols of guilt—deviation, wandering, captivity,—all the myths—chaos, blinding, mixture, fall,—speak of the situation of the being of man in the being of the world. The task, then, is, starting from the symbols, to elaborate existential concepts—that is to say, not only structures of reflection but structures of existence, insofar as existence is the being of man.[46]

Ricoeur's phenomenology of fault makes recourse to creation stories in order to build a normative conception of human nature as "existence." Eliade's analysis of the creation stories does not build a normative conception of human nature, but instead puts us in the position of admiring or rejecting a way of life that is in many ways presented as foreign to our own. In Eliade we are at one with creation substantively, but alienated methodologically; in Ricoeur we are alienated substantively, but are nonetheless capable of knowing ourselves to be so alienated.

Ricoeur's hermeneutic phenomenology of existence exemplifies several aspects of both traditional and modern versions of natural law. First, Ricoeur affirms that there is a human nature, that this nature is humanly knowable, and that human nature has a moral dimension: in this case, a dimension of evil. Secondly, Ricoeur's anthropology is one of existence; the moral dimensions of human nature are called "structures of existence." Here Ricoeur is typical of contemporary anthropologies that have felt the influence of Heidegger. I want to distinguish between the content of this existential anthropology and its range of functions within an overall theory.

The content of Ricoeur's anthropology, as I have indicated, emphasizes that we are not utterly at home in the created world. Thus Ricoeur learns from the creation stories not that we can directly participate in creation by repetition of the sacred archetypes (Eliade), but that we carry with us a fault or fracture. A major function of creation stories, and of closely related myths—Edenic paradise and its fall, tragic tales of gods and mortals, Gnostic myths of the exiled soul—is to express this fracture in a way that makes it available to thought.

Despite its roots in cosmogonic sources, however, Ricoeur's "ontology of finitude and evil that elevates the symbols to the rank of existential concepts"[47] seems vulnerable to Karl Barth's criticisms of natural law and natural theology. In his *magnum opus,* the *Church Dogmatics,* Barth rejects what he takes to be the fundamental project of Roman Catholic moral theology, the effort to found an ethics on an account of human existence, saying that "The order of obligation built on the order of being cannot as such be a real order of obligation . . . as introduced in Jesus Christ."[48] This "divine image of being, the god-concept of ancient philosophy, . . . can do many things, as is the case with such demon-figures. But it cannot in the true sense of the word command."[49]

Here Barth is half right and half wrong. Barth is correct in saying of an ontological ethics, such as Ricoeur's hermeneutic phenomenology of existence in *The Symbolism of Evil,* that it does not generate an "ought" in the sense of a "command," and correct again in regarding this incapacity as a defect. But Barth is wrong in attributing this defect to any defining feature of natural law or natural theology, Catholic or otherwise. It would be more accurate to say that an interpretation of cosmogony yields an ontology, even a profound understanding of the value-relatedness of existence, but not yet a full theory of natural law, until it generates or provokes an ought in an experience of being commanded. Insofar as he explores cosmogony to illuminate our general normative *situation* in relation to nature—created, yet distanced from creation by a fracture variously conceived in the symbolism of stain or defilement, and in mythic narratives of tragedy, fall, or exile—Ricoeur has employed a conception of human nature in one of the ways that a theory of natural law requires. Insofar as his theory leaves us in a confessional state, expressing our guilt but unable to define courses of action that we ought to pursue, Ricoeur has failed to employ a conception of human nature in a second way required by a complete theory of natural law. In fact, since Ricoeur's conception of human nature as existence does not include definite experiences of obligation, *a fortiori* it cannot conceive of failures to meet those obligations; since it cannot conceive of those failures, it cannot fully understand the experience of estrangement or stain that defines the fracture peculiar to human nature. Hence the absence of one anthropological function in the theory prevents the other function from fulfilling its aim.

Although I cannot develop the idea here, I believe that cosmogonic stories have tended to produce the requisite ought or command in three distinct ways. On Eliade's assumptions, all creation exerts a claiming value in that all creation embodies and renews the sacred world-creating activity. This generates universal "moral considerability":[50] All things are sacred, hence all things make claims upon us to the kind of treatment that sacredness merits. A second and quite different ethic is generated by those mythic stories that deny, in Blake's phrase, that "Every thing that lives is holy." Leviticus, for example, brands many animals as "abominations" that may not be eaten. Such schemes repose ethical value not in created objects as such, but in the sacred order that the creator imposes against a backdrop of the profane and chaotic. Here, cosmogonic stories function to identify courses of action that are impure or polluting.[51] Finally, cosmogonic stories often are read in such a way as to express impatience with the disjunctive order of the created world: an order that divides light from dark, heaven from earth, male from female, "our kind" from "the other kind," and so on. On such readings, the ultimate moral message sent by cosmogonic stories is an injunction not to preserve but to transcend the binary oppositions embedded in the cosmos, in a *coincidentia oppositorum* or marriage of contraries. This aim of suspending the cosmic oppositions in an acosmic union has always won many adherents, to whom this end has no doubt represented the pinnacle of human creativity: For in it, human unifying action proves ultimately more creative than the very acts of world-creation.[52]

B. The Imago Dei Argument

To these basic cosmogonic themes, the biblical faiths have added an anthropogonic narrative that has proved to be extraordinarily important in the development and justification of basic political positions. In Genesis 1:26–27, God makes humanity in the divine image and likeness. This story of the creation of humanity in the *imago dei* has seemed to many to offer a foundational insight into human dignity and into the rights and duties appropriate to that dignity.[53] Genesis itself appears at several points to argue from the *imago dei* to certain basic legal relations. For example, after God has preserved Noah's family and the representative animals from the flood, God declares "Whoever sheds the blood of man, by man shall his blood be shed; for God made man in his own image."[54] In that same proclamation to Noah, God delivers the bounty of the earth to humanity, repeating the connection that the first chapter of Genesis establishes between the *imago dei* and human "dominion" over all living things.[55]

In its more subtle roles, the *imago dei* argument has functioned as a moment in human moral and metaphysical self-reflection. It has, for example, served to illuminate the idea of

our natural communality or sociality. Thus, the God who creates us is in some sense plural: "Then God said, 'Let *us* make
man in *our* image, after *our* likeness,' " etc.[56] "So God created
man in his own image, in the image of God he created him;
male and female he created them."[57] Interestingly, the latter
passage, which returns to the more typical language in which
God is spoken of as singular, suggests that the image of God is
"male and female." Thus God is at once one and several, same
kind and different kinds. The Christian conception of the Trinity
preserves this intuition, and makes it available to the perennial
philosophical effort to understand the relation between personhood and communality. Indeed, the Trinitarian formula, which
holds that God is three *persons,* is an often-overlooked source
of the idea of personhood. Here we see how the *imago dei* argument has provided a vehicle for our most basic efforts to
understand the structures of our existence.[58]

While the *imago dei* argument raises a number of interesting
questions, I shall restrict my attention here to two matters central to my overall interpretation of natural law. First, I will illustrate, by recourse to the Declaration of Independence, one
way in which the *imago dei* argument associates a political theory (in this case, a theory of natural rights) with a conception
of human nature. Second, I will indicate how an *imago dei* argument might make the "cosmogonic life," or a conception of
human nature as self-creation, available to political theory.

The Declaration of Independence makes theological claims
at central points in its argument for natural rights and for the
legitimacy of national rebellion. The American people are said
to be entitled by "the laws of nature and of nature's God" to a
separate and equal station among the powers of the earth. Then
follow famous propositions that few will be heard to contest,
even today: "We hold these truths to be self-evident, that all
men are created equal; that they are endowed by their Creator
with certain inalienable rights; that among these are life, liberty, and the pursuit of happiness." Cosmogonic ethics, and the
imago dei argument in particular, provide a frame of reference
within which these propositions might be understood.[59]

What might the Declaration mean by asserting that we are
endowed by our Creator with certain inalienable rights? It might
mean that God sends us off into the world with an endowment

of rights, just as our parents might send us off to school with lunch money in our pockets. This is surely the most direct connection that it would be possible to draw between nature and political institutions or relations: a connection so direct that it is actually not a connection at all, but an identity. Rights on this view do not need to be justified, since they simply *exist* as a part of the natural endowment.

Yet the Declaration assumes that rights do need to be justified, and also to be provided with some content. It is to satisfy these needs of basic political thought, for justification and for content, that the Declaration pursues the course of cosmogonic ethics. The basic notion is that rights are an endowment appropriate to the nature that God has given us. Worth noting, here, are the references to God as Creator, and to the inalienability of the fundamental natural rights. I will try to show why these references to the Creator and to inalienability are related to one another, and to the basic logic of the *imago dei* argument: the reasoning that holds that because we are made in the image and likeness of God, we owe one another the sort of respect or deference that God's image merits.

In the proposition "We are endowed by our Creator with certain inalienable rights," the references to the Creator and to inalienability illuminate one another. To see this, it is necessary to recognize that in the familiar framework of secular liberal thought, inalienability seems exceptional. Constraints on my capacity to transfer my possessions—where "possessions" includes both my primary status as right-holder, and the secondary things to which I have a right by virtue of my primary status as right-holder—are disfavored in secular liberal thought, since they restrict freedom of choice and preclude certain gains which flow from free trade.[60] By contrast, natural rights viewed anthropogonically are "birthrights": endowments which come down to us, and which we must in turn hand down to those who follow.

> Now Naboth the Jezreelite had a vineyard in Jezreel, beside the palace of Ahab king of Samaria. And after this Ahab said to Naboth, "Give me your vineyard, that I may have it for a vegetable garden, because it is near my house; and I will give you a better vineyard for it; or, if it seems good to you, I will give you its value in money." But Naboth said to Ahab, "The Lord forbid that I should give you the inheritance of my fathers."[61]

From the biblical point of view, the most important rights of all—precisely the rights that it will make sense to think of as natural rights—are those bound by inalienability. They are precluded from sale by their history, their lineal descent from those with whom God entrusted them, and by their future, the role they will play in the destiny to which God is calling the chosen people. Theologically, inalienability expresses the central idea that the endowment of rights is above all a vocation: a calling to fulfill the destiny for which people were created. Hence, rights grounded in the *imago dei* argument cannot have the wholly optional character that they exhibit when derived from liberal state-of-nature premises.

The linkage between inalienability and appeals to the Creator is further evidenced when the *imago dei* argument is modified or attacked by lapsarian theological assumptions. In certain forms of Christianity, especially those shaped by Reformation theology, the sense of defilement and of a corresponding fracture in creation is expressed doctrinally in a conception of the Fall which denies that the image and likeness of God survives sufficiently intact to serve as a foundation for rights and responsibilities. This stress upon the depravity of human nature both presupposes and generates alienability. Alienability is presupposed because if the Fall strips us of anything, we must have been able to give it away or sell it. That is, we sold our eternal life in exchange for knowledge of good and evil (on one possible interpretation of the Fall). At the same time, this interpretation sets the stage for a kind of cosmic or ontological alienability. Since we have lost the *imago dei,* we must be saved (if at all) not by reference to our nature but instead by means of grace. This requires substitutional atonement. We sinners must be free to give up our burdens and place them on Christ's shoulders; Christ, in turn, must be free to give up the life he merits in his blameless state, in order to bear the sins of humanity.

To gain a better appreciation of what is (and what is not) at stake in the quarrel between Reformation theology and the *imago dei* argument, it will be helpful to take a closer look at the views of Karl Barth, and the quarrel over "natural theology." I have already indicated how Barth attacks an ethics such as Ricoeur's, which is based on the sort of anthropological argument that I have called a hermeneutic phenomenology of existence. If Barth was unwilling to ground ethics on any account of the fractured nature of our existence, he was *a fortiori* unwilling to ground ethics in any purported human capacity to recognize remnants of our original, pre-fractured nature.

As worked out by Protestant theologian Emil Brunner, for example, natural theology begins with the characteristic *imago dei* deduction.[62] Brunner believed that some of the *imago dei* survived the Fall and the debilitating effects of sin. Human personhood and subjectivity, the ability to communicate with God, to bear responsibility for one's acts, all remain of the *imago dei*. This gives God a basis on which to build what Roman Catholic theology had called the natural law, but what Brunner called the "ordinances." Thus Brunner described the state as God's "ordinance of preservation," albeit touched by sin, and matrimony as the yet-unsullied "ordinance of creation." Brunner regarded his own theological efforts as faithful applications of the natural law teachings of Luther and Calvin.[63] "It is the task of our theological generation," said Brunner, "to find our way back to a true *theologia naturalis*."[64]

Barth rejected Brunner's natural theology both vehemently and systematically: the former in Barth's reply to Brunner, succinctly entitled "Nein!" (No!),[65] and the latter in the many volumes of Barth's *Church Dogmatics*.[66] In part, the basis of Barth's rejection of natural theology is the difficulty of validating generalizations about human nature. This is a familiar objection to all anthropologically based ethical proposals, but Barth clearly links the objection to his characteristic insistence that ethics yield commands.

> No doubt there are such things as moral and sociological axioms which seem to underlie the various customs, laws and usages of different peoples, and seem to appear in them with some regularity. And there certainly seems to be some connection between these axioms and the instinct and reason which both believers and unbelievers have indeed every reason to allow to function in the life of the community. But what are these axioms? Or who among us 'sinners through and through' decides what they are? If we consulted instinct and reason, what might or might not be called matrimony? Do instinct and reason really tell us what is *the* form of matrimony, which would then have to be acknowledged and pro-

claimed as a divine ordinance of creation? . . . And who or what raises these constants to the level of commandments, of binding and authoritative demands, which, as divine ordinances, they would obviously have to be?[67]

The key words in this argument are "commandments" and "demands." Barth requires that ethics be understood as the commands of God and that those commands be understood in such a way as to make them free of all contentful or justificatory connection with human nature. For Barth, in fact, what we know of human nature—indeed, everything that we know—we know by virtue of God's gift of faith. To conceive of ethics in any other way is to commit "intellectual works-righteousness."

The predictable result of Barth's severing any connection that the divine commands might have to human nature is that Barth simply wages natural law by other means. And he does it with a vengeance. Having rejected natural theology's way of establishing an ethics of marriage by reference to created human nature, for example, Barth nonetheless manages to restate the old natural law affirmations, and to reinvent *Bradwell v. Illinois.* Barth finds that "coitus without coexistence is demonic";[68] marriage is the *telos* of relations between men and women;[69] man is related to woman by "taking the lead as the inspirer, leader, and initiator in their common being and action."[70] Male or female religious orders are "obviously disobedience";[71] homosexuality is a sickness and a perversion; "It is always in relationship to their opposite that man and woman are what they are in themselves."[72] Of course, these ethical imperatives are not to be taken as "orders" or "ordinances" (Brunner), or as "mandates" (Bonhoeffer). That would be to misunderstand them in the fashion of natural theology. Instead, they must be understood as part of "the constancy of the divine command," which provides ethics a "formed reference."[73]

Clearly, traditional natural law teachings are just as liable as Barth's divine-command theology to produce the familiar sexist account of marital order. In fact, it is evident that Barth has borrowed much of the content of his marital ethics precisely from those traditional teachings.[74] Yet there is a crucial difference. While an old-fashioned natural law sexist would make the human nature claims up front, where they can be challenged (at least in principle) as a false and distorted view of nature, Barth's claims about human nature (e.g., "it is always in relationship to their opposite that man and woman are what they are in themselves") are dressed up as divine commands. They have the force, not of reasoned inferences from observation and experience, but of protracted dogmatic harangue. They cannot be attacked by recourse to nature. The very movement to attack them as unnatural is branded by Barth as demonic; one rejects natural theology, says Barth, as one rejects the abyss.[75]

These criticisms of Barth must be conjoined to Barth's own criticisms of Ricoeur's project of building an ethics upon an analysis of the structures of existence. Put rather crudely, an ethics such as Barth's, which denies all validity to anthropological inquiry and argument unmediated by divine command, is just as incomplete as an ethics such as Ricoeur's, which purports to grasp the fractured character of human nature without reference to objective failure to meet the requirements of moral law. Barth's insistence on the promulgation of the law, and Ricoeur's phenomenology of existential fault, would appear to complete one another within a larger account of human moral experience.

C. The Anthropogonic Life

The *imago dei* argument has embraced anthropologies as different as the Aristotelian teleological conception of human nature adopted in Thomistic natural law, and the liberal proprietary conception associated with modern natural rights. Since *imago dei* is a rather formal argument, its capacity to be adapted to the needs of quite different anthropologies and ideologies is not surprising. What is surprising, however, is the infrequency with which the formal content of *imago dei* is rendered substantive in an anthropogonic anthropology. By this I mean to point out the rather obvious, if unorthodox, fact that if we are made in the image and likeness of God, and if the God in whose image and likeness we are made is anthropogonic and cosmogonic (human-making and world-making), then our nature must be that we are human-making and world-making. This view of our nature might be called a conception of the anthropogonic life.

To see how the *imago dei* might support the anthropogonic life, let us consider the following two passages. The first is a summary by Leo Strauss of the six-day creation story in Genesis; the second is a rabbinic commentary arising in a separate context.

> God created everything in six days. . . . The creatures of the first three days cannot change their places; the heavenly bodies change their places but not their courses; the living beings change their courses but not their 'ways'; men alone can change their 'ways'. Man is the only being created in God's image.[76]
>
> R. Joshua b. Levi said: A procession of angels pass before man and the heralds proclaim before him saying: 'Make room for the image of God.'[77]

Here we see an *imago dei* argument for human nature as self-creation or self-transformability, coupled with an account of the normative or political consequences that flow from human nature so described. The first passage interprets the creation story as depicting a progression from lower to higher creatures, culminating in humans. The first creatures cannot move at all; the planets move, but only in fixed orbits; animals move outside of fixed orbits, but only in accordance with their predispositions. Only humanity can be self-creating, and in that sense mirror God the creator. The second passage describes, in the symbol or metaphor of "making room," the dignity or worth of the creature who is God's image. This symbol or image nicely captures the specific normative content that might be associated with creatures who can be self-creating, who can "change their ways." One might conceive of the angels and heralds as rights, moving ahead of these self-transforming beings, in order to open a zone for their self-transformative movement.

Historically, the main line of thought pressing toward a vision of anthropogonic life had circumvented the *imago dei* argument. This line of thought is the Gnostic cosmology. According to Gnostic creation myths, we are trapped within the material creation of an inferior deity. Our mission is to liberate ourselves from the created exile, through knowledge and manipulation of secret cosmic events that will transform the physical into the spiritual. On these assumptions, the anthropogonic life consists not in revering but instead in displacing the creator god.

Of the two principle modern worldviews that embody Gnostic assumptions, namely romanticism and existentialism, only romanticism has retained the technique with which I have been concerned throughout this section: employment of creation stories to associate an ethics with a conception of human nature. As Paul Cantor has demonstrated, central texts such as Blake's *The Book of Urizen* and Mary Shelley's *Frankenstein* gave modern form to the Gnostic idea that liberation and salvation consist in denying the circumscribing claims of the creator god.[78] Existentialism, by contrast, shuns creation-stories as a genre. Nonetheless, as Hans Jonas has shown, existentialist writings often retain the basic themes, such as homelessness, aloneness, and anguish, that earlier Gnosticism had expressed in cosmogonic narrative.[79] Moreover, existential writings often stress the anthropogonic notion that we overcome ourselves or make ourselves.[80] Even as existentialism denies that there is such a thing as human nature, and *a fortiori* denies that there can be an ethics grounded in human nature, it asserts that we in fact have an anthropogonic nature, and that this nature is a kind of dignity or worth. This is the sense, as Sartre understood, in which existentialism is a modern humanism.

> If man as the existentialist sees him is not definable, it is because to begin with he is nothing. He will not be anything until later, and then he will be what he makes of himself. Thus there is no human nature, because there is no God to have a conception of it. Man simply is. Not that he is simply what he conceives himself to be, but he is what he wills, and as he conceives himself after already existing—as he wills to be after that leap toward existence. Man is nothing else but that which he makes of himself. That is the first principle of existentialism. And this is what people call its 'subjectivity,' using the word as a reproach against us. But what do we mean to say by this, but that a man is of a greater dignity than a stone or a table.[81]

Here we see Sartre expressly rejecting the metaphysics and the ethics of the *imago dei*. God has not made us, has fashioned no conception of us which governs us by defining our essence. Therefore we have no nature. Instead, we are a self-transformative "leap;" we are what we make of ourselves. Hence we are different from the things in the world: from stones or tables. (We are different from stones and tables in much the way that the creature of the sixth day differs from creatures of the first three days; the former can change its "ways.") This difference is a "dignity": a deservingness, or worth.

While the existentialists have celebrated their agonistic crown of creation, they have taught us little about the content, meaning, or experience of its special dignity. Instead, they have largely repeated the same formula, without elaboration. Consider these claims by Ortega.

> Here we come upon the formidable and unparalleled character which makes man unique in the universe. We are dealing—and let the disquieting strangeness of the case be well noted—with an entity whose being consists not in what it is already, but in what it is not yet, a being that consists in not-yet-being. Everything else in the world is what it is. An entity whose mode of being consists in what it is already, whose potentiality coincides at once with his reality, we call a "thing."

> *Man, in a word, has no nature; what he has is—history.* Expressed differently: what nature is to things, history, *res gestae,* is to man.[82]

Ortega does not speak of human dignity; instead, he says that human being is a "formidable and unparalleled character." He draws the usual contrast between this "character" and the reality of the "thing." He defines the character in terms of "not-yet-being," but he appears reluctant to say more. He cannot say more, in fact, because to do so would be to defeat the claim he is most intent on making (and which he again shares with Sartre): the claim that "Man has no nature."

More than any other modern, self-consciously atheistic philosopher, it was Ernst Bloch who expounded the ontology of the not-yet-being (Bloch's *noch nicht Sein*), and who attempted to draw its consequences for an ethic human dignity *(menschliche Würde).*[83] Bloch's more complete account of human self-transformability, and of its moral significance, stems from his acceptance of Marxian eschatology. While Sartre's existentialism looked to Marxism primarily as a source of critical resolve, Bloch's inherited from Marxism its hopeful picture of human self-creation through a life of struggle. Yet Bloch palpably existentializes this hope; human life in the state of future bliss no longer consists of hunting in the morning and fishing in the afternoon.

> As the 'wretched snags' of social life are removed, as capitalism is abolished, all the socially irremovable problematics of the soul loom larger than ever. . . . At this point men will be free to deal with those uniquely practical concerns and questions which otherwise come only at the hour of death. . . . The goal, the eminently practical goal, and the basic motive of socialist ideology is this: to give to every man not just a job but his own distress, boredom, wretchedness, misery and darkness, his own buried, summoning light; to give everyone's life a Dostoyevskyan touch.[84]

Here human self-creation is given an interpretation at once historical and personal. This historical side lies in abolishing the 'wretched snags' of social life; the personal side lies in existential struggle. Thus Marx allows us to "make room" for Kierkegaard's dread and Heidegger's being-toward-death, for life with a "Dostoyevskyan touch." These "problematics of the soul," this "buried, summoning light," recall for us those perennial Gnostic yearnings which surpass every material limitation in their striving for transformation. In this way, Bloch, despite his resolute atheism, returns us to the theistic conception of human nature as self-creation.

Indeed, it is Bloch who renders explicit the otherwise suppressed premise in the *imago dei* syllogism which concludes with the claim that human nature is anthropogonic. Let us look again at Leo Strauss's interpretation of the initial account of creation in Genesis.

> God created everything in six days. . . . The creatures of the first three days cannot change their places; the heavenly bodies change their places but not their courses; the living beings change their courses but not their 'ways'; men alone can change their 'ways'. Man is the only being created in God's image.[85]

Strauss surely seems to be safe in contrasting the mobility of the creations of the latter three days with the immobility of the creations of the first three days, and in suggesting that this account of creation in Genesis stresses not only the superiority of mobility over immobility, but of human mobility (change of 'ways') over lesser forms of mobility (change of courses and places). But what licenses the inference that this human mobility or self-transformability is made in the image of God? Alternatively, if one supplies the missing passage—the declaration, in Genesis 1:27, that "God created man in his own image"— what must one assume about God?

Ernst Bloch's ontology of the not-yet-being supplies the answer. Bloch translates God's word of self-revelation in Exodus 3:14, *"Ehyeh asher ehyeh,"* as "I will be what I will be."[86] The syllogism is now complete. God's nature is to become, to "change ways;" humans are made in the image of God; therefore human nature is to "change ways."

Without crediting Bloch, who stood firmly in the philosophical traditions he most resolutely opposed, Strauss also translates the Sinaitic revelation as "I shall be what I shall be."[87] Why does Strauss prefer this translation to its traditional alternative, which has God say "I am who I am"?[88] Because the traditional translation of God's self-revelation, according to Strauss, misconceives the passage in question as offering "the metaphysics of Exodus." Strauss goes on to say that "It is indeed the fundamental biblical statement about the biblical God, but we hesitate to call it metaphysical, since the notion of *physis* [nature] is alien to the Bible."[89] In *Natural Right and History,* Strauss claims that "The Old Testament, whose basic premise may be said to be the implicit rejection of philosophy, does not know 'nature': the Hebrew term for 'nature' is unknown in the Hebrew Bible."[90] In his essay on "Natural Law," Strauss says that "The notion of nature is not coeval with human thought; hence there is no natural law teaching, for instance, in the Old Testament."[91]

When he says that the Hebrew Bible lacked a notion of nature, what he means is that the Bible lacked philosophy. "Philosophy as distinguished from myth came into being when nature was discovered, or the first philosopher was the first man who discovered nature."[92] Lacking nature and hence philosophy, Biblical ethics must be rooted not in knowledge but in obedience, submission to God's command. "According to the Bible, the beginning of wisdom is fear of the Lord; according

to the Greek philosophers, the beginning of wisdom is wonder."[93]

Strauss's distinctions between fear and wonder, obedience and
knowledge, eliminate in their rigid and simplistic dualism the
very space in which the idea of natural law should be located.
To reopen that space, I have sketched in this section some of
the complex ways in which creation stories have made conceptions of nature and of human nature available to moral experience and to political thought. Strauss to the contrary notwithstanding, examples of these conceptions are to be found in the
Hebrew Bible[94] and also in the New Testament.[95]

Yet Strauss's mistake, in associating natural law exclusively
with "Athens" and not at all with "Jerusalem," is not to be corrected simply by reversing the poles. The point is to understand the idea, not to assign it to one side or the other of a
quarrel between Hebraism and Hellenism, ancients and moderns, or Catholics and Protestants. Yet if we are to understand
the idea, we must see how it has felt the imprint of these oppositions.

VI. Beyond "Creation Science"

The importance of creation stories is evidenced by recent attempts by certain religious groups to require that the biblical
account of human origins be taught in the public schools. To
many of those who have contested these efforts, or who view
them with distaste and concern, renewed enthusiasm for creation stories confirms a view of religion that places it squarely in
the realm of the irrational, indeed of the antirational. In this
view, fundamentalist advocacy of so-called creation science exemplifies three of religion's most dangerous attributes: its refusal to accept a rational and empirical attitude toward nature,
its credulous and unquestioning submission to supposed divine
commands, and its readiness to impose those commands on
others.

Whether these are truly attributes of religion (or of the biblical religions), and whether the religious interest in creation
stories furthers these tendencies, are questions that cannot be
answered without careful attention to the natural law tradition.

And when that attention is paid, the complexity of any adequate answer to such questions becomes apparent.

The aspiration toward natural law, as I conceive it, has always regarded nature as an educator as well as a promulgator. Natural right has served as a means not of concealing but of exposing the lines of justification; natural command has tried not to suppress but to evoke and express fundamental moral experience. In these respects, natural law represents an attitude toward nature that is as opposed as the scientific attitude, although in different ways and for different reasons, to a view of nature that enlists it in the service of arbitrary and unquestionable commands.

Yet the origins of the idea of natural law reflect the fact that religion has by no means uniformly and unambiguously adopted the attitude toward nature that this idea represents. The biblical faiths, in any event, have stamped the idea of natural law with views of nature that seek to circumscribe or defeat it as the opposite of law, grace, or redemption.

Natural law provides a context within which the normative meanings of creation stories may be located. Such stories may serve to unite natural right and natural command in subtle and instructive ways, as the history of the *imago dei* argument attests. Or they may serve to entrench commands, as in *Bradwell v. Illinois,* or to strip nature of its legitimating functions, as in some Gnostic myths.

If today's creation science hearkens a return to *Bradwell,* with its fixed and unquestionable roles within which human lives are to be immured, then we must oppose this "science." Creation stories as a genre, however, are not forever wedded to pseudoscience, or committed to the ratification of predetermined commandments. At their most instructive, they provide ethical naturalism a narrative form whose genius is precisely its capacity to avoid the rigidity and simplification to which naturalistic ethics might otherwise be subject. Stories that tell of cosmic creativity, of fundamental changes in the order of the world, of the breath of life breathed into all the dwellers in the sublunary sphere, will never be exhausted by those interpreters who see in them only a way to fix us in immutable roles according to the "law of the Creator."

NOTES

I am indebted to my teacher Mordecai Finley, to my colleague Barry Seltser, and to the University of Southern California's Faculty Research and Innovation Fund.

1. See *McLean v. Arkansas Board of Education,* 529 F. Supp. 1255 (E. D. Ark. 1982), and *Aguillard v. Edwards,* 765 F. 2d 1251 (5th Cir. 1985), invalidating under the establishment clause state statutes requiring "balanced treatment" of "creation-science" and "evolution-science."

2. Leo Strauss, *Natural Right and History* (Chicago: University of Chicago Press, 1953).

3. Compare Alasdair MacIntyre, *After Virtue* (Notre Dame: University of Notre Dame Press, 1981), chaps. 1–5, to Strauss, *Natural Right,* chaps. 1, 5, 6. Compare MacIntyre's criticism of the fact/value distinction and discussion of Weber in *After Virtue,* chaps. 7, 8, to chap. 2 of *Natural Right.* Compare MacIntyre's treatment of the virtues, chaps. 9–18, esp. chap. 17, to Strauss's discussion of classical natural right in chap. 4 of *Natural Right.* Interestingly, MacIntyre does not cite Strauss.

4. Certain forms of utilitarian thought also exhibit the consequences of relying entirely upon natural right, at the expense of natural command. That is, utilitarian thought sometimes builds a complex argument that can endorse political institutions and adjudicate within such institutions, but at the same time loses contact with ordinary moral experience. In my terms, utilitarianism is an ethical theory that is built on the justificatory moment but not on the presentational moment; it fails to present the ethical as a subject-matter.

5. Jer. 31:31–33; cf., Heb. 8:10. All biblical quotations in this chapter are from the Revised Standard Version (RSV).

6. Rom. 2:14–15.

7. For a summary and critique of the conventional wisdom that denies that the Hebrew Bible embodies any notion of natural law, see John Barton, "Natural Law and Poetic Justice in the Old Testament," *Theological Studies* 30 (1979): 1, and Douglas A. Knight, "Cosmogony and Order in the Hebrew Tradition," in *Cosmogony and Ethical Order,* eds. Robin Lovin and Frank Reynolds (Chicago: University of Chicago Press, 1985), p. 133. For a comparable discussion of the popular notion that Pauline and Reformation thought excludes natural law, see John T. McNeill, "Natural Law in the Teaching of the Reformers," *Journal of Religion* 26 (1946): 168;

idem, "Natural Law in the Thought of Luther," *Church History* 10 (1941): 211; and the extremely thoughtful essay by David Little, "Calvin and the Prospects for a Christian Theory of Natural Law," in *Norm and Context in Christian Ethics,* eds. Gene Outka and Paul Ramsey (New York: Scribners, 1968), pp. 175–97.

8. Qu'ran 7:54, quoted in Sheryl L. Burkhalter, "Completion in Continuity: Cosmogony and Ethics in Islam," in eds. Lovin and Reynolds, *Cosmogony and Ethical Order,* p. 228.

9. Certain verses in the Psalms, however, draw a connection between God's law and "the light of God's countenance." Psalm 4, verse 7: "There are many who say, 'O that we might see some good! Lift up the light of thy countenance upon us, O Lord!" Consider these lines from Psalm 119 (verses 131, 134-5): "With open mouth I pant, because I long for thy commandments. . . . Redeem me from man's oppression, that I may keep thy precepts. Make thy face shine upon thy servant, and teach me thy statutes." Here God's "commandments," "precepts," or "statutes" are associated with God's face. On the one hand, God's face is too holy and terrible to be seen directly (Is. 6:2, Ex. 4:5–6, 1 Kings 19:13); but on the other hand, insofar as we are made "in the image and likeness of God" (the *imago dei* argument discussed in section V.B. of this chapter), we are able to "see some good" when "the light of God's countenance" illuminates us.

10. Fritz Meier, "The Transformation of Man in Mystical Islam," in *Man and Transformation,* ed. Joseph Campbell (Princeton: Princeton University Press, 1980), p. 37. Moojan Momen, *An Introduction to Shi'i Islam: The History and Doctrines of Twelver Shi'ism* (New Haven: Yale University Press, 1985).

11. Robert Cover, "Nomos and Narrative," *Harv. L. Rev.* 97 (1983): 4, 11. In "Nomos and Narrative" and in several of his last essays, including "Bringing the Messiah Through Law" (published in this volume), Professor Cover developed a natural law theory that associates law with diffused communal narratives, and contrasted that theory with an Austinian positivism that associates law with centralized commands. In "Meaning and Ending," *Yale L. J.* 96 (1987): forthcoming, I discuss Professor Cover's ideas about the contribution that narratives make to the ethical naturalism in natural law. "Meaning and Ending" considers natural law from the vantage-point of stories about endings, while the present essay considers natural law from the vantage-point of stories about beginnings.

12. *The Babylonian Talmud: Seder Nezikin,* vol. 1 (London: Soncino Press, 1935), Baba Mezia 59b, pp. 352–53.

13. Job 31:13-15

14. Job 31:38-40. For discussion of these and other examples of ethical appeals to a natural order in the Hebrew Bible, see Barton, "Natural Law and Poetic Justice," and Knight, "Cosmogony and Order."

15. For a major effort to draw a sharp distinction between Hebraic and Hellenic conceptions of human nature, at the expense of the latter, see Reinhold Niebuhr, *The Nature and Destiny of Man,* 2 vols. (New York: Scribners, 1964).

16. Aristotle, *Nicomachean Ethics,* V.7,1134b18-1135a5.

17. Aristotle, *Politics,* 1.2,1252b27-1253a3.

18. On teleology as a form of perfectibility, see John Passmore, *The Perfectibility of Man* (New York: Scribners, 1970), p. 46ff.

19. John Finnis, *Natural Law and Natural Rights* (Oxford: Clarendon Press, 1980), p. 103.

20. C. G. Jung, "Transformation Symbolism in the Mass," in *The Mysteries,* ed. Joseph Campbell (Princeton: Princeton University Press, 1955), p. 279.

21. Ibid., pp. 311–12.

22. Quoted in Hans Jonas, *The Gnostic Religion* (Boston: Beacon Press, 1963), p. 45.

23. Michael Moore, "A Natural Law Theory of Interpretation," *So. Calif. L. Rev.* 58 (1985): 277, 283–86.

24. Ibid., p. 286.

25. Michael Moore, "Moral Reality," *Wisconsin L. Rev.* 1982 (1982): 1061, 1144.

26. Ibid., p. 1146.

27. Ronald Dworkin, "Hard Cases," in *Taking Rights Seriously* (Cambridge: Harvard University Press, 1977), pp. 81–130.

28. Ronald Dworkin, " 'Natural' Law Revisited," *Univ. of Florida L. Rev.* 34 (1982): 165.

29. Ibid.

30. Ibid., p. 185.

31. Michael Moore has discussed Dworkin's conventionalism in "Metaphysics, Epistemology, and Legal Theory," *So. Calif. L. Rev.* 60 (1987): 453.

32. "A realist must deny . . . any identification of her theory of justification with her theory of truth. For what is distinctive about realism is the belief that propositions can be true even if we, at present, have no rational grounds for believing or asserting that they are true." Ibid., p. 455.

33. Finnis, *Natural Law and Natural Rights,* especially parts one (pp. 3–55) and three (pp. 371–413); John Finnis, *Fundamentals of Ethics* (Oxford: Oxford University Press, 1983), especially chaps. 1, 2 (pp. 1–55).

34. See Germain Grisez, "The First Principle of Practical Reason: A Commentary on the *Summa theologiae*, 1–2, Question 94, Article 2," *Natural Law Forum* 10 (1965): 168.

35. Finnis, *Fundamentals of Ethics*, chap. 1.

36. Finnis, *Natural Law and Natural Rights*, pp. 29–31.

37. Finnis (*Fundamentals of Ethics*, p. 7), like Moore, denatures *physis* by regarding it as equivalent to objectivity or moral reality.

38. For Augustine's ethics of love, see *De Doctrina Christiana (On Christian Instruction)* in *The Nicene and Post-Nicene Fathers*, ed. Philip Schaff, vol. 4 (Grand Rapids: Eerdmans, 1956), esp. pp. 38–57. I understand Finnis's account of practical reasoning to distinguish itself from Augustine's ethics of love in two respects. First, the hierarchical ordering that is essential to Augustine's *ordo amoris* violates Finnis's principle of the equal priority of all basic human goods. Second, Augustine's view that love is the common theme of all faith and ethics violates Finnis's principle of the mutual irreducibility of the basic human goods.

39. See Martin Buber, "What is Man?" in his *Between Man and Man* (New York: Macmillan, 1965), p. 119.

40. *Bradwell v. The State [Illinois]*, 83 U.S. (16 Wall.) 130 (1873), at 141 (Bradley, J., concurring in the judgment).

41. The best available work on the ethical meanings of cosmogonic stories is Lovin and Reynolds, eds. *Cosmogony and Ethical Order*. Jung and his followers also have studied creation myths with a view to recovering their moral meanings. See e.g., Erich Neumann, *The Origins and History of Consciousness* (Princeton: Princeton University Press, 1973), pp. 5–127. See also G. van der Leeuw, "Primordial Time and Final Time," in *Man and Time*, ed. Joseph Campbell (Princeton: Princeton University Press, 1983), pp. 324–50.

42. Among Eliade's many books, see Mircea Eliade, *The Myth of the Eternal Return: Or, Cosmos and History* (Princeton: Princeton University Press, 1971), idem, *The Sacred and the Profane* (New York: Harcourt, Brace and World, 1959), and idem, *Patterns in Comparative Religion* (New York: Meridian, 1958).

43. See generally Ninian Smart, *The Phenomenon of Religion* (New York: Seabury Press, 1973); G. van der Leeuw, *Religion in Essence and Manifestation* (Princeton: Princeton University Press, 1986).

44. Paul Ricoeur, *The Symbolism of Evil* (Boston: Beacon Press, 1967).

45. Ibid., p. 9.

46. Ibid., pp. 356–57.

47. Ibid., p. 357.

48. Karl Barth, *Church Dogmatics*, vol. 2, t. 2, *The Doctrine of God* (Edinburgh: T. and T. Clark, 1957), p. 532.

49. Ibid., p. 533.

50. Kenneth Goodpaster, "On Moral Considerability," *Journal of Philosophy* 75 (1978): 308–25.

51. The outstanding text here is Mary Douglas, *Purity and Danger* (London: Routledge and Kegan Paul, 1966). See especially chap. 3, "The Abominations of Leviticus." Edmund Leach, *Genesis as Myth and Other Essays* (London: Jonathan Cape, 1969), pp. 7–83. Leach "decodes" the mythic stories of Genesis, to retrieve their normative messages.

52. On the *coincidentia oppositorum* and the quest for acosmic union, see Mircea Eliade, *The Two and the One* (New York: Harper and Row, 1965); Victor Turner, "Liminality and Communitas," in his *The Ritual Process* (Ithaca: Cornell University Press, 1969), chap. 3.

53. " 'There is one thing that the Pope [John Paul II] has against the modern world, and that is that it has forgotten about the first two chapters of the Book of Genesis,' said Joaquin Navarro Valls, a Spanish layman who is the chief Vatican spokesman. 'The world has forgotten that human beings get their life and their dignity not from themselves, but from God.' " E. J. Dionne, Jr., "As Pope Confronts the Dissenters, Whose Catholicism Will Prevail?" *New York Times,* 23 December 1986, pp. Al, A8.

54. Gen. 9:6.

55. Gen. 9:2–3; 1:27–30.

56. Gen. 1:26; cf. 3:22, 11:7.

57. Gen. 1:27.

58. See Saint Augustine, *De Trinitate* (On the Trinity), in *The Nicene and Post-Nicene Fathers,* vol. 3, pp. 1–228; especially bk. 1, chap. 4; bk. 8, chaps. 8–10; bk. 10, chaps. 10–12. See also John Macmurray, *Persons in Relation* (Atlantic Highlands, N.J.: Humanities Press, 1979), pp. 127–46; Ronald Garet, "Communality and Existence: The Rights of Groups," *So. Calif. L. Rev.* 56 (1983): 1001.

59. I claim only that the cosmogonic context helps make sense out of the natural-law claims of the Declaration, not that this context was an element of Jefferson's authorial intentions or of the Declaration's meaning to any of its many audiences.

60. See Margaret Jane Radin, "Market-Inalienability," *Harv. L. Rev.* 100 (1987): forthcoming, and works therein cited.

61. 1 Kings 21:1–4. This passage is one of two that Leo Strauss uses as epigraphs to Strauss, *Natural Right.*

62. Emil Brunner, "Nature and Grace," in *Natural Theology,* ed. John Baillie (London: Centenary Press, 1946), p. 30.

63. Ibid., p. 36. On the question of whether the Reformers should be regarded as embodying a notion of natural law, see McNeill, "Natural Law in the Teaching of the Reformers"; idem, "Natural Law

in the Thought of Luther"; Little, "Calvin and the Prospects for a Christian Theory of Natural Law."

64. Brunner, "Nature and Grace," p. 59.

65. Karl Barth, "Nein!" ("No!"), in ed. Baillie *Natural Theology*, p. 71.

66. For example, see Karl Barth, *Church Dogmatics* vol. 3, t. 4, *The Doctrine of Creation* (Edinburgh: T. and T. Clark, 1961), p. 22. See Louis C. Midgley, "Karl Barth and Moral Natural Law: The Anatomy of a Debate," *Natural Law Forum* 13 (1968): 108.

67. Barth, "Nein!," in *Natural Theology*, p. 86.

68. Barth, *Church Dogmatics* vol. 3, t. 4, *Doctrine of Creation*, p. 133.

69. Ibid., p. 140.

70. Ibid., p. 170.

71. Ibid., p. 165.

72. Ibid., p. 163.

73. Ibid., pp. 18–22.

74. Barth departs from the tradition in several respects. He distinguishes himself from Roman Catholic teachings by holding the parental aspect of marriage subordinate to the conjugal and by rejecting the celibate religious orders. He distinguishes himself from Luther by carefully avoiding the latter's tendency to treat marriage as an obligation.

75. Barth, "Nein!," in *Natural Theology*, pp. 74–75.

76. Leo Strauss, "Jerusalem and Athens," in *Studies in Platonic Political Philosophy* (Chicago: University of Chicago Press, 1983), pp. 152–53.

77. *Midrash Rabbah: Deuteronomy* (London: Soncino Press, 1939), p. 92.

78. Paul Cantor, *Romantic Man: Creature and Creator* (Cambridge: Cambridge University Press, 1984).

79. Jonas, "Epilogue: Gnosticism, Nihilism, and Existentialism," in his *The Gnostic Religion*.

80. For example, see Friedrich Nietzsche, *Thus Spoke Zarathustra*, trans. Walter Kaufmann (New York: Penguin, 1978), p. 12 ("Zarathustra's Prologue") and p. 115 ("On Self-Overcoming"): *"I teach you the overman.* Man is something that shall be overcome. What have you done to overcome him?" "And life itself confided this secret to me: 'Behold,' it said, "I am *that which must always overcome itself."*

81. Jean-Paul Sartre, "Existentialism is a Humanism," in *Existentialism from Dostoevsky to Sartre,* ed. Walter Kauffman (Cleveland: World Publishing, 1956), pp. 290–91.

82. José Ortega y Gasset, "Man Has No Nature," in ed. Kaufmann, *Existentialism from Dostoevsky to Sartre*, pp. 154–55, 157. The selection is from Ortega's *History as a System* (1961).

83. For a general introduction to Bloch's thought, see Paul R. Mendes-Flohr, " 'To Brush History against the Grain': The Eschatology of

the Frankfurt School and Ernst Bloch," *Journal of the American Academy of Religion* 51 (1983): 631. Bloch's major work on the natural law, *Naturrecht und menschliche Würde,* has recently been translated into English: Ernst Bloch, *Natural Law and Human Dignity,* trans. Dennis Schmidt (Cambridge: MIT Press, 1986).

84. Quoted in Mendes-Flohr, " 'To Brush History Against the Grain,' " p. 643.

85. Strauss, "Jerusalem and Athens," pp. 152–53.

86. Ernst Bloch, *A Philosophy of the Future* (New York: Herder and Herder, 1970), p. 130.

87. Strauss, "Jerusalem and Athens," p. 162. Strauss presents this element of his argument substantially after he has apparently concluded his discussion of the Creation. Thus the reader is forced, as one always is when reading Strauss, to guess just what message Strauss was trying to hide by bisecting the syllogism.

88. The Hebrew *ehyeh* is the first person singular of the verb "to be." Tense is not specified. Hence *Ehyeh asher ehyeh* is variously translated "I am who [or what] I am," "I will be who I will be," or even "I am who I will be," or "I will be who I am." See W. Gunther Plaut, et. al. *The Torah: A Modern Commentary* (New York: Union of American Hebrew Congregations, 1981), pp. 404–6.

89. Strauss, "Jerusalem and Athens," p. 162.

90. Strauss, *Natural Right,* p. 81.

91. Leo Strauss, "Natural Law," in *Studies in Platonic Political Philosophy* (Chicago: University of Chicago Press, 1983), p. 138.

92. Strauss, *Natural Right,* p. 82.

93. Strauss, "Jerusalem and Athens," p. 149.

94. Knight, "Cosmogony and Order"; Barton, "Natural Law."

95. Hans Dieter Betz, "Cosmogony and Ethics in the Sermon on the Mount," in eds. Lovin and Reynolds *Cosmogony and Ethical Order,* p. 158.

12

POLITICS AND RELIGION IN AMERICA: THE ENIGMA OF PLURALISM

JOHN LADD

One of the central issues in the relationship of politics and religion is the status, scope, and limits of religious toleration. Although the principle of toleration is generally taken for granted
by most Americans in an almost ritualistic fashion, they tend to
ignore the controversial character of the principle itself: what
it means, how it is to be applied, what its limitations are, and,
in general, how it is grounded in moral and political philosophy. When asked about the moral basis of toleration the general answer is that toleration comes from pluralism, and ours is
a pluralistic society. Q.E.D. It is obvious, however, that the
magical quality of the word "pluralism" does nothing to advance the argument philosophically. The purpose of this essay
will be not simply to defend pluralism but to explain what it
might mean. I shall begin with the notion of toleration.

Perhaps the best way to approach the notion of toleration is
to ask what problems the principle of toleration is supposed to
solve. As a philosophical enterprise, our task will be to identify
and sort out these problems as a propaedeutic to a further inquiry into the concept of toleration and indirectly of pluralism.
This essay will therefore be more concerned with raising questions than with providing answers. My conclusions, such as they
are, will be highly speculative and controversial. As such, they

are intended to be provocative rather than definitive. In discussing concepts like toleration, I shall be primarily concerned with ethical issues and shall deliberately avoid legal and constitutional issues, which are authoritatively and lucidly presented by David Richards elsewhere in this volume.

I. POLITICS AND RELIGION: AN AMBIVALENT RELATIONSHIP

It will be useful to begin our inquiry with a few general comments on the relation between politics and religion. It is commonplace that throughout Western history this relationship has been a rocky one; sometimes politics has won out and more often religion has had the final say. As far as toleration is concerned, when we reflect on the great number of holy wars that have been fought and are still being fought in the name of the Almighty (or Allah) against unbelievers or infidels, one might easily come to wonder whether the concept of religious toleration is not, indeed, an oxymoron, that is, a contradiction in terms. A religious faith, by its very nature, might be thought to require intolerance of other religions as well as of atheism.

Admittedly, some religions do have some principle or other of tolerance, of humanity, love and mercy, built into them. In this regard, one cannot deny that the Judeo-Christian Deity is not always a jealous God and a God of Vengeance but sometimes also a God of Love. Different sects have different views of the matter.

Nevertheless, even when a religion supports toleration, it does so on its own terms, so to speak. It is never toleration *tout court*— without strings attached. The religion that preaches and practices tolerance of other religions always reserves the right to be the final arbiter of what is to be tolerated. This point is well illustrated in the following quotation from Saint Thomas Aquinas:

> Human government derives from divine government and should imitate it. Now God, in His omnipotence and sovereign goodness, sometimes permits evil to be done in the world, though he could prevent it; lest, by so doing, a greater good be destroyed or even greater evils might follow. So also in human government those who are in power, rightly permit certain evils lest some good be brought to nothing or perhaps greater evils take place. . . .

Therefore, though infidels may sin by their rites, they are to be tolerated either because of some good that comes from them or because of some evil which is avoided. Thus, from the fact that the Jews observe their rites, in which our own faith was foreshadowed of old, there derives this benefit that we obtain testimony to our faith . . . so they are tolerated in their rites. But the rites of other infidels, which have nothing of truth or usefulness in them, are to be in no-wise tolerated; except perhaps to avoid some evil, such as avoidance of scandal or the discord that might arise from their suppression.[1]

II. Religion in America

In the present essay, I shall be chiefly concerned with religion and politics in the United States. My approach, however, will be philosophical rather than historical or sociological. I shall focus on the American tradition, as embodied in our private and political life as well as in our law, because it is an especially challenging one for a philosopher, inasmuch as it combines two ostensibly incompatible strands, namely, the general affirmation of religion as a necessary foundation of politics and morality along with the equally strong affirmation of the separation of church and state, exemplified by the disestablishment of religion prescribed in the First Amendment.

To observers from abroad and to almost anyone brought up on classical Western political philosophy, this simultaneous combination of religiousness and depoliticization of religion is a stumbling block. On the face of it, it seems contradictory and hypocritical, or at least paradoxical. On the other hand, many writers, notably Tocqueville, have tried to tie these two strands together. In what follows, I shall try to show a way around the paradox.

In order to put the general issue of politics and religion in America in context, I simply cite some well-known facts. First, Americans are more explicitly religious than their counterparts in other parts of the civilized world. Thus, public opinion polls attest to the fact that in contrast, say, to continental Europe, four times as many people in the United States attend church and some 90 percent of the population claim to believe in God.[2] This reverence for religion is found not only among the general populace, but it is also part of the American tradition going back to the Founding Fathers. It is affirmed in George Washington's Farewell Address and is repeated by all of our presidents down through Ronald Reagan, as well as by many other leaders. All of them have repeated over and over again that the American nation is a religious nation "under God."

Along with the high value placed on religion is the fact that our society embraces a remarkably large number of religious groups: easily more than two hundred different sects, and the number is growing every day. Pluralism is the predominant theme of the sociology of religion in the United States. This pluralism, which should be called *de facto* or descriptive pluralism, may provide a partial historical or sociological explanation of the popular acceptance of the principle of toleration. Americans have become accustomed to religious differences and are therefore more tolerant of them. The explanation might, of course, go the other way around, namely, that toleration leads to the multiplication of religious groups. No doubt there is some truth in both explanations. Be that as it may, it is important to observe that no single religious group (sect) commands the majority of the population nation-wide, although in some states, such as Rhode Island, the majority of the population belongs to one group, Roman Catholic. One is tempted to suppose that where every religious group is in the minority, there is likely to be more toleration than where one of them is in the majority. Some historical evidence supports this hypothesis, for in numerous instances the religion of the dominant majority has been oppressive.

III. Conflicts due to Religion

Returning to our original question about toleration: How does the issue of toleration arise in a society such as ours—or how might it arise? How does it become a problem? The obvious answer is that toleration becomes an issue when there are critical conflicts between religious groups or between religious groups and government (or society). In order to gain a deeper understanding of what is involved in the concept of toleration, it will be worthwhile to ask what some of these conflicts are and where they come from.

First, there are traditional differences and disagreements over the particulars of religious practice, religious doctrine and rites, where one party adheres to an article of faith that the other party rejects. European history provides what Hegel would call a slaughter-bench of religious divisions of this sort, e.g., over the Divine Presence in Holy Communion, baptism, creation and salvation. Conflicts over purely religious matters of this sort are, however, relatively uncommon in the United States, where the usual way of dealing with them is to split off from the old group and to establish a new one. Basically, theological conflicts of this kind are not taken as seriously in the United States as they once were and still are elsewhere. Indeed, I suspect that the average American would have difficulty in identifying the theological differences between various well-known sects such as Catholicism, Lutheranism, Methodism, Unitarianism and even Judaism; all that he would be able to do is to identify the different kinds of religious ceremonies practiced by each group. The American political tradition regarding purely religious differences has remained substantially the same as Locke's, namely, that it is none of the state's business to meddle in these purely religious matters. Toleration, or if you wish, religious liberty, is the word of the day.

More prominent differences between religious bodies occur over the regulation of conduct, particularly in the sexual sphere (abortion, divorce, homosexuality, pornography, intermarriage), in education, and in the distribution of resources (e.g., aid to parochial schools). These differences play themselves out in the political arena, because they involve matters of legislation and judicial decision. Here, of course, is where the principle of toleration comes under fire or, perhaps more correctly, becomes a matter of tug-of-war between opposing parties. The principle of toleration often seems to be lost and the principle of separation of church and state is bent to serve the purposes of particular religious bodies.

In these conflicts, the aim of one party is to exploit the resources of the state for its own (divinely sanctioned) ends, while the aim of the other party is to resist this use of the state's resources and to use them instead for its own ends. In this way religious conflicts turn into political conflicts. All of this is so familiar that it hardly seems worthwhile mentioning except to bring out the need for differentiating the kinds of conflict that challenge or support, as the case may be, the principle of toleration.

IV. Different Aspects of Religion

At this juncture, we must turn more directly to a discussion of religion. The concept of religion as it enters into American life, society, and politics is a complicated one with many different aspects. At risk of oversimplification, it is possible to identify three of these aspects, each of which represents a different way of categorizing religion: First, it can be regarded as a social institution; second, it can be regarded as a set of ecclesiastical organizations (churches); and third it can be regarded as a body of doctrines of a particular kind. Careful attention to the differences between these three aspects of religion is necessary if we want to avoid confusion and arguing at cross-purposes in our examination of ethical issues in the relationship between politics and religion. For it should be obvious that the issues that concern us in this essay, e.g., issues relating to toleration, are quite different as we move from one of these aspects of religion to another.

V. Religion as a Social Institution

In considering religion in America we must start with it as a social institution. Tocqueville says "Religion is the first political institution [of American society]"[3] His theory was that religion acted as a counterforce to "purify, control and restrain that excessive and exclusive taste for well-being," the "pursuit of prosperity," and the thinking of oneself that grows out of equality. It provides a sort of social unifying force. (The details are unimportant.)

Going beyond Tocqueville, one must note the function that religion plays in community life by providing churches as unifying social groups. In the small communities from which the American ethos springs, local churches in some ways play a role that is similar to the role of the extended family in other societies. The local church provides a social bond between individuals, a focus for their activities, and a source of identification. In typical small communities throughout the United

States, of which the fictitious Lake Wobegon would be an example, the natives are identified by their church affiliations: the Smiths are Catholics, the Joneses are Congos, the Browns are Methodists, the Johnsons are Lutheran, and so on. Thus, simply for their social role in American life, if for nothing else, religions are important to Americans in a way that they generally are not in other societies. An attack, or imagined attack on religion, therefore, is very much like an attack on the family or other social institutions such as schools or hospitals.

The social role of religion, or perhaps better of religions, in community life provides the backdrop of political life and explains why a politician is committing political suicide if he comes out against religion. This social fact may be the substance of religious utterances of public officials that otherwise would seem vacuous, if not silly. Considering the other fact, namely, that there are usually a number of different churches, religions or sects, present in each community, it is easy to understand why, for practical reasons, Americans find tolerance of different religions to be reasonable and desirable. One's neighbors may belong to different churches from oneself, but that is unimportant when it comes to doing business with them or associating with them. Good neighbors are, and are expected to be, tolerant of each other even though their religious loyalties are different. Just as family life ought to be kept out of politics, so church life also ought to be kept out of politics. Everyone is better off if it is.

Even if the picture that I have drawn is not entirely accurate, the emphasis on social role brings out an important aspect of religion in America that tends to escape the theorist and even the lawyer, despite the fact that it is an important part of the background of American politics. In the other two aspects of religion, religious and political conflicts are more discernible and intransigent.

VI. RELIGIONS AS ORGANIZATIONS

Most religious groups in this country, although not all, are also organized bodies. That is, they have an organizational structure providing a more or less formal governance with established procedures and rules, an authority structure, a specification of membership, and a budget. In this sense, religions (sects, churches)—large and small, national and local—may be categorized as voluntary associations.[4] As organizations, these religious groups have the usual interest that organizations have, such as organizational integrity, independence, and economic viability. Their special interests often place them in competition with other religious groups, with other kinds of voluntary associations and with the state. Money, power and prestige are as much a sine qua non for religious organizations as they are for other voluntary organizations, such as businesses or labor unions.

One could plausibly argue that many, if not most, clashes between religious groups and between religious groups and the government are organizational conflicts, that is, conflicts of interest, and as such arise out of competitive struggles for power, money and prestige. They may draw on religious doctrines to promote and defend their claims but, to borrow a phrase from Gramsci, the doctrines provide only the form, while the content comes from struggles over conflicts of interest. Surely the conflicts between the popes and emperors in the Middle Ages were, in the ultimate analysis, conflicts of interest, power struggles to determine who was to have the upper hand.

VII. Religion as Doctrine

In the final analysis, the real stumbling block to toleration in the relationship between politics and religion comes, as I have suggested, from religious doctrine. Although it is obviously dangerous to make sweeping statements about religious doctrine in general, we must start off with the assumption that religion always involves, in one way or another, the belief in God, that is, the belief in the existence of a transcendental, supernatural being who is the source of morality and goodness. Admittedly, some authors, for purposes of their own, stretch the notion of religion to encompass ultimate value-systems of every sort, that is, ideologies, but for our purposes this general use of "religion" obscures what I take to be the critical aspect of the problem with which we are concerned, namely, the implications of peculiarly transcendental doctrines for the notion of toleration and for the relationship between politics and religion in general.

In characterizing religious doctrine, I shall try to identify features that apply to the largest variety of religious groups, at least in the United States. These features are intended to apply across the board to all religions, in the designated sense, and can be used to distinguish religious associations from other kinds of associations and religious value-systems from other kinds of value-systems.

First, religion in the sense of doctrine represents, in one way or another, an ultimate and absolute type of value-system. As such, it claims superiority over all other value-systems and is ultimate and final in the sense that there is nothing beyond it on which its value rests or from which it is derived. In sum, every religion claims *primacy*.

Second, as I have already emphasized, religious value-systems presuppose and are based on beliefs about a transcendental reality, a diety. Thus, religions presuppose the existence of another, super-sensible reality, over and beyond the ordinary world that we live in, and they hold that this super-sensible reality provides the foundation of values, morality and ethics in general. It is unnecessary to mention further theological and philosophical ramifications concerning such subtleties as the exact ontological relationship between values and, say, God's will. It suffices to observe that religions hypothesize some sort of necessary relationship between a transcendental Being and values and take this transcendental Being to be the basis of morality and values. Their derivation from a transcendental Being confers on morality and values a peculiarly strong kind of peremptoriness, inviolateness and sacredness. This transcendental basis makes their claim to primacy uniquely powerful.

The appeal to the Deity as the foundation of morality and politics is, accordingly, a very forceful appeal. The transcendental basis makes the values proceeding from it more exigent in a number of ways, including emotionally and psychologically, than values that do not have a transcendental basis, e.g., the values of an atheist or naturalist. For someone who does not share the beliefs on which a theological morality is grounded, it is easy to underestimate their power in the life of believers— their authority to command renunciation, sacrifice, and martyrdom, as well as often to justify inhumanity towards other human beings in the service of a vengeful God.[5]

It is important to recognize that the transcendental basis of religion is used not only to support the claims of religious value-systems to primacy in the sense of claiming priority over ordinary wordly values, but also to support the demand that ordinary moral norms sometimes be superseded or cancelled entirely. Characteristically, religious doctrine is used to rationalize the *suspension* of the rules of ordinary morality, for example, in relation to violence or deception, in favor of values based on religious belief, say, a Divine Command. Despite frequent denial, I find that the notion of the "suspension of the ethical," introduced by Kierkegaard to justify the sacrifice of Isaac, is paralleled in other religious writers who are less extreme, including Thomas Aquinas. Inquisitions, *autos da fe,* Crusades and terrorism are not necessarily doctrinal aberrations; rather they may be rational corollaries of a particular religious doctrine. The point that I am making is that, when the chips are down, there is a built-in element of fanaticism in every religion.

A third element of religion conceived as religious doctrine is what may be called the presupposition of special and generally limited access to moral and religious truths. These truths are accessible only to the faithful, the believers, and not to others. Religions differ in their views about the conditions of access, which may be defined not only in theoretical but also in practical terms, depending on such things as the robustness of a faith. A fairly typical way of handling access to religious truth is to prescribe the acceptance of an authority of some kind or other, such as a book, an institution, a priest or a prophet, as a necessary and perhaps sufficient means of access to the Deity and to the truths of religion and ethics.

Although some theologians, notably Roman Catholic adherents of the doctrine of Natural Law, *claim* that the 'truths' in question are accessible to any rational person, their practice does not jibe with the theory; for they constantly resort to authorities of one kind or another to supply the correct interpretation of the Natural Law. As I have argued elsewhere, the anti-abortionist claim that life begins at the moment of conception is, in fact, a religious doctrine that presupposes particular religious premises whose acceptance is contingent on membership in a specific religious group.[6] In general, then, I argue that owing to its transcendental basis, the notion of limited access, e.g., access only to the faithful, is built if not theoretically at least practically into the concept of religion, all claims to the contrary not withstanding.

The limited-access presupposition means that in fact, even if not in theory, all religious doctrines are addressed to *limited audiences,* to use Chaim Perelman's terms.[7] The barriers to universal access are of many kinds: Some are part of the doctrine, such as having faith, being a priest or being among the elect, and some are the result of the way a religious doctrine is established and disseminated. With regard to the latter, it is not a coincidence that different religions tend to be associated with different cultures, languages, and geographic areas. Religions tend to be local and ethnocentric. A religion is a "live option," to use William James's term, generally only for people who live where the religion is alive; for those living outside and under different circumstances, the religion in question tends to have little or no meaning.

Fourthly and finally, religious doctrines of every kind draw a line between insiders and outsiders, the faithful and others. More often than not, the distinction is sacramental in addition to being factual. Those who have access are insiders, those who do not have it are outsiders. Doctrine maintains that certain privileges, such as salvation, as well as certain obligations, such as fasting, pertain only to insiders and not to outsiders.

VIII. Outsiders

In addition to defining conditions of membership, privileges and obligations, every religious doctrine typically has a theory of how insiders are to treat outsiders, including those who subscribe to different and contrary doctrines. Often a double moral standard applies to insiders and outsiders; thus, insiders may be permitted by doctrine to exercise violence on outsiders—or even to burn them as heretics and infidels. The quotation from Aquinas illustrates an insider's view of how to treat outsiders.

Obviously many will disagree with this account of religious doctrine. They might object that it is too simple-minded. Some might say that it applies only to fanatical religions. Others might say that it reveals a profound ignorance of what true religion is all about. Nevertheless, although it may not seem fair to an insider, it is primarily intended to reflect how a religion, perhaps any religion, appears to an outsider. It is supposed to represent the *outsider's point of view*.

If the proposed account of religious doctrine is correct, it follows that it is a mistake, perhaps one with serious consequences, to underestimate or even to deny the realities of religious doctrines, especially those of organized groups. Religious doctrines make religions very powerful, for reasons that I have given. They also make them potentially dangerous; for religious doctrines by their very nature need to separate and insulate insiders from outsiders. This makes them impregnable. Consequently, whether it be explicitly or merely implicitly so, the fact of limited access (credibility) of any religious doctrine coupled with the other two characteristics—claims to primacy and a transcendental foundation—make every religion a potentially formidable threat to other religions, to the state, and to the principle of toleration.

IX. TOLERATION FOR OUTSIDERS

The issue of toleration is an issue for outsiders. From the inside point of view there is no problem, for, as I have argued, religious doctrine has to include teachings about how to pass judgment on and how to handle outsiders, the infidel. Treatment of outsiders, as prescribed from the insider's point of view, may be invidious or benign. Some doctrines, such as Aquinas's, prescribe a limited tolerance for outsiders. Evangelical religions may view outsiders as potential converts, and their doctrine requires that every effort be made to convert them.

In any event, however, the treatment or tolerance prescribed by a particular religious doctrine for outsiders is unlikely to coincide with the outsiders' view of the matter. But, and this is the nub of the issue of toleration, *all of us are at one time or other outsiders*, for the insiders of one religion are outsiders with respect to other religions. In a pluralistic society such as our own and in a pluralistic world peopled by strange religions, it is impossible for insiders of one religion to avoid having to rub shoulders with insiders of other religions, which for them are outsiders and which in turn look on them as outsiders!

Regarded from the point of view of outsiders rather than of

insiders, the principle of toleration takes on a different character. The challenge is an uneasy one. The rest of this essay will be about ways of dealing with this challenge.

X. How Is Toleration Possible?

So far I have argued that, from an insider's point of view, religious doctrine is very powerful indeed, and it tolerates differing opinions only on its own terms. Compromise, which is a necessary ingredient in political life, is inconsistent with the absolutism of religious doctrine. It is only when religion becomes embodied in organizations that compromise and political wheeling and dealing become acceptable. But our concern here is with doctrine.

For historical reasons, our nation has been fortunate in not having had to deal with religious confrontations in extremist terms, for mainstream Protestantism, which has been the dominant religious force, makes religion a matter of private conscience and, for the most part, eschews political involvement on narrowly religious terms. Our society, unlike the societies from which the original colonists came, has not been beset by violent religious divisions. Furthermore, there has been a kind of consensus on basic moral issues between the various religious groups, barring the extremists, that has made political life viable. But there is no reason to think that this agreeable relationship will persist forever: Already signs of breakdown appear in struggles over abortion and homosexuality, and, as I have argued, the seeds of intolerance and perhaps of violence are embedded within the very concept of religious doctrine.

Accordingly, the norm of de facto tolerance that is accepted and practised by most Americans on the grounds that religion is a matter of private choice for the individual and as such not to be challenged by outsiders may not be as certain a way out as it is generally assumed to be. Indeed, the relativism or subjectivism that is implied in the so-called privatization of religion is, as I have argued here and elsewhere, basically nonsense.[8] It cannot be used to substantiate the principle of religious tolerance unless one wishes to make religion a matter of private taste like eating olives or listening to rock 'n roll. My argument thus far has been that that kind of "downgrading of religion" is unrealistic and dangerous. We must, for reasons I have given, take the claims of religious doctrine seriously and deal with them realistically.

XI. SECULARISM

A quite different approach to the problem of toleration is represented by secularism, which affirms the primacy of the political over religion. This, of course, is the position of Hobbes, Bodin and of secular philosophers in general. Another version of secularism, which might be called "liberalism," claims primacy for rights, such as the rights to property and liberty, which are regarded as having priority over the claims of religion. Secularism, in its various forms, is generally identified with the philosophy of the Enlightenment. There are, of course, numerous philosophical groundings of the primacy of the political. It obviously appeals to atheists. (Bayle). But even some religious doctrines recognize a limited kind of primacy of the political in worldly affairs: "The powers that be come from God." The latter doctrine, associated with Lutheranism, suffers from a certain kind of internal absurdity which emerged clearly when it had to confront National Socialism.

Secularist doctrines, like their religious counterparts, are absolutist; the main difference is that they ascribe primacy to political, secular values rather than to religious values. Lacking a transcendental foundation and the kind of ideological immunities that characterize religious doctrines, secularist doctrines are less powerful ideologically and conceptually than religious doctrines. Their chief appeal is to intellectuals, agnostics and atheists. For reasons such as these, it is doubtful that a secularist answer to the problem of toleration can stand up, in practice, against the formidable threats of religion that have been mentioned. As evidence of the relative weakness of secularism, one might note that both Washington and Jefferson doubted that "a civil society founded on the rights of man could sustain itself in the absence of extraneous support provided by religious belief."[9]

It might also be noted that secularist philosophies can be intolerant in their own particular way, even though they expressly deny being so. Religionists often feel, perhaps justifiably, that they are outsiders in a secular world. That is why they have invented the term "secular humanism," to suggest that secularism is really just another religion. So-called secular humanism cannot, however, be a religion in our sense, because it is not founded on a belief in God. But since secularism, like religious doctrines, is a doctrine of primacy—in the sense that I have explained earlier—it may more accurately be categorized as a kind of absolutism, along with religions and other sorts of ideology.

XII. Absolutism and Pluralism

We now seem to have reached an impasse, namely, how to deal with conflicting and incompatible absolutisms—including atheism, naturalism, and liberalism as forms of absolutism—in addition to religious absolutisms. The problem with absolutism in general, as I have argued elsewhere, is that it provides no way for insiders to deal rationally with outsiders who do not accept the insider's premises: "If you don't accept my basic premises, e.g. about God, or man, I cannot argue with you."[10] Furthermore, it provides no way of coping with the claims of outsiders that do not fit into the framework of one's own insider's system or that might even be in some ways inconsistent with it: "You are not talking a language, e.g. about God or the soul, that I can understand."[11]

At this point, we might wish to return to pluralism, not of the de facto descriptive variety—which is not at issue—but of what might be called de jure or ethical pluralism. Although there is much talk about pluralism in this sense, most of it, as I have already suggested, is obscure and confused. More often than not the label "pluralism" is adopted as a philosopher's stone that can be used to turn prejudice into tolerance without explaining the mystery of how it is done.[12]

Pluralism is sometimes considered to be the "philosophical" theory that different points of view or different value-systems are equally valid or valuable. Pluralism in this sense comes close to, and is perhaps identical with, ethical relativism, which I have already mentioned.[13] It is difficult to understand, both theoretically, what equal validity in this context could mean and, practically, how it could be applied. How, for example, can the

principle of equal validity be applied to religious doctrines that
hold, on the one hand, that creationism should be taught in the
schools and, on the other hand, that it should not be taught in
the schools because it is unscientific? What does it mean to say
that both positions are "equally valid"? A position like this kind
of pluralism that requires the rejection of the law of non-con-
tradiction hardly merits serious attention—either theoretically
or practically.[14]

The ostensible paradox of pluralism just mentioned arises from
its being given an absolutist interpretation, that is, it assumes
that the different value-systems held to be equally valid are absolutist positions as well as the principle of equal validity itself.

XIII. Critique of Absolutism

Let us now turn to absolutism. An absolutist, by definition, is
one who denies the validity of positions that do not follow from,
or are inconsistent with his own. To oversimplify, the absolutist
takes a deductive system like geometry as his theoretical model,
and the concepts of deducibility and inconsistency are defined
in terms of that mode. It is precisely this kind of model, which
is generally associated with some form or other of ethical foun-
dationalism, that must be rejected if we want to make any head-
way in dealing with the problem of toleration. I have argued
against it on ethical grounds elsewhere.[15]

An idea of how we might proceed in dismantling absolutism
is to replace categorical truth claims or absolute imperatives with
presumptions. For example, with regard to a claim that is outside
one's own system, one would start by assuming that there might
be some truth in it and that; therefore, it must not be dismissed
out of hand. The fact that someone seriously believes in a value
creates a presumption and poses a challenge to the rest of us
as outsiders to give it due consideration as a possible option.
Accordingly, one might admit that there is something of value
in a religious doctrine even though one does not, and cannot,
accept it in toto, and the item in question is not part of one's
own previously adopted value-system. A presumption of this
kind might be what some people have in mind when they are
willing to concede that religion is indispensable for American
democracy, while at the same time they are unwilling to en-

dorse any one particular religion or sect. Respect for religion in general does not require the acceptance of a particular religion or, for that matter, of any religion at all. Clearly, one could even be an atheist and accept the value of religion in this general way.

Going backward, we can now see that if we take religion and particular religious doctrines pragmatically, that is, as presumptions or as "experiments in living"[16], we will be able to free ourselves from the closed absolutism of dogmatic, authoritarian religious doctrine and will still be able, even from the point of view of an outsider, to acknowledge the possibility of something good in religion, whether it be religion in general or a particular religion. This, as a matter of fact, is the pragmatic attitude that I believe most people in America take towards particular religions, that is, they prefer to approach them not in the absolutist way but as experiments in living with other people in a shared world of suffering and hope.

Further development of a non-absolutist form of pluralism may provide a theoretical answer to the question of toleration that has been the concern of this essay and along with it a further clarification of the relation of politics and religion in our society. But here we must not forget Spinoza's dictum: "All things excellent are as difficult as they are rare." True toleration, which consists not merely in abstention from violence but also in acknowledging and respecting values and religions other than our own, is one of those excellent things that is both difficult and rare.

NOTES

1. Thomas Aquinas, *Summa Theologica*, IIaIIae, question 10, article 11, Translation adapted from Aquinas, *Selected Political Writings*, ed. A. P. D'Entrèves (Oxford: Basil Blackwell, 1948).
2. More details can be found in Robert Bellah et al., *Habits of the Heart.* New York: Harper and Row, 1986), especially chap. 9.
3. Alexis de Tocqueville, *Democracy in America,* trans. George Lawrence (Garden City, N.Y.: Anchor Books, Doubleday, 1969), p. 292.
4. See *Voluntary Associations:* NOMOS XI, eds. J. Roland Pennock and John W. Chapman. (New York: Atherton Press, 1969).
5. For illustrations of fundamentalist beliefs about a vengeful God,

see A. G. Mojtabai, *Blessed Assurance: At Home with the Bomb in Amarillo, Texas* (Boston: Houghton Mifflin, 1986).

6. See John Ladd, "Euthanasia, Liberty, and Religion," *Ethics* 93 (October 1982): 129–38. The Catholic Bishops' Pastoral Letter on War and Peace of May 3, 1983, entitled *The Challenge of Peace: God's Promise and Our Response,* illustrates the same point, namely, it is a discussion couched in Natural Law language that in fact relies almost exclusively on papal authority in its argumentation.

7. Chaim Perelman, *The Realm of Rhetoric* (Notre Dame: University of Notre Dame Press, 1982).

8. John Ladd, Introduction to *Ethical Relativism* (Lanham, Md.: University Press of America, 1985).

9. Walter Berns, "Religion and the Founding Principle," in *The Moral Foundations of the American Republic,* 3rd ed., ed. Robert H. Horwitz, p. 213. (Charlottesville: University Press of Virginia, 1986).

10. See John Ladd, "The Poverty of Absolutism" in *Edward Westermarck: Essays on His Life and Works,* ed. Timothy Stroup. *Acta Philosophica Fennica,* vol. 34 (Helsinki: Societas Philsophical Fennica, 1982).

11. Ibid.

12. The philosopher's stone was a reputed stone that alchemists could use to turn other substances into gold.

13. Ladd, Introduction to *Ethical Relativism.*

14. There may be other senses of pluralism that are consistent and meaningful. See, for example, John Hick, *Problems of Religious Pluralism* (New York: St. Martin's Press, 1985), p. 34. Pluralism, for Hick, means that "There is a plurality of saving human responses to the ultimate divine Reality."

15. The arguments are set forth in greater detail in Ladd, "Poverty of Absolutism."

16. See Alexander MacBeath, *Experiments in Living* (London: Macmillan, 1952).

INDEX